CAMBRIDGE
University Press

CAMBRIDGE
Global English

for Cambridge Primary English as a Second Language

Teacher's Resource 6

Nicola Mabbott with Helen Tiliouine

Series Editor: Kathryn Harper

CAMBRIDGE
UNIVERSITY PRESS

University Printing House, Cambridge CB2 8BS, United Kingdom

One Liberty Plaza, 20th Floor, New York, NY 10006, USA

477 Williamstown Road, Port Melbourne, VIC 3207, Australia

314–321, 3rd Floor, Plot 3, Splendor Forum, Jasola District Centre, New Delhi – 110025, India

103 Penang Road, #05–06/07, Visioncrest Commercial, Singapore 238467

Cambridge University Press is part of the University of Cambridge.
It furthers the University's mission by disseminating knowledge in the pursuit of
education, learning and research at the highest international levels of excellence.

www.cambridge.org
Information on this title: www.cambridge.org/9781108963848

First published 1993
Second edition 2022

20 19 18 17 16 15 14 13 12 11 10 9 8 7 6 5

Printed in Great Britain by CPI Group (UK) Ltd, Croydon CR0 4YY

A catalogue record for this publication is available from the British Library

ISBN 978-1-108-96384-8 Paperback with Digital Access

Additional resources for this publication at www.cambridge.org/9781108963848

Cambridge University Press has no responsibility for the persistence or accuracy
of URLs for external or third-party internet websites referred to in this publication,
and does not guarantee that any content on such websites is, or will remain,
accurate or appropriate. Information regarding prices, travel timetables, and other
factual information given in this work is correct at the time of first printing but
Cambridge University Press does not guarantee the accuracy of such information
thereafter.

....

....

⟩ Contents

Digital resources

⤓ The following items are available on Cambridge GO. For more information on how to access and use your digital resource, please see inside front cover.

Active learning

Assessment for Learning

Developing learner language skills

Differentiation

Improving learning through questioning

Language awareness

Metacognition

Skills for Life

Letter for parents

Lesson plan template

Curriculum framework correlation

Scheme of work

Audio files and audioscripts

Progress tests 1–3 and answers

Progress report

Learner's Book answers

Workbook answers

Wordlist

You can download the following resources for each unit:

Differentiated worksheets and answers

Photocopiables

Sample answers

End-of-unit tests and answers

› Introduction

Welcome to the new edition of our Cambridge Global English series.

Since its launch, the series has been used by teachers and learners in over 100 countries for teaching the Cambridge Primary English as a Second Language curriculum framework.

This exciting new edition has been designed by talking to Global English teachers all over the world. We have worked hard to understand your needs and challenges, and then carefully designed and tested the best ways of meeting them.

As a result of this research, we've made some important changes to the series, while retaining the international and cross-curricular elements which you told us you valued. This Teacher's Resource has been carefully redesigned to make it easier for you to plan and teach the course. It is available in print for all Stages.

The series still has extensive digital and online support, including Digital Classroom which lets you share books with your class and play videos and audio. This Teacher's Resource also offers additional materials, including tests, available to download from Cambridge GO. (For more information on how to access and use your digital resource, please see inside front cover.)

The series uses successful teaching approaches like active learning and metacognition and takes a 21st-century skills approach, with a focus on developing critical thinking skills. This Teacher's Resource gives you full guidance on how to integrate them into your classroom.

Formative assessment opportunities help you to get to know your learners better, with clear learning intentions and success criteria as well as an array of assessment techniques, including advice on self and peer assessment.

Clear, consistent differentiation ensures that all learners are able to progress in the course with tiered activities, differentiated worksheets, open-ended project tasks and advice about supporting Learner's different needs.

All our resources are written for teachers and learners who use English as a second or additional language. In this edition of Global English we focus on four aspects of language:

- there is more grammar presentation and practice in the Workbook and on the Digital Classroom
- we have introduced scaffolded writing lessons with models of a range of text types
- we have included a range of literature
- and we have worked to ease the transition between stages, especially between primary and secondary.

We hope you enjoy using this course.

Eddie Rippeth

Head of Primary and Lower Secondary Publishing, Cambridge University Press

> About the authors

Jane Boylan

Jane Boylan is a freelance author, consultant, and creator of ESL materials for print and digital resources. She has worked for a range of publishers and educational organisations, creating and developing language learning materials for young learners and teachers of English. She has taken a leading role in educational resource projects for specific cultural contexts in East Asia, the United Arab Emirates, Pakistan, West Africa and Kazakhstan, consulting on content development and classroom application. Formerly, Jane worked on British Council teacher development projects primarily in East Asia, managing, writing and delivering a diverse range of training courses to state sector primary and secondary teachers of English. Earlier in her career, she worked as an English language teacher in Spain, Portugal, Thailand and Vietnam.

Claire Medwell

Passionate about quality English teaching, **Claire Medwell** is a teacher, teacher trainer and independent materials writer. She has 26 years of experience in ELT and ESL specializing in infant and primary learners.

Her publications include Cambridge Global English Stages 4–6 and the New Fun Skills 1 and 2.

Nicola Mabbott

Nicola Mabbott is a linguist who began her teaching career in Nottingham, England in 1998, teaching English as a Foreign Language to young adults. Since then, she has taught learners of all abilities and ages (from preschool age to retired adults) in Italy. She also regularly works as a Tutor in English for Academic Purposes.

Nicola has been writing for a variety publishers in the UK and Italy – mostly resources for teachers of EFL to young learners and adolescents – for over 10 years. These resources include games, quizzes, communicative activities, worksheets, self study resources, short stories and reading and listening activities for school course books.

Nicola has a passion for language and languages and also works as a translator.

Kathryn Harper

Kathryn Harper is a freelance writer, publisher and consultant. Early on in her career, she worked as an English Language teacher in France and Canada. As an international publisher at Macmillan and Oxford University Press, she published teaching materials for Europe, the Middle East, Africa, Pakistan and Latin America. Her freelance work includes publishing reading schemes, writing electronic materials, language courses and stories for markets around the world. Her primary French whiteboard course for Nelson Thornes, *Rigolo*, won the 2008 BETT award. She also volunteers as an English teacher for child refugees and as a mentor for young African writers.

Helen Tiliouine

Helen Tiliouine is an experienced teacher and writer of test materials. She has been involved in writing a range of ESL and ELT test materials, including *Cambridge Global English Teacher's Resource tests, Cambridge English Prepare! Test generator,* and *Complete First for Schools*. She is an experienced examiner.

Alison Sharpe

Alison Sharpe is a freelance teacher, writer and publisher. She started her career teaching English in Japan, Taiwan and the UK. She then worked for many years at Cambridge University Press and Oxford University Press publishing learning, teaching, exams and assessment materials for teachers and students all around the world. As a freelancer, she has been involved in a wide range of projects, including developing online teacher training materials, the assessment of children's writing and editing language learning materials for young learners and adults. She is also currently a part time tutor of academic literacy at Oxford University's Department of Continuing Education.

> How to use this series

The Learner's Book is designed for learners to use in class with guidance from the teacher. It offers full coverage of the curriculum framework. The cross-curricular content supports success across the curriculum, with an international outlook. There is a focus on critical thinking, reading and writing skills with a literature section in every unit and a scaffolded approach to the development of written skills, with model texts. End-of-unit projects provide opportunities for formative assessment and differentiation so that you can support each individual learner's needs.

Digital Access with all the material from the book in digital form is available via Cambridge GO.

The write-in Workbook offers opportunities to help learners consolidate what they have learned in the Learner's Book and is ideal for use in class or as homework. It provides plenty of differentiated grammar practice at three tiers so that learners have choices and can support or extend their learning, as required. Activities based on Cambridge Learner Corpus data give unique insight into common errors made by learners.

Digital Access with all the material from the book in digital form is available via Cambridge GO.

In the print Teacher's Resource you'll find everything you need to deliver the course, including teaching ideas, answers and differentiation and formative assessment support. Each Teacher's Resource includes:

- a print book with detailed teaching notes for each topic
- a digital edition with all the material from the book plus editable unit and progress tests, differentiated worksheets and communicative games.

The Digital Classroom is for teachers to use at the front of the class. It includes digital versions of the Learner's Book and Workbook, complete with pop-up answers, helping you give instructions easily and check answers. Zoom in, highlight and annotate text, and support better learning with videos, grammar slideshows and interactive activities.

A letter to parents, explaining the course, is available to download from Cambridge GO (as part of this Teacher's Resource).

> How to use this Teacher's Resource

This Teacher's Resource contains both general guidance and teaching notes that help you to deliver the content in our Cambridge Global English resources. Some of the material is provided as downloadable files, available on **Cambridge GO**. (For more information about how to access and use your digital resource, please see inside front cover.) See the Contents page for details of all the material available to you, both in this book and through Cambridge GO.

Teaching notes

This book provides **teaching notes** for each unit of the Learner's Book and Workbook. Each set of teaching notes contains the following features to help you deliver the unit.

The **Unit plan** summarises the lessons covered in the unit, including the number of learning hours recommended for the lesson, an outline of the learning content and the Cambridge resources that can be used to deliver the lesson.

Lesson	Approximate number of learning hours	Outline of learning content	Learning objectives	Resources
1 What connects us with the people around us?	1.5–2.0	Talk about feelings that connect us.	6Ld.04 6So.01 6Ug.07	Learner's Book Lesson 1.1 Workbook Lesson 1.1 **Digital Classroom:** Video – What makes us who we are?; Activity – Present perfect – talking about the past

The **Background knowledge** feature provides information which helps the teacher to familiarise themselves with the cross-curricular and international content in the unit.

Learner's prior knowledge can be informally assessed through the **Getting started** feature in the Learner's Book.

The **Teaching skills focus** feature covers a teaching skill and suggests how to implement it in the unit.

BACKGROUND KNOWLEDGE

It is useful to have a good understanding of a range different literary genres (historical fiction, traditional folk and fairy tales and myths, science fiction, mystery stories, fantasy fiction, adventure stories, etc.).

TEACHING SKILLS FOCUS

The challenge with active learning is to stop yourself telling learners things that they could discover for themselves.

Reflecting the Learner's Book, each unit consists of multiple lessons.

At the start of each lesson, the **Learning plan** table includes the learning objectives, learning intentions and success criteria that are covered in the lesson.

It can be helpful to share learning intentions and success criteria with your learners at the start of a lesson so that they can begin to take responsibility for their own learning.

LEARNING PLAN

Learning objective	Learning intentions	Success criteria
6Ld.04	• **Listening:** Understand a range of instructions.	• Learners can understand, with support, details of a conversation about emotional reactions.

There are often **common misconceptions** associated with particular grammar points. These are listed, along with suggestions for identifying evidence of the misconceptions in your class and suggestions for how to overcome them. At Cambridge University Press, we have unique access to the Cambridge Learner Corpus to help us identify common errors for key language groups. ◉

Misconception	How to identify	How to overcome
Learners use the present simple/past simple instead of the present perfect. For example:	Write sentences on the board using the present perfect and one other tense. Elicit the different implications of using the two tenses. For example:	Ask concept check questions. For example: • Is there a connection implied between past and present? • Is the focus on the time or the experience?

For each lesson, there is a selection of **starter ideas**, **main teaching ideas** and **plenary ideas**. You can pick out individual ideas and mix and match them depending on the needs of your class. The activities include suggestions for how they can be differentiated or used for assessment. **Homework ideas** are also provided, with home–school link suggestions to enable learners to continue their learning at home.

Starter ideas

Have you ever felt …? (10 minutes)

• Write the adjectives from Activity 1 on the board (*happy, excited, nervous, angry, interested, scared*).

• Elicit a model dialogue about one of the adjectives. For example:

A: Have you ever felt really excited?

B: Yes, I have.

A: When?

B: Last year.

A: What about?

B: My holiday to India.

• Discuss which questions and answers are in the past simple and which are in the present perfect.

• In pairs, learners ask and answer questions using the other adjectives.

Getting started (10 minutes)

• Look at the pictures on page 11 and answer question a. Write the names of the activities/events on the board and ask learners how the activities/events make them feel.

• Write the word 'identity' on the board. Build up suggestions about what makes up a person's identity; for example, what we are like, what we are good at/enjoy doing, what makes us happy/sad, etc.

The **Language background** feature contains information to help you present the grammar in the unit.

LANGUAGE BACKGROUND

Present perfect

- The **present perfect** tense describes events when the time of the event is not important, or to show a connection between the present and the past.

The **Cross-curricular links** feature provides suggestions for linking to other subject areas.

CROSS-CURRICULAR LINKS

Geography: Here are some question examples for a short quiz to interest learners in the subject:

- *Is London an example of a town, city or county?* (city)

> **Differentiation ideas:** This feature provides suggestions for how activities can be differentiated to suit the needs of your class.

> **Critical thinking opportunity:** This feature provides suggestions for embedding critical thinking and other 21st-century skills into your teaching and learning.

> **Assessment ideas:** This feature highlights opportunities for formative assessment during your teaching.

> **Digital Classroom:** If you have access to Digital Classroom, these links will suggest when to use the various multimedia enhancements and interactive activities.

Answers: Answers to Learner's Book exercises can be found integrated within the lesson plans and Learner's Book and Workbook answer keys are also available to download.

Note: Some texts used in the Learner's Book and Workbook have been abridged, so please be aware that learners may not be presented with the full version of the text.

Digital resources to download

This Teacher's Resource includes a range of digital materials that you can download from Cambridge GO. (For more information about how to access and use your digital resource, please see inside front cover.) This icon ⬇ indicates material that is available from Cambridge GO.

Helpful documents for planning include:

- **Letter for parents:** a template letter for parents, introducing the Cambridge Global English resources.
- **Lesson plan template:** a Word document that you can use for planning your lessons.
- **Curriculum framework correlation:** a table showing how the Cambridge Global English resources map to the Cambridge Primary English as a Second Language curriculum framework.
- **Scheme of work:** a suggested scheme of work that you can use to plan teaching throughout the year.

Each unit includes:

- **Differentiated worksheets:** these worksheets cater for different abilities. Worksheet A is designed to support learners who don't feel confident about the topic. Worksheet B is designed for learners who have a good general understanding of the topic. Worksheet C is aimed at learners who want a challenge. Answer sheets are provided.
- **Photocopiable resources:** these include communicative language game, templates and any other materials that support the learning objectives of the unit.
- **Sample answers:** these contain teacher comments, which allow learners and teachers to assess what 'good' looks like in order to inform their writing.
- **End-of-unit tests:** these provide quick checks of the learner's understanding of the concepts covered in the unit. Answers are provided. Advice on using these tests formatively is given in the Assessment for Learning section of this Teacher's Resource.
- **Project checklists:** checklists for learners to use to evaluate their writing and project work.

Additionally, the Teacher's Resource includes:

- **Progress test 1:** a test to use at the beginning of the year to discover the level that learners are working at. The results of this test can inform your planning. Answers are provided.
- **Progress test 2:** a test to use after learners have studied Units 1–5 in the Learner's Book. You can use this test to check whether there are areas that you need to go over again. Answers are provided.
- **Progress test 3:** a test to use after learners have studied all units in the Learner's Book. You can use this test to check whether there are areas that you need to go over again, and to help inform your planning for the rest of the year. Answers are provided.
- **Progress report:** a document to help you formatively assess your classes' progress against the learning intentions.
- **Audioscripts:** available as downloadable files.
- **Answers to Learner's Book questions**
- **Answers to Workbook questions**
- **Wordlist:** an editable list of key vocabulary for each unit.

In addition, you can find more detailed information about teaching approaches.

🎧 **Audio** is available for download from Cambridge GO (as part of this Teacher's Resource and as part of the digital resources for the Learner's Book and Workbook).

📹 **Video** is available through the Digital Classroom.

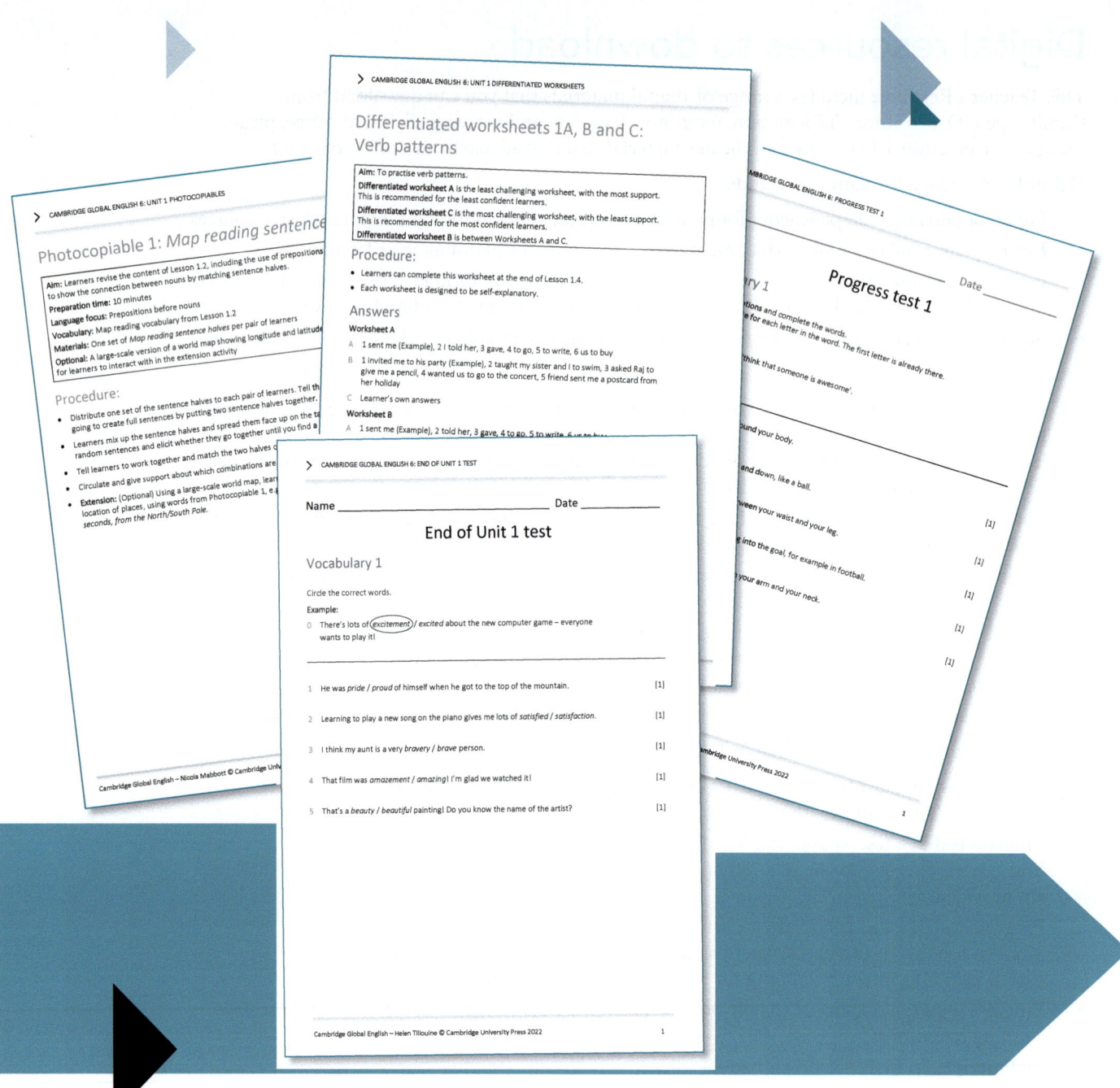

> CAMBRIDGE GLOBAL ENGLISH 6: UNIT 1 DIFFERENTIATED WORKSHEETS

Differentiated worksheets 1A, B and C: Verb patterns

Aim: To practise verb patterns.

Differentiated worksheet A is the least challenging worksheet, with the most support. This is recommended for the least confident learners.

Differentiated worksheet C is the most challenging worksheet, with the least support. This is recommended for the most confident learners.

Differentiated worksheet B is between Worksheets A and C.

Procedure:
- Learners can complete this worksheet at the end of Lesson 1.4.
- Each worksheet is designed to be self-explanatory.

Answers

Worksheet A

A 1 sent me (Example), 2 I told her, 3 gave, 4 to go, 5 to write, 6 us to buy

B 1 invited me to his party (Example), 2 taught my sister and I to swim, 3 asked Raj to give me a pencil, 4 wanted us to go to the concert, 5 friend sent me a postcard from her holiday

C Learner's own answers

Worksheet B

A 1 sent me (Example), 2 told her, 3 gave, 4 to go, 5 to write, 6 us to buy

---

> CAMBRIDGE GLOBAL ENGLISH 6: UNIT 1 PHOTOCOPIABLES

Photocopiable 1: Map reading sentence

Aim: Learners revise the content of Lesson 1.2, including the use of prepositions to show the connection between nouns by matching sentence halves.

Preparation time: 10 minutes

Language focus: Prepositions before nouns

Vocabulary: Map reading vocabulary from Lesson 1.2

Materials: One set of *Map reading sentence halves* per pair of learners

Optional: A large-scale version of a world map showing longitude and latitude for learners to interact with in the extension activity

Procedure:
- Distribute one set of the sentence halves to each pair of learners. Tell them going to create full sentences by putting two sentence halves together.
- Learners mix up the sentence halves and spread them face up on the ta random sentences and elicit whether they go together until you find a
- Tell learners to work together and match the two halves o
- Circulate and give support about which combinations are
- **Extension:** (Optional) Using a large-scale world map, lear location of places, using words from Photocopiable 1, e.g seconds, *from the North/South Pole.*

Cambridge Global English – Nicola Mabbott © Cambridge Univ

> CAMBRIDGE GLOBAL ENGLISH 6: PROGRESS TEST 1

Progress test 1   Date

ry 1

tions and complete the words.
e for each letter in the word. The first letter is already there.

think that someone is awesome'.

ound your body.

and down, like a ball.

een your waist and your leg.   [1]

into the goal, for example in football.   [1]

y your arm and your neck.   [1]

                                                                       [1]

                                                                       [1]

                                                                       [1]

Cambridge University Press 2022   1

> CAMBRIDGE GLOBAL ENGLISH 6: END OF UNIT 1 TEST

Name _____ Date _____

End of Unit 1 test

Vocabulary 1

Circle the correct words.

Example:

0 There's lots of (excitement) / *excited* about the new computer game – everyone wants to play it!

1 He was *pride* / *proud* of himself when he got to the top of the mountain.   [1]

2 Learning to play a new song on the piano gives me lots of *satisfied* / *satisfaction*.   [1]

3 I think my aunt is a very *bravery* / *brave* person.   [1]

4 That film was *amazement* / *amazing*! I'm glad we watched it!   [1]

5 That's a *beauty* / *beautiful* painting! Do you know the name of the artist?   [1]

Cambridge Global English – Helen Tiltouine © Cambridge University Press 2022   1

> About the curriculum framework

*This series supports the Cambridge Primary English as a Second Language curriculum frameworks (0057) from 2020. You should always refer to the appropriate curriculum framework document to confirm the details of the framework and for more information. Visit **www.cambridgeinternational.orglprimary** to find out more.*

The Cambridge Primary English as a Second Language curriculum framework is designed to enable young learners from an ESL background (who speak little or no English at home) to communicate effectively and with confidence in English. Cambridge Global English is designed to deliver this curriculum. It does this by developing the skills to access and understand a wide range of information, media and texts. It achieves this by focussing on active learning, developing critical thinking skills and intellectual engagement with a range of topics.

Our scheme is designed to fully support teachers to deliver the framework by providing an integrated approach to planning and teaching to develop effective communication skills in English. The five strands, and their respective learning objectives, work together to support the development of knowledge, skills and understanding in:

- Reading
- Writing
- Use of English
- Listening
- Speaking.

The new curriculum framework includes some important changes. For example, there is a new sub-strand of learning objectives within the Speaking strand, with new learning objectives concerning fluency and accuracy of pronunciation.

> About the assessment

Information concerning the assessment of the Cambridge Primary English as a Second Language curriculum framework is available on the Cambridge Assessment International Education website: **www.cambridgeinternational.org/primary**.

The resources provide support for the Cambridge Primary English as a Second Language curriculum framework from 2020.

> Approaches to learning and teaching

The following are the teaching approaches underpinning our course content and how we understand and define them.

Active learning

Active learning is a teaching approach that places student learning at its centre. It focuses on how students learn, not just on what they learn. We, as teachers, need to encourage learners to 'think hard', rather than passively receive information. Active learning encourages learners to take responsibility for their learning and supports them in becoming independent and confident learners in school and beyond.

Assessment for Learning

Assessment for Learning (AfL) is a teaching approach that generates feedback which can be used to improve learner's performance. Learners become more involved in the learning process and, from this, gain confidence in what they are expected to learn and to what standard. We, as teachers, gain insights into a learner's level of understanding of a particular concept or topic, which helps to inform how we support their progression.

Differentiation

Differentiation is usually presented as a teaching approach where teachers think of learners as individuals and learning as a personalised process. While precise definitions can vary, typically the core aim of differentiation is viewed as ensuring that all learners, no matter their ability, interest or context, make progress towards their learning intentions. It is about using different approaches and appreciating the differences in learners to help them make progress. Teachers therefore need to be responsive, and willing and able to adapt their teaching to meet the needs of their learners.

Language awareness

For many learners, English is an additional language. It might be their second or perhaps their third language. Depending on the school context, students might be learning all or just some of their subjects through English.

For all learners, regardless of whether they are learning through their first language or an additional language, language is a vehicle for learning. It is through language that students access the learning intentions of the lesson and communicate their ideas. It is our responsibility, as teachers, to ensure that language doesn't present a barrier to learning.

Metacognition

Metacognition describes the processes involved when learners plan, monitor, evaluate and make changes to their own learning behaviours. These processes help learners to think about their own learning more explicitly and ensure that they are able to meet a learning goal that they have identified themselves or that we, as teachers, have set.

Skills for Life

How do we prepare learners to succeed in a fast-changing world? To collaborate with people from around the globe? To create innovation as technology increasingly takes over routine work? To use advanced thinking skills in the face of more complex challenges? To show resilience in the face of constant change? At Cambridge, we are responding to educators who have asked for a way to understand how all these different approaches to life skills and competencies relate to their teaching. We have grouped these skills into six main Areas of Competency that can be incorporated into teaching, and have examined the different stages of the learning journey and how these competencies vary across each stage.

These six key areas are:

- Creativity – finding new ways of doing things, and solutions to problems
- Collaboration – the ability to work well with others
- Communication – speaking and presenting confidently and participating effectively in meetings
- Critical thinking – evaluating what is heard or read, and linking ideas constructively
- Learning to learn – developing the skills to learn more effectively
- Social responsibilities – contributing to social groups, and being able to talk to and work with people from other cultures.

Cambridge learner and teacher attributes

This course helps develop the following Cambridge learner and teacher attributes.

Cambridge learners	Cambridge teachers
Confident in working with information and ideas – their own and those of others.	**Confident** in teaching their subject and engaging each student in learning.
Responsible for themselves, responsive to and respectful of others.	**Responsible** for themselves, responsive to and respectful of others.
Reflective as learners, developing their ability to learn.	**Reflective** as learners themselves, developing their practice.
Innovative and equipped for new and future challenges.	**Innovative** and equipped for new and future challenges.
Engaged intellectually and socially, ready to make a difference.	**Engaged** intellectually, professionally and socially, ready to make a difference.

Reproduced from Developing the Cambridge learner attributes with permission from Cambridge Assessment International Education.

 More information about these approaches to learning and teaching is available to download from Cambridge GO (as part of this Teacher's Resource).

❯ Setting up for success

Our aim is to support better learning in the classroom with resources that allow for increased learner autonomy while supporting teachers to facilitate student learning. Through an active learning approach of enquiry-led tasks, open-ended questions and opportunities to externalise thinking in a variety of ways, learners will develop analysis, evaluation and problem-solving skills.

Some ideas to consider to encourage an active learning environment are as follows:

- Set up seating to make group work easy.

- Create classroom routines to help learners to transition between different types of activity efficiently, e.g. move from pair work to listening to the teacher to independent work.

- Source mini-whiteboards, which allow you to get feedback from all learners rapidly.

- Start a portfolio for each learner, keeping key pieces of work to show progress at parent–teacher days.

- Have a display area with learner work and vocab flashcards.

Planning for active learning

We recommend the following approach to planning. A blank lesson plan template is available to download to help with this approach.

1 **Plan learning intentions and success criteria:** these are the most important feature of the lesson. Teachers and learners need to know where they are going in order to plan a route to get there.

2 **Plan language support:** think about strategies to help learners overcome the language demands of the lesson so that language doesn't present a barrier to learning.

3 **Plan starter activities:** include a 'hook' or starter to engage learners using imaginative strategies. This should be an activity where all learners are active from the start of the lesson.

4 **Plan main activities:** during the lesson, try to: give clear instructions, with modelling and written support; coordinate logical and orderly transitions between activities; make sure that learning is active and all learners are engaged; create opportunities for discussion around key concepts.

5 **Plan assessment for learning and differentiation:** use a wide range of Assessment for Learning techniques and adapt activities to a wide range of abilities. Address misconceptions at appropriate points and give meaningful oral and written feedback which learners can act on.

6 **Plan reflection and plenary:** at the end of each activity and at the end of each lesson, try to: ask learners to reflect on what they have learned compared to the beginning of the lesson; build on and extend this learning.

7 **Plan homework:** if setting homework, it can be used to consolidate learning from the previous lesson or to prepare for the next lesson

To help planning using this approach, a blank lesson plan template is available to download from Cambridge GO (as part of this Teacher's Resource).

For more guidance on setting up for success and planning, please explore the Professional Development pages of our website **www.cambridge.org/education/PD**

> 1 My world

Unit plan

Lesson	Approximate number of learning hours	Outline of learning content	Learning objectives	Resources
1 What connects us with the people around us?	1.5–2.0	Talk about feelings that connect us.	6Ld.04 6So.01 6Ug.07	Learner's Book Lesson 1.1 Workbook Lesson 1.1 **Digital Classroom:** Video – What makes us who we are?; Activity – Present perfect – talking about the past
2 Where in the world am I?	1.5–2.0	Discover how to find locations on a world map.	6Rd.03 6Uv.02	Learner's Book Lesson 1.2 Workbook Lesson 1.2 ⬇ Photocopiable 1 **Digital Classroom:** Activity – Prepositions before nouns
3 Inspiring people	2.0–2.5	Talk about someone who we admire.	6Sc.02 6Sc.06 6Sc.05 6Sor.01	Learner's Book Lesson 1.3 Workbook Lesson 1.3 **Digital Classroom:** Video – Giving a class presentation
4 A first time for everything	1.5–2.0	Describe our feelings about a first-time experience.	6Wca.03 6Ug.07 6Rm.01 6Us.07	Learner's Book Lesson 1.4 Workbook Lesson 1.4 ⬇ Photocopiable 2 ⬇ Photocopiable 3 ⬇ Differentiated worksheets 1A, B and C ⬇ Unit 1 sample answer **Digital Classroom:** Activity – Noun or adjective?; Slideshow – First-time experiences; grammar presentation – Verb patterns
5 *A Girl Called Owl*	1.5–2.0	Read about a girl with an unusual name.	6Rm.01 6Rm.02	Learner's Book Lesson 1.5 Workbook Lesson 1.5 **Digital Classroom:** Activity – *A Girl Called Owl*
6 Project challenge	1.0–1.5	Project A: A presentation about something or someone special to you. Project B: Design an 'Our names' poster for your classroom.	6Sc.06 6Sc.02 6Wca.03 6Sc.01	Learner's Book Lesson 1.6 Workbook Lesson 1.6 ⬇ Unit 1 project checklists

(continued)

Cross-unit resources

⬇ Unit 1 Audioscripts
⬇ End of Unit 1 test
⬇ Progress test 1
⬇ Unit 1 Progress report
⬇ Unit 1 Wordlist

BACKGROUND KNOWLEDGE

In Lesson 1.1, learners play the Connections game. This involves them drawing pictures or writing words that they connect with particular emotions. They then compare their ideas with a partner and find connections – things they have in common with the other players.

Lesson 1.2 focuses on geography and finding locations on a world map. There are a number of different criteria for distinguishing continents, mostly resulting in five, six and seven continent models.

- Five-continent models combine North and South America and exclude Antarctica. This five-continent model is used in the United Nations and the five-ring symbol of the Olympic games.

- Six-continent models consider Eurasia as a single continent.

- The seven-continent model is now widely accepted and commonly taught in English-speaking countries.

In this lesson, there is quite a lot of geographical vocabulary, for example the text discusses invisible *longitude and latitude* lines, which are used to pinpoint the exact location of a place, such as for navigational purposes.

In Lesson 1.3, the title *Inspiring people* has a double meaning – *people who inspire others* or the act of *inspiring* others.

The reading in Lesson 1.5 is from *A Girl Called Owl*, by Amy Wilson. *A Girl Called Owl* was nominated for the CILIP Carnegie medal, a children's book award in the UK. The author has a background in journalism and studied creative writing at Bath Spa University in the UK. She has written other children's titles, including *Shadows of Winterspell*, *Snowglobe* and *A Far Away Magic*.

TEACHING SKILLS FOCUS

Differentiation

Differentiation in the class is the process of making an activity more or less challenging for the different skills of your learners. This can help maximise the potential of learners of different abilities. If an activity is too demanding, there is the danger of some learners becoming de-motivated and 'switching off'. However, if the lesson isn't challenging enough, other learners may become bored.

This resource has suggestions throughout about using differentiation with the activities in the Learner's Book. Each unit also has one set of worksheets and two photocopiable activities.

Differentiation and the worksheets

- Each worksheet has three differentiated versions.
- The 'A' worksheets are the least challenging. They have the most support and usually the fewest activities.
- The 'C' worksheets are the most challenging, with the least support.
- The 'B' worksheets are between worksheets A and C.

If you set the worksheets for homework, you could set Worksheet B for most of the class and Worksheet A for learners who are struggling with the particular learning point. You could set Worksheet C for learners who need to be challenged more.

CONTINUED

Differentiation and the photocopiable activities

Unlike the worksheets, there is only one standard version of the photocopiable activities.

To get the most out of the photocopiables, you could devise strategies, like adapting them to the different levels of competence of your learners. Here are some ideas:

1 Adapt the content, e.g. shorten/add content.

2 Adapt the learning process, e.g. give a model dialogue and extra prompts/fewer prompts.

3 Adapt expectations of what learners will be able to achieve, e.g. how many questions they will be able to work through.

4 Put different abilities into pairs or groups, e.g. to benefit less confident speakers who can follow the lead of their partners/group members.

5 Add extra tasks to challenge more confident speakers, or give less confident speakers fewer tasks or more time.

Your challenge

- Look through the photocopiable activities and think about your learner's strengths and weaknesses.

- Consider other ways you can tailor the activities to add extra support for less confident speakers.

- Are there any extra tasks you could add to challenge more confident speakers?

1.1 Think about it: What connects us to others?

LEARNING PLAN

Learning objectives	Learning intentions	Success criteria
6Ld.04 6So.01 6Ug.07	• **Listening:** Understand a range of instructions. • **Speaking:** Express opinions, feelings and reactions. • **Use of English:** Use present perfect forms to express recent, indefinite and unfinished past. • **Vocabulary:** *happy, excited, nervous, angry, interested, scared, win, bully, scratch, awesome, cool, mean, harm, pollution, starve*	• Learners can understand, with support, details of a conversationabout emotional reactions. • Learners can express opinions, feelings and reactions. • Learners can express feelings and reactions using the present perfect (to describe events in the recent past).

21st-century skills

Emotional development: Describe what makes us feel happy, angry or excited.

Materials: Learner's Book pages 11–13; Workbook pages 8–9 and 10–11; blank A4 sheet of paper for each learner for Activity 7

LANGUAGE BACKGROUND

Present perfect

- The **present perfect** tense describes events when the time of the event is not important, or to show a connection between the present and the past.

I've only ever been to the seaside twice in my life. (Unspecified time – focus on the experience, not when.)

CONTINUED

- We use the **past simple** when we are referring to a specific situation in the past, or we mention or speak about the time the action happened.

  The first time I saw the sea was on a school trip. (definite time)

  When did you see the sea for the first time?

- We often use the **present perfect** with *just*, to talk about events in the recent past.

Where have you been?

I've (just) come back from the shop. I've brought some bread for us to eat.

- We use the **present perfect** with *ever* and *never* if we are focusing on a period of time that has not finished. (See Lesson 1.4 and **Photocopiable 2** for this use of the present perfect.)

Have you ever been to Vietnam? No, never.

Common misconceptions

Misconception	How to identify	How to overcome
Learners use the present simple/past simple instead of the present perfect. For example: We ~~became~~ **have become** good friends since then. Next Saturday, I have a day off so I ~~decide~~ **have decided** to go on a picnic. Tomorrow is my birthday. I ~~invite~~ **have invited** all my friends and family.	Write sentences on the board using the present perfect and one other tense. Elicit the different implications of using the two tenses. For example: Present perfect: • We **have become** good friends since then. • **Have** you ever **been** to Vietnam? Past simple: • We **became** good friends after that. • When **did** you go to Vietnam?	Ask concept check questions. For example: • Is there a connection implied between past and present? • Is the focus on the time or the experience? • Or are we more interested in *when* it happened? See Activities 1–3 on pages 10–11 in the Workbook. Use **Photocopiable 2** after Lesson 1.4.

Starter ideas

Have you ever felt …? (10 minutes)

- Write the adjectives from Activity 1 on the board (*happy, excited, nervous, angry, interested, scared*).

- Elicit a model dialogue about one of the adjectives. For example:

  A: Have you ever felt really excited?

  B: Yes, I have.

  A: When?

  B: Last year.

  A: What about?

  B: My holiday to India.

- Discuss which questions and answers are in the past simple and which are in the present perfect.

- In pairs, learners ask and answer questions using the other adjectives.

Getting started (10 minutes)

- Look at the pictures on page 11 and answer question a. Write the names of the activities/events on the board and ask learners how the activities/events make them feel.

- Write the word 'identity' on the board. Build up suggestions about what makes up a person's identity; for example, what we are like, what we are good at/enjoy doing, what makes us happy/sad, etc.

- Check learners understand the expression *make me feel.*

- For question b, elicit and build up a list of ideas from learners about what makes up their identities.

- Check learners understand the meaning of *have in common.* Have a general discussion about what the learners think they have in common and what makes them different.

Answers

a Main image: hands holding a globe showing planet Earth. Left image: boys on a bike ride adventure; central image: boys on a stage performing a play; right image: a family celebration, maybe a birthday. Learner's own answers.

b Learner's own answers. Suggested answers may include: Identity describes features, characteristics and information that make you who you are, and make you an individual who is unique and different from others. Factors that make up your identity can be your name, date of birth, where you live, your nationality, culture, race, religion, physical appearance, likes and dislikes.

c Learner's own answers.

› **Digital Classroom:** Use the video 'How do they feel?' to explore the subject of feelings and identity. The i button will explain how to use the video.

Main teaching ideas

1 How do the photos make you feel? (10 minutes)

- **Emotional development:** Learners work alone and match each photo with the emotion(s) it makes them feel. Make it clear that the aim of the activity is to compare learner's different/ unique feelings and that there aren't any 'right' or 'wrong' answers.

- Learners compare their ideas with a partner.

› **Differentiation ideas:** For learners who need more support with this task, create a sentence starter worksheet or write the sentences on a mini-whiteboard. For example: *My cat makes me feel …*; *I'm happy when …*; *That makes me feel …*; *What about …?* This should also help give them confidence for Activity 7.

Answers

Learner's own answers.

 ### 2 Which pictures do the children talk about? (10 minutes)

- Tell learners they are going to listen to two children talking about the pictures. Elicit predictions about the kinds of things the boys might say about each picture.

- Tell learners to focus on understanding which pictures the children are talking about and which emotions they match with each image.

- If necessary, replay the audio and pause after each speaker.

- Circulate and offer support while learners tell their partners whether the children's ideas are the same or different to their own.

Audioscript: Track 1

See Learner's Book page 12

Boy 1: Let's look at the photos… The cat… mmm. The cat photo makes me feel nervous. It looks like my Grandma's cat. That cat always jumps on me and scratches me!

Boy 2: Really? I love the cat but I love most animals – they make me feel happy. But the picture of the polar bear makes me feel angry. It looks like a photo from a documentary I watched in class. It was about how pollution causes ice to melt in the Arctic and then polar bears can't hunt and eat and then they starve. It was horrible. I get angry when pollution harms wild animals.

Boy 1: Yeah, me too actually… What about this picture? It looks like they're playing Minecraft. I love Minecraft – it's awesome!

Boy 2: I don't play it. Why is it awesome?

Boy 1: Because you can build really cool buildings and whole new worlds! I get excited when I make things on Minecraft. You can make things that you could never make in real life.

Boy 2: Hey, look at that scorpion – that's so cool!

Boy 1: Nooo… That makes me feel scared – once my uncle got bitten by a scorpion in the desert and he had to go to hospital!

Answers

The children talk about images b, c, d and e.
Image b (cat): nervous/happy
Image c (boys playing computer game): excited
Image d (polar bear on melting ice): angry
Image e (scorpion): interested ('that's so cool!'), scared

3 What ideas do the children have in common? Which ones are different? (10 minutes)

- Focus on the examples on page 12 of the Learner's Book and ask more confident speakers to complete the sentences.

- Circulate and offer support while learners make similar sentences with a partner about what ideas the children have in common and which are different.

- Give class feedback and build up sentences on the board for less confident speakers to refer to.

Answers

In common: Both boys get angry when they look at the polar bear photo because the ice is melting around it, causing it problems with hunting and eating.
Different:
- The cat makes Boy 1 feel scared (because his grandma's cat scratches him) but makes Boy 2 feel happy because he loves most animals.
- Boy 1 feels excited when he looks at the photo of the boys playing a computer game because it reminds him of playing Minecraft. Boy 2 doesn't know the game.
- Boy 2 is interested in the scorpion photo; he thinks it is 'cool'. However, the photo makes Boy 1 feel scared because his uncle once got bitten by a scorpion and had to go to hospital.

4 Listen to the children's teacher describe the Connections game. (5–10 minutes)

- Tell learners they are going to play a game called the Connections game. They will need a blank sheet of paper and a pencil to play it. Encourage predictions about what the game may involve and what its purpose could be.

- Learners listen to the teacher to check their predictions.

Audioscript: Track 2

See Learner's Book page 13

Teacher: Listen everyone. We're going to play the Connections game! First, you take a piece of paper and divide it into six parts. Then, in each part, I

want you to draw something or write a word that you connect with one of the emotions: happy, excited, nervous, angry, interested, scared. We are going to find out what connects us. Look at my example here … I have drawn a car. Why do you think I've drawn … [fade out]

Answers

To play the game: Divide a piece of paper into six parts. Draw something or write a word that you connect with one of these emotions: happy, excited, nervous, angry, interested or scared.
Purpose of the game: To find out things that connect us through our feelings and emotions.

5 Listen to two students discussing their words. (5–10 minutes)

- Read the sentences before listening to the recording.

- Learners listen to the conversation and complete their questions they hear.

- If learners need extra support, listen again for two ideas the children have in common.

Audioscript: Track 3

See Learner's Book page 13

Boy 1:   Have you finished yet?

Boy 2:   Yes, I have. Let's have a look at yours … Oh look, we've both drawn a football. Why have you drawn a football?

Boy 1:   Because I really like watching football with my dad. I love it when we go to watch games. I get really excited with the big crowds and the chanting. What about you?

Boy 2:   Yeah, I like watching football too, but I prefer playing it. I get nervous before a match, but I feel really happy when we win. Why have you written 'mean'?

Boy 1:   Because mean people make me angry. You know, mean kids who bully other kids.

Boy 2:   Yeah, me too. I've written 'bully' – that's similar to yours …

Answers
Completed questions and answers (in brackets):

a *Have* you finished yet? (Yes, he has.)

b Why have you *drawn* a football? (Because he likes watching football with his dad.)

c Why *have* you *written* 'mean'? (Because mean people make him angry.)

Two ideas in common: both children have drawn a football because they like watching and playing football; both have written 'mean' and 'bully' because mean people make them angry.

> **Digital Classroom:** Use the activity 'Present perfect – talking about the past' to reinforce the use of the present perfect in questions. The i button will explain how to use the activity.

Use of English – Present perfect (5–10 minutes)

- Write sentences on the board from the audio that use the present perfect, for example:

  I have drawn a car. Why do you think I've drawn …?

  Have you finished yet?

  Yes, I have. We've both drawn a football. Why have you drawn a football?

- Ask concept-check questions such as: *What is the focus of the sentences? Is it a) they have drawn a football or b) the fact that it is a finished action?*

- Elicit that the focus is on the fact *they have drawn a football* and the time is not important.

- Explain what the present perfect tense is and when learners might use it.

Workbook

For further practice, please see Activities 1–3 on pages 10–11 in the Workbook.

---

6 Look at these words from the children's conversations. Which words are positive and which are negative? How do you know? (10 minutes)

- Demonstrate the activity. Focus on the first word (*win*) and see if learners can remember where it was in the conversation. Elicit the meaning of the word and whether it is positive or negative. Briefly discuss why we know it's a positive word (we associate positive feelings with it).

- If necessary, repeat with other words until you are satisfied that learners understand the activity.

- Learners work with a partner and do the same for the other words.

> **Differentiation ideas:** If some learners need more support with this task, download the audioscript. Working in small groups, show each word in context and check learners understand its meaning. Then answer the questions as a group.

- Give class feedback on the correct answers.

Answers
Suggested answers:
Positive: win, awesome, cool
Negative: bully, scratch, mean, harm, pollution, starve
We think of words as positive or negative according to the ideas and feelings that we associate with them. Those feelings usually come from our experiences or prior knowledge of something.

---

7 Play the Connections game! (10–15 minutes)

- Tell learners it's now their turn to play the Connections game.

- Distribute a blank sheet of A4 paper to each learner.

- Circulate and offer support as learners follow the instructions on page 13 of the Learner's Book to play the game.

> **Differentiation ideas:** Challenge learners by asking them to write two or three words in each part.

Answers
Learner's own answers.

Plenary ideas

Reflection (5 minutes)

- In groups, learners reflect on what they have learned in the lesson about identity and things they have in common with their partners. Did anything surprise them?

- Ask them to share their ideas and write some notes on the board.

Homework ideas

- Learners choose two emotions and write about what makes them feel these emotions.

> **Assessment ideas:** As a class, write a short checklist so that learners can self-assess their homework before handing it in. For example: Have I used the new vocabulary from the lesson? Have I used the correct tense? Have I checked my spelling?

Workbook

Learners do Activities 1–4 on pages 8–9.

1.2 Geography: Where in the world am I?

LEARNING PLAN

Learning objectives	Learning intentions	Success criteria
6Rd.03	• **Reading:** Understand, with support, most of the detail of an argument in short and extended texts.	• Learners can understand, with support, specific information in a text about finding locations on a world map.
6Uv.02	• **Use of English:** Use an increasing range of prepositions preceding nouns and adjectives in prepositional phrases.	• Learners can write coordinates and interesting information about places on the map, using phrases with prepositions before nouns.
	• **Vocabulary:** *street, district, town, city, county, province, country, continent, global, international, national, local, North Pole, the equator, latitude, longitude, South Pole*	

21st-century skills

Cross-curricular link: Geography: Learners discuss cities, continents, lines of longitude and latitude, and poles.

Materials: Learner's Book pages 14–15; Workbook pages 10–11; a national map of your country/state; **Photocopiable 1**

Common misconceptions

Misconception	How to identify	How to overcome
Learners often use the wrong preposition. Below are two common examples: • They use of + *origin* instead of from + origin. For example: *They can provide us with food **of from** any part of the world.* • They wrongly use *the same with* instead of *the same as*. For example: *She is the same age **with as** me.*	Make a list on the board of typical mistakes learners of this level make when speaking or writing.	Create a worksheet consisting of sentences containing problematic prepositions. Leave a gap for the preposition and get learners to fill it in.

Starter ideas

Quiz (10 minutes)

- Interest learners in the subject of the lesson by preparing a short quiz. Try to pre-teach as many words from the lesson (see Vocabulary box) as possible.

> ### CROSS-CURRICULAR LINKS
>
> Geography: Here are some question examples for a short quiz to interest learners in the subject:
>
> - *Is London an example of a town, city or county?* (city)
> - *Is Asia an example of a continent or district?* (continent)
> - *Do longitude lines run horizontally or vertically from the North Pole to the South Pole?* (vertically)
> - *What are the most northern and southern points of the Earth called? Bars or poles?* (poles)

Main teaching ideas

1 Where is your place in the world? (10 minutes)

- Discuss how we know where we are in the world, and why it is important.
- Focus on the envelope and elicit the meaning of the words in the boxes. Point out that not all addresses have a district, especially if the address is in a town or village and not a city. The district can often be omitted in city addresses too.
- Allow learners time to match the words to the lines of the address in pairs.
- Give feedback and then help learners to match the words to the lines of their own address.

Answers

31 New Street – street; *Fenton* – district; *York* – town/city; *North Yorkshire* – county; *UK* – country; *Europe* – continent.
Learner's own answers.

2 Where do you live on a local, national, international and global scale? (10 minutes)

- The Planet Earth text used in this lesson is very challenging and extends beyond the level of the Cambridge Primary English as a Second Language curriculum framework.
- Elicit which part of where learners live is considered *local* and what is considered *national* and *international*.
- Look together at the world map and identify the names of the seven continents. Then challenge learners to point to their country on the world map.
- Ask: *Do longitude lines run horizontally or vertically from the North Pole to the South Pole?* (vertically)
- Point out the latitude and longitude lines and encourage learners to see their importance in pinpointing exact locations.

Answers

Local: street/district/town/city. Learner's own answers.
National: Learner's own answers.
International: Learner's own answers.
Global: The seven continents are Africa, Antarctica, Asia, Australia, Europe, North America, South America. Learner's own answers.

3 How do you pinpoint exact locations on a world map? Read and listen to the text. Label the Earth. (5–10 minutes)

- Build on Activity 2 by reminding learners that it's important to have a way of finding exact locations on a map (using latitude and longitude lines).
- Tell learners that they are going to read and listen to an *infographic* text – an information text that accompanies a visual and is usually quite brief. In this case, the visual is the world map on page 15 of the Learner's Book. If possible, project or pin up a large-scale version of the map that learners can interact with.
- Read and listen to the infographic text (on page 15 of the Learner's Book).

- Ask learners to tell the class what they remember from the text.

- Then invite learners to work in pairs and small groups to label the map with the equator, South Pole, longitude and latitude.

> **Differentiation ideas:** If learners need support with this task, give them the four labels with definitions to help them work out where each label goes.

- Replay the recording, or alternatively ask readers to read the text out loud, pausing if necessary to give learners the chance to complete the map.

Audioscript: Track 4

See Learner's Book page 14

Answers
Learner's own answers.

4 Read the text again and look at the world cities on the map. Match each city to a coordinate. Which countries are the cities in? (5–10 minutes)

- Read the text again together. Focus on the last two paragraphs and, if necessary, explain what a coordinate is.

- Ask learners to make a note of the countries the cities are in.

> **Differentiation ideas:** If learners need more support with this task, work with them in a smaller group. Demonstrate how to match the first city to a coordinate and then ask them to try. Supporting learners with this task will help them with Activities 5 and 7.

CROSS-CURRICULAR LINKS

Geography: Challenge learners to name two other cities in each country and write their coordinates.

Answers
a Bangkok (Thailand)
b Sydney (Australia)
c Istanbul (Turkey)
d Rio de Janeiro (Brazil)

Key words: map-reading (5 minutes)

- Ask learners to close their books. Write the five words on the board then read the definitions.

- Encourage learners to match each word to a definition.

- Learners open their books and see how many they knew/guessed correctly. Discuss any definitions that learners find difficult to understand.

Use of English – Prepositions before nouns (5–10 minutes)

- Elicit why propositions are used in a sentence.

- Build up a list of prepositions that learners know on the board.

Workbook

See also Activities 1–3 on pages 12–13 in the Workbook.

- Ask learners to complete **Photocopiable 1**.

> **Digital Classroom:** Use the activity 'Prepositions before nouns' to revise prepositions before nouns. The i button will explain how to use the activity.

5 Read the Use of English box. Find other examples of prepositions before nouns in the text (5–10 minutes)

- Learners work individually to find ten examples of prepositions before nouns in the reading text.

> **Differentiation ideas:** If learners need more support with this task, ask them to find five examples. Extend the activity by asking more confident learners to find two more examples.

Answers
Other examples include: of places, At one end, In the middle, in degrees, to the south, from the North Pole, to the South Pole, of an orange, in degrees, to the east, to the west, between the lines

6 **Work in small groups. Find your town or city on the world map. Find the nearest lines of latitude and longitude. (10–15 minutes)**

- Check learners know the meaning of *famous buildings*, *mountain ranges* and *volcanoes*.

- Learners then find three interesting places with the same latitude and three with the same longitude as their town/city. Tell them to look not only for cities but also for famous buildings, mountain ranges and volcanoes.

- Check learners have found their six places. Encourage them to use prepositional phrases in their sentences when they write their interesting information. Circulate and offer support.

〉 **Differentiation ideas:** Learners could work on the activity in multi-ability groups. Learners who are more confident with this task can provide support with writing coordinates and using prepositional phrases.

〉 **Assessment ideas:** When learners have finished writing their sentences, ask them to exchange them with another group. They give each other feedback on their use of prepositional phrases and how well they communicate their ideas.

Answers
Learner's own answers.

Plenary ideas

What can you remember? (5–10 minutes)

- Ask learners what they have enjoyed about the lesson and what they have found challenging. Ask if they enjoyed learning about longitude and latitude and using coordinates to find their town/city.

Homework ideas

Using an atlas, website (under adult supervision) or globe, learners find the locations of three more places and make a mini-quiz for their friends. They should include the co-ordinate and an interesting fact about each place.

Workbook
Learners do Activities 1–3 on pages 10–11.

1.3 Talk about it: Inspiring people

LEARNING PLAN

Learning objectives	Learning intentions	Success criteria
6Sc.02, 6Sc.06	• **Speaking:** Describe people, places and objects, and routine past and present actions and events; begin to produce and maintain stretches of language comprehensibly, allowing for hesitation and reformulation, especially in longer stretches of free production.	• Learners can deliver a presentation, describing a person they admire, describing past and present actions and using sequencing words and phrases.
6Sc.05	• **Speaking:** Pronounce familiar words and phrases clearly; begin to use intonation and place stress at word, phrase and sentence level appropriately.	• Learners can pronounce familiar words ending in: -*tion* and -*sion*.
6Sor.01	• **Speaking:** Link sentences using an increased range of connectives. • **Vocabulary:** *admire, media, protest, activist, campaign, ban*	• Learners can link sentences using an increased range of connectives.

21st-century skills

Communication: Give a presentation about someone we admire.

Materials: Learner's Book pages 16–17; Workbook pages 12–13; pictures of inspiring people that learners could write about; internet access to research the presentation

Starter ideas

Different heroes (10 minutes)

- Tell learners that this lesson is about people who are inspiring.

- Show pictures of people that learners could write their presentation about, for example cultural icons (past and present), sports stars, people in entertainment. Make sure these are people who have done admirable things such as charity work, rather than just being famous.

- Ask learners to name the people and tell you something about what they have achieved. Establish that these are all people who have done good things and that we call them *heroes* or *idols*.

Main teaching ideas

1   **Do you have a hero? Who do you admire and why? Look at the photo of Malala Yousafzai. What do you know about her? Why is she famous? (5–10 minutes)**

- Circulate and offer support while learners tell a partner about a person they admire and explain why they admire him/her.

- Elicit and build up a list of things that learners know about Malala Yousafzai. Don't worry if your learners don't know much – guide them by asking questions. Elicit/pre-teach words from the text, e.g. *(famous) activist, campaigns for girls' education, the right (to go to school), attacked for her beliefs* and *supporters.*

- Make sure learners know that Malala is an *activist for girls' education* and they understand what this means.

Answers

Learner's own answers.

Sample answer: Malala Yousafzai is famous for her international work supporting girls' education worldwide. She has been an activist in her native country of Pakistan since she was 11 years old. When she was 15, she was attacked by a Taliban gunman for protesting against the Taliban's ban on girls' education in Pakistan.

Answers

Aliya asks her audience a question and gives them information to listen out for. This gives them a reason to listen: they have to reply and this makes sure they are listening to her.

2 **Listen to Part 1 of Aliya's presentation about Malala Yousafzai. (5–10 minutes)**

- Before listening to Part 1 of Aliya's presentation about Malala Yousafzai, encourage predictions about how she will make her audience want to listen to her presentation.

- Play the audio for learners to check their predictions.

Audioscript: Track 5

See Learner's Book page 16

Aliya:	Good morning everyone. Today I'm going to talk about a famous person that I admire. But first, I want you all to guess who it is. Here are some clues:
	Did you know that … there are more than 130 million girls in the world who can't go to school?
	This person is a famous activist, who campaigns for girls' education.
	She believes that every girl in the world has the right to go to school.
	She was attacked for her beliefs and nearly died; but she recovered and carried on fighting for girls' education.
	She is now world famous. She has many famous supporters too, including the former US president, Barack Obama.
Classmate:	I know! It's Malala.
Aliya:	Yes, that's right!

3 **Listen to Part 2 of Aliya's presentation. Answer the questions. (5–10 minutes)**

- Before listening to the presentation, read the four questions and elicit predictions.

- Make clear to learners that they just need to listen out for the answers to the four questions; they do not need to understand every word.

- Play the recording and ask learners to answer questions a–d.

- If necessary, replay the recording, pausing after the information that is relevant to each question.

> **Differentiation ideas:** Challenge more confident learners to add more detail to their answers for questions b and d.

- Give class feedback on the correct answers.

Audioscript: Track 6

See Learner's Book page 16

Aliya:	So today I'm going to talk about Malala Yousafzai. As I said in my introduction, she is a famous activist for girls' education. Malala was born in a village in Pakistan in 1997. Her father was a teacher and Malala loved going to school. Malala's father believed strongly that all girls should have an education. But when Malala was 11 years old, her village was invaded by a group called the Taliban. They took control and banned all the girls from going to school.
	Malala and her father were angry about this decision and they protested against it. Malala wrote a blog, using a false name, about how much she wanted to go back to school. She talked to the media and even made a documentary with an American journalist. Because of this, people guessed that she was also the blogger. She became well-known in

Pakistan and abroad for supporting girls' education. By this time, she was still only 13 years old!

When Malala was 15, she was shot by a Taliban soldier on her way home from school. The Taliban were angry about her speaking against their rules. She was very badly hurt but she survived the attack. She was taken to hospital in Pakistan, and then to England. She slowly recovered and her family moved to England to live. This terrible event made more people all over the world support her campaign for girls' education.

It took months and months for Malala to recover. But she was determined to carry on her fight. Since then, with her father, she created the Malala Fund, to help every girl go to school and have opportunities. In 2014, when she was only 17, she became the youngest person ever to win the Nobel Peace Prize. This is a very important award for people who have done great things to help other people.

Answers

a   Malala's father

b   She protested against it. (Extension: She wrote a blog, talked to the media and made a documentary with an American journalist.)

c   She was shot by a Taliban soldier because the Taliban were angry about her protests (speaking against their rules).

d   Malala carried on her fight (after she recovered from the attack). (Extension: she created an organization called the Malala Fund, which supports girls' education projects worldwide).

---

4   **Listen to Part 3 of Aliya's presentation. Why does she admire Malala? How does she finish her presentation? (5–10 minutes)**

•   Before listening, elicit that we normally sum up what we have already spoken about.

•   Play the audio to see if this is what Aliya does to finish her presentation and for learners to find out why Aliya admires Malala.

•   Challenge learners to explain why Aliya thinks Malala is brave.

Audioscript: Track 7

See Learner's Book page 16

Aliya: To sum up, I chose to talk about Malala because I think she is very brave. She stood up for what she believed in, even though it was very dangerous and people tried to stop her. I admire her because she has done so much to support other girls. She understands that it is very important for all girls to have an education. We are the future!

To finish my presentation, I'm going to show you a video of one of Malala's projects …

Answers

Aliya admires Malala because she thinks she is very brave (Extension: because she stood up for what she believed in despite the dangers) and she has done so much to support girls' education.

She finishes the presentation with a video about one of Malala's projects.

---

5   **Listen to Parts 1–3 again. Match the three parts with the headings below. (10–15 minutes)**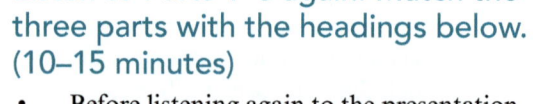

•   Before listening again to the presentation, read the three headings and elicit ideas from learners about which headings go with the three parts.

•   Replay the recording and check.

- Then have a brief discussion about what learners thought of the presentation. Did it work well? Would they do anything differently? What questions would they ask the presenter?

> **Differentiation ideas:** Learners complete Differentiated worksheet 1A, B or C.

Audioscript: Track 8

See Learner's Book page 16

(Tracks 5–7 combined)

Answers
a Part 2   b Part 3   c Part 1

6 Match words from the presentation to their definitions. (5–10 minutes)

- Read the words together and check learners know the correct pronunciation.
- Focus on the first word *admire*, and read the definitions.
- Elicit that the correct definition is number 2.
- Circulate and offer support while learners match words from the presentation to their definitions.

Answers
a activist   d media
b admire   e protest
c ban   f campaign

7 Listen and repeat the *-tion/-sion* words from the presentation. What sound do you hear at the end of the words? (5 minutes)

- Play the recording and encourage learners to repeat the *-tion/-sion* words.
- Elicit the correct sound at the end of the words.

Audioscript: Track 9

See Learner's Book page 17

Speaking tip and 8 Word study (5–10 minutes)

- Write examples of *sequencing words* on the board, like the ones in the answers. Elicit that we use these expressions to help our audience follow our presentations.
- Focus on the phrases in the Learner's Book and elicit their meaning.
- Learners discuss in pairs when the phrases in the Speaking tip are used.
- Give class feedback on the answers.

Answers
a Today I'm going to talk about …
b As I said in my introduction …, By this time …, Since then …
c To sum up …

> **Digital Classroom:** Use the video 'Giving a class presentation' to support learners in preparing and delivering a presentation. The i button will explain how to use the video.

9 Prepare a presentation about someone you admire. (30 minutes + time for learners to present their presentations)

- **Communication:** Learners prepare a presentation about someone they admire, using what they have learned from Aliya's presentation to help them.
- Make sure all the learners have decided on a person to write their presentations about.
- Support learners as they research interesting facts about the person and make notes. If using the internet in class is not practical, take learners to the library or you could provide a choice of texts for learners to research from.
- Once learners have done their research, circulate and offer support while they organise their notes into sections. Encourage them to use the headings in Activity 5 to help them.
- Offer support with adding sequencing words and thinking of a way to get the attention of their audience at the beginning.
- Allow time for learners to practise their presentations with a partner. Circulate and offer practical suggestions about pace and pronunciation.

• Learners perform their presentations to the class.

> **Assessment ideas:** To help ensure that learners listen attentively to their classmates' presentations, invite them to write down a question to ask each presenter at the end and one interesting fact from each presentation.

Plenary ideas

Consolidation (10–15 minutes)

• Choose one learner to ask a question after each presentation.

> **Assessment ideas:** Provide verbal feedback to learners on their pronunciation, use of sequencing words and ability to link sentences using an increased range of connectives.

Homework ideas

If lesson time is limited, the research could be set as homework and the presentations done in the next lesson.

Workbook

Learners do Activities 1–3 on pages 12–13.

1.4 Write about it: A first time for everything

LEARNING PLAN		
Learning objectives	**Learning intentions**	**Success criteria**
6Wca.03 6Ug.07	• **Writing/Use of English:** Plan, write, edit and proofread short texts, with little or no support; use present perfect forms to express recent, indefinite and unfinished past.	• Learners can plan, write, edit and proofread a short description of a first-time experience, using the present perfect for experiences.
6Rm.01	• **Reading:** Understand, with support, most of the main points of short and extended texts.	• Learners can understand the main points of short descriptions of first-time experiences.
6Us.07	• **Use of English:** Use the patterns verb + object + infinitive (e.g. *have something to do*) and *give/take/send/bring/show* + direct/indirect object; present perfect with 'Have you ever ...?'.	• Learners can use the patterns verb + object + infinitive and *give/take/send/bring/show* + direct/indirect object.
	• **Vocabulary:** *amazement/amazing, beauty/beautiful, terror/terrifying, pride/proud, bravery/brave, excitement/excited, satisfaction/satisfied*	
21st-century skills		
Creative thinking: Explore why an experience was special.		

Materials: Learner's Book pages 18–19; Workbook pages 14–15; Unit 1 sample answer; **Photocopiables 2 and 3, Differentiated worksheets 1A, B and C**

Starter ideas

A time I felt satisfied/proud *and* Something I achieved (10 minutes)

- Write these prompts on the board and check learners know what they mean.

- Elicit achievements like *learning to swim, speaking in front of the class, speaking English for the first time.*

- Ask a couple of learners to explain why they are proud of their achievements. For example: *I was afraid of the water, so I felt satisfied when I learned to swim. Going on a roller-coaster for the first time was an achievement because I was afraid!*

Main teaching ideas

1 Have you done anything recently you have never done before? How did the experience make you feel? (10 minutes)

- Focus on the first question in the rubric. Elicit that this is the present perfect tense, which is used to express an experience at an unspecified time. Elicit that the second question is in the past simple, which is used to refer to a specific (singular) experience.

- Learners answer the questions in pairs or small groups.

> **Differentiation ideas:** Support less confident speakers by giving them a worksheet with some sentence starters, or by writing them on a mini-whiteboard. Make sure there are present prefect and past simple sentences and elicit why each tense is used. For example: *Recently, I have… ; Learning to…. made me feel…; I enjoyed/didn't enjoy…; Last week/year I tried* [verb]+*ing.*

Answers
Learner's own answers.

2 These children are describing a first-time experience. Find key words to describe what each child did, why it was special and their feelings about the experience. (10 minutes)

- Explain that it is not always necessary to understand and translate every word of a text, but it is useful to identify key words. Check that learners understand that key words show the main information in the text.

- Read the Activity 2 rubric and look at the pictures. Before reading, encourage learners to make predictions about what the key words might be.

- Learners check their predictions – ask them to skim the text for key words to describe what each child did, why it was special and their feelings about the experience. Then tell learners to compare their ideas with a partner.

- Focus on specific sentences and check learners understand which words are the key words.

> **Differentiation ideas:** If learners need support with this task, work with them in a smaller group while the other learners complete the main task. Write the key words for Olivia's experience on the board and ask learners to find them in the text. Ask learners how they would feel doing the activities in the pictures and then elicit the adjectives in the text. Elicit the nouns that go with the adjectives, e.g. *excitement* and *pride*. This should help learners with the next activity.

Answers
Suggested answers:
Olivia – first time / sea / school trip / amazement / beautiful / huge
Santok – rollercoaster / scared / exciting / terrifying / sense of pride
Cody – proud / learned to swim / excitement / six / fear of water / satisfied

3 **Copy and complete the table with adjectives and nouns from the descriptions. Then talk about an experience or feeling you've had. (10–15 minutes)**

- Ask a learner to explain what adjectives and nouns are and to give an example of each one.

- Look at the first adjective together and elicit the noun 'amazement'. Then ask learners to copy and complete the table.

- Circulate and support learners.

> **Differentiation ideas:** If learners need support with this task, give them a list of the missing nouns and adjectives, with a few distractors, so it becomes a matching activity.

- When you have given class feedback on the correct answers, learners talk to a partner about an experience or feeling they've had using the words in the table.

> **Assessment ideas:** While learners are talking in pairs, circulate and check their pronunciation and the use of the adjectives and nouns in the table.

Answers

Nouns: amazement, pride, excitement
Adjectives: beautiful, terrified, brave, satisfied

> **Digital Classroom:** Use the activity 'Noun or adjective?' to revise nouns and adjectives. The i button will explain how to use the activity.

> **Digital Classroom:** Use the slideshow 'First-time experiences' to give learners ideas for talking about an experience or feeling they've had. The i button will explain how to use the slideshow.

4 **Match questions a–c to the children's answers in Activity 2. Then ask and answer the questions with your partner. (10 minutes)**

- Circulate and offer support while learners do the matching activity in pairs. Give class feedback on the answers.

- Circulate and offer support while learners ask and answer the questions with a partner. Give class feedback on common errors.

Answers
a descriptions 2 and 3, b description 1,
c descriptions 2 and 3

Language focus – Verb patterns (5–10 minutes)

- Read the Language focus box together. Identify what function the components have in each clause and the order they are in.

- Build up a list of examples on the board.

> **Digital Classroom:** Use the grammar presentation 'Verb patterns' to revise the patterns verb + object + infinitive (e.g. *have something to do*) and *give/take/send/bring/show* + direct/indirect object. The i button will explain how to use the grammar presentation.

5 **Look in description 3 in Activity 2. Can you find another example of the verb pattern *verb + object + infinitive (with to)*? (5 minutes)**

- As a class, look for another example in description 3 (Cody, 12).

- Circulate and offer support while learners practise this verb pattern in pairs, using other family members and activities. For example: *My mum/sister/brother taught me to read/play football*, etc.

Answers
My dad taught me to swim …

6 **Writing tip and 6 Write a description of a first-time experience (20–30 minutes)**

- Make sure learners remember what key words are. Read the Writing tip together.

- Ask a learner to explain what a verb is and to give a couple of examples.

- **Creative thinking:** Engage learners in the activity – explain that they are going to build on their conversations from Activity 4 and explore in more detail why an experience was special.

- Circulate and offer support while learners write key words about their special experiences. Make sure they have written nouns, verbs and adjectives.

- Continue to offer support while learners use the questions in the Learner's Book to plan their description and build their sentences using their key words.

> **Assessment ideas:** Before beginning Step 2, show learners the answer for Unit 1 without the mark scheme comments. Evaluate the strengths and weaknesses of its organisation, as well as the use of different verb tenses, verbs, adjectives and nouns. Also look at the checklist on **Photocopiable 3**, so that learners know what they are aiming for with their description.

- Allow learners time to complete Step 2.

> **Assessment ideas:** When learners have finished their description, ask them to work through the checklist on **Photocopiable 3** again to self-assess their work. When they have made any updates, ask them to swap the description with a partner. Encourage them to find similarities and differences in their descriptions. Learners then proofread each other's work and circle any errors.

Plenary ideas

Reflection (10 minutes)

- Learners share their thoughts on the writing process they used. Will they use any of the strategies they've looked at in this lesson in their writing from now on? Can they share any other tips that work well for them?

- Discuss what learners enjoyed about writing the descriptions. What were the challenges?

- Learners could complete **Photocopiable 2**.

Homework ideas

Ask learners to write a brief description of a first-time experience of a family member/relative, using the suggestions in Workbook Activity 5.

Workbook

Learners do Activities 1–5 on pages 14–15.

1.5 Read and respond: *A Girl Called Owl*

LEARNING PLAN		
Learning objectives	**Learning intentions**	**Success criteria**
6Rm.01, 6Rm.02	• **Reading:** Understand, with support, most of the main points of short and extended texts. Read independently a range of short, simple fiction and non-fiction texts with confidence and enjoyment. • **Vocabulary:** *swoop, feathers, inherited, whirly, masses, intense, rotate*	• Learners can read and enjoy a story about a girl with an unusual name, understanding the main points.
21st-century skills		
Social responsibilities: Discuss how our differences can be positive.		

Materials: Learner's Book pages 20–23; Workbook pages 16–17

Starter ideas

Names (5–10 minutes)

- Explain that the story learners are going to read is about a girl with an unusual name. Have a general discussion about names that are popular in learner's countries.

- Then introduce some popular British names with an obvious meaning; for example Grace, Violet, Hope, Rose, Daisy, Robin, Hunter, Patience. Ask learners if they know what they mean in their language. Are they boys' or girls' names?

Main teaching ideas

1 What do you think about your name? (5–10 minutes)

- Learners work in groups of 3–4 and talk about whether they like their name, if their name has a special meaning and if there any special reasons why they were given their name.

- Circulate and offer support.

- Ask a learner from each group to tell the class something interesting about a group member's name.

2 Read and listen to Parts 1 and 2 of the story. What is the girl's name? What does her name mean? Are the sentences that follow each section true or false? (10 minutes)

- Focus on the pictures and the title. Then read and listen to Parts 1 and 2 of the story. Check learners understand the meaning of *sketching* and *paying attention*.

- Ask learners what the girl's name is and what her name means.

- Read the ten sentences together. Check learners understand them and ask if they can remember if any of the sentences are true or false without looking at the text.

- Make it clear that it is not necessary for learners to understand every word of the text at this stage. Learners reread the text in small groups and decide if the sentences are true or false.

> **Differentiation ideas:** Learners could work on the activity in multi-ability groups. More confident readers could point out where relevant information is to work out whether the sentences are true or false.

- Give class feedback – make sure that learners are clear which sentences are true and false in preparation for the next activity.

Audioscript: Track 10

See Learner's Book pages 20–22

Answers

The girl's name is Owl. An owl is a type of bird (a bird of prey).

a False, b True, c False, d True, e True, f False, g True, h False, i False, j True

> **Digital Classroom:** Use the activity 'A Girl Called Owl' to reinforce comprehension of the story from the Learner's Book. The i button will explain how to use the activity.

3 Work in pairs. Can you correct the false sentences? (10 minutes)

- Circulate and offer support while learners correct the false sentences in pairs.

> **Differentiation ideas:** Learners could focus on changing two or three of the five false sentences.

- Give class feedback.

Answers

a Owl doesn't like her name.

c She has the same shaped nose as her mum.

f She finds it annoying that her friends like her mum.

h Her mum loves her drawings.

i Mallory thinks Owl should change and draw another type of bird.

Reading tip and 4 Answer the questions. Find sentences in the story to support your answers. (10 minutes)

- Write the verb 'infer' on the board and check learners understand what it means. Then read the Reading tip together. This is beyond the requirements of the Cambridge Primary English as a Second Language curriculum framework.

- Demonstrate Activity 4. Make it clear to learners that these are inference questions. Read the first question and ask learners to find the part of the text where the information is given. Discuss possible answers together.

- Circulate and offer support while learners answer the questions and look for the sentences in the story to support their answers.

> **Differentiation ideas:** Learners could just focus on underlining the relevant sentences in the story. Extend the activity by asking learners to write at least two sentences for each answer.

- Give class feedback on the answers.

Answers

Sample answers:

a The story infers that Owl thinks the other children's questions are silly and annoying ('I like owls. I think they're beautiful, but you know, my head doesn't rotate 360 degrees. I can't fly. I don't hunt at night. All these are questions the other kids have asked me, over the years.')

b No, not always. The story infers that Owl gets annoyed because her mum doesn't seem to understand how her unusual name can make her feel embarrassed (e.g. about other children's questions) ('All these are questions the other kids have asked me, over the years. Mum laughs when I tell her.') At other times, Owl doesn't want to join in when her mum is having fun, even if she wants to laugh too ('… when she laughs, it's difficult not to join in. I do try my very best not to join in.') Owl also says that she gets annoyed because her friends love her mum ('My friends love her. Which is annoying.') The last two points imply that Owl resents her mum in some ways, even though she loves her.

c She tells us that she draws owls all the time ('I draw them, over and over'), in many different forms ('Little ones, big ones, owls with crazy whirly eyes, owls swooping down from the sky'). Her school books and bedroom are full of owl pictures ('They're in all the borders of my lined school books. They're on Post-it notes around my bedroom. I have sketches of them, paintings, even little clay figures.') For another person, the effect could be quite disturbing ('Actually, if you walked into my bedroom, you'd probably run back out again, screaming. They're a bit intense.')

d The story infers that her name is something that Owl thinks about a lot. She seems interested to know why she is called 'Owl' ('And there had to be a reason. A reason Mum called me Owl.'); during her life, there has been a lot of interest about her name from other children.

5 **Work out the meaning of the words in blue in the story by looking at other words in the sentence. Then match them to the definitions. (10 minutes)**

- Focus on the first blue word, *feathers*.
- Read the other words around it in the story and elicit that *feathers* is a noun.
- Read through the definitions and elicit which of them refer to a noun. This eliminates a, c and g, which refer to verbs, and e, which refers to a quantity expression.
- Focus on the remaining definitions (b, d and f). Reread the sentence containing the word *feathers* and elicit that the correct answer is b.
- Circulate and offer support as learners match the remaining definitions.
- Give class feedback on the correct answers.

Answers

a	swooping	e	masses
b	feathers	f	intense
c	inherited	g	rotate
d	whirly		

6 **Talk about the questions in groups. (10 minutes)**

- Circulate and support learners while they discuss the two questions in groups.

› **Differentiation ideas:** Provide less confident speakers with a prompt sheet, or write the prompts on a mini-whiteboard. For example, for question 2 you could include: *Maybe she …, She might have … .*

- After a few minutes, ask one learner from each group to share their answers with the class.

Answers

Learner's own answers.

7 **Values: Accepting our differences. (5 minutes)**

- Check that learners know the meaning of 'stand out from the crowd'.
- **Social responsibilities:** Discuss how our differences can be a good thing by eliciting positive reasons for and consequences of

'standing out from the crowd'. Possible advice is that people won't forget Owl's name/it is memorable; when people say her name, she knows they are referring to her. Encourage learners to share their ideas.

Answers
Learner's own answers

8 In what ways can we feel different to other people? How can this be a good thing? (10–20 minutes)

- As a class, create a mind map about the ways in which people can feel different to others. Examples may include different abilities, races, religions, etc. Remember to be sensitive to your learners.

- Next, brainstorm positive things that everyone has in common and needs, despite their differences Ask: *What things do we all have in common? What things do we all want and need?* Examples could include love, kindness, friends, to have fun, to share things, to be included, to do activities together etc.

- Finally, discuss why difference is important. Elicit and build up a list of advantages, and think about the disadvantages if we were all the same. Guide the discussion to show learners how accepting each other's differences, and focusing on what we have in common, helps us to understand each other better and live together more happily and peacefully.

Answers
Learner's own answers.

Plenary ideas

Diversity agenda (10 minutes)

- As a class, agree on a diversity agenda. For example:

  We respect people of different colours/abilities/religions.

  We are kind to each other.

  We help each other.

  We have fun together

Homework ideas

- Learners write their own story about someone who feels 'different'.

Workbook

Learners do Activities 1–6 on pages 16–17.

> **Assessment ideas:** Write a short checklist as a class so that learners can self-assess their work before handing it in. For example: *Have I used full sentences? Have I used new vocabulary from the lesson?*

1.6 Project challenge

LEARNING PLAN

Learning objectives	Learning intentions	Success criteria
6Sc.06 6Sc.02	• **Speaking:** Begin to produce and maintain stretches of language comprehensibly, allowing for hesitation and reformulation, especially in longer stages of free production. Describe people, places and objects, and routine past and present actions and events.	• Learners can deliver a presentation about something or someone special to them. • Learners can create a poster describing the history of their first name and present the poster to their class.
6Wca.03 6Sc.01	• **Writing/Speaking:** Plan, write, edit and proofread short texts, with little or no support. Give detailed information about themselves and others.	

21st-century skills

Collaboration: Participate actively in a group project

Materials: Learner's Book pages 24–25; Workbook page 18; access to the internet or to library resources; examples of other learner's work; poster card; Unit 1 project checklist; End of Unit 1 test

Starter ideas

Raise interest in the projects (10–15 minutes)

• Tell learners they are either going to deliver a presentation about something or someone special to them (Project A) or design an 'Our names' poster for their classroom (Project B).

• If possible, raise interest in the projects by showing examples of learner's work on a similar topic.

• In a fun way, revise the unit's new vocabulary from the vocabulary box in each lesson, which learners could use for the challenges. For example, you could make a word search or crossword. Alternatively, write some letters from the words on the board with spaces, or create anagrams and ask the class to guess the words.

Main teaching ideas

Introduce the projects (60 minutes)

• **Collaboration:** Encourage learners to choose one of the projects and then follow the steps for their chosen project. For Project A, learners work individually or with a partner. For Project B, learners work in groups, managing and sharing the tasks in the project.

Project A: A presentation about something or someone special to you

• Make sure each learner has chosen a presentation topic.

• Circulate and offer support while learners research their topics using the internet or library resources. You could provide a choice of texts or websites.

• Read the guidelines in Step 3 together and support learners when they are planning their presentations, helping them out with the vocabulary they need.

• Before learners write their presentations, encourage them to revisit Aliya's presentation from Lesson 1.3 again, and check they have information for all parts of the presentation.

• Learners add photos, videos, drawings or other suitable props to their presentations.

- Finally, learners use Step 3 as a checklist to check they have included everything in their presentation.

- Before learners deliver their presentations, check that those who are working with a classmate have divided the presentation tasks equally.

- Learners deliver their presentations.

> **Assessment ideas:** Learners use the Unit 1 project checklist to evaluate other learner's presentations. Encourage them to complete at least one interesting fact that they learned from the presentation.

Project B: Design an 'Our names' poster for your classroom

- **Collaboration:** Learners participate actively in groups of about four to complete this project.

- Start by reading the options for the first step together. Encourage learners to decide which suggestion to follow and put them into groups.

- Circulate and offer support while learners research their chosen option using the internet or library resources.

- Offer support while learners write their paragraphs. If learners have chosen Option A, check they have found information about the age, history and meaning of their first names. If they have chosen Option B, check they have found the most popular names and written notes about their history.

- Distribute poster card and encourage learners to design bright headings and to add their information from Step 2. Circulate and offer support while learners add the information and decorate their posters.

- Learners check they have included everything on the poster and decide which part of the poster they are going to present.

- Learners present their posters.

> **Assessment ideas:** Learners use the Unit 1 project checklist to evaluate other learner's posters. Encourage them to complete at least one interesting fact that they learned from the poster.

- Display the posters on the wall of your classroom.

Plenary ideas

Reflection (10–15 minutes)

- Ask learners what they enjoyed about their project work.

- As a class, learners discuss what they found most challenging about the projects and whether there is anything they would do differently next time.

> **Workbook**
>
> Learners do Activities 1–12 on page 18.

1.7 What do you know now?

What makes us who we are?

- **Learning to learn:** Learners have the opportunity to reflect and evaluate their own learning success.

- Reintroduce the question from the start of the unit: *What makes us who we are?* Discuss learner's responses to the question now and compare them with their comments at the beginning of the unit. How much has changed?

- Ask learners to work on the tasks in pairs.

- Demonstrate the first two tasks by eliciting example sentences about the adjectives and recent activities using the present perfect correctly (and the past simple where necessary).

- For tasks 3–6, encourage learners to look back through the unit if they can't remember. Circulate and offer support.

- When learners have finished the questions, give class feedback on the answers. Build up a list of interesting sentences for 1 and 2. Vote for the most interesting recent experience in 2.

Answers

1 Learner's own answers.

2 Learner's own answers.

3 Learner's own answers. Sample answer: *Latitude* and *longitude* are lines on the surface of a map

or globe. They tell us exactly where places are in the world. The lines of latitude run horizontally around the world; lines of longitude are vertical.

4 amazement, excitement, terror, beauty, satisfaction, pride

5 Aliya admires Malala because she supports girls' education. She thinks Malala is brave because she spoke out about what she believed in when she was a young girl in Pakistan, and it was dangerous to do this.

6 Owl has white-blond hair that flicks around her face, like feathers. Her eyes are pale brown ('almost yellow') and her nose is shaped a little like a bird's beak.

Look what I can do!

• There are seven 'can do' statements. Learners read through the statements and tick the things they can do. Encourage them to reflect on how well they can do these things. Also invite them to think of ways they can improve further, for example what strategies they can use or learn to use.

• If learners find it challenging to read the statements, look through the unit with them and support them to find the relevant information.

• Finally, ask learners to work through the questions on page 19 of the Workbook. Encourage them to talk about what they enjoyed and also about any further support they might need.

> 2 Sport

Unit plan

Lesson	Approximate number of learning hours	Outline of learning content	Learning objectives	Resources
1 What can we get from sport?	2.0–2.5	Talk about different types of sport.	6Lm.01 6Sc.03	Learner's Book Lesson 2.1 Workbook Lesson 2.1 **Digital Classroom:** video – Sports; activity – Sports and sports equipment
2 Eat for strength and energy!	1.5–2.0	Find out how food helps us to do sport.	6Rd.01 6Ug.09	Learner's Book Lesson 2.2 Workbook Lesson 2.2 ⬇ Photocopiable 4 **Digital Classroom:** slideshow – Thinking drinks!; grammar presentation – Conditional 1
3 Ready to go!	1.5–2.0	Give instructions for sports exercises using modal verbs.	6Sc.04 6Ug.12 6Ld.01 6Wc.01	Learner's Book Lesson 2.3 Workbook Lesson 2.3 ⬇ Photocopiable 5 **Digital Classroom:** activity – Parts of the body; animation – Warm-up exercises; activity – Should, need or mustn't?
4 Our favourite sports stars	2.0–2.5	Write a biography about a sports star.	6Wc.02	Learner's Book Lesson 2.4 Workbook Lesson 2.4 ⬇ Photocopiable 6 ⬇ Unit 2 sample answer **Digital Classroom:** activity – High flyer!
5 An extract from *Off Side*	2.0–2.5	Read and enjoy a story about a football match.	6Rm.02 6Sc.05	Learner's Book Lesson 2.5 Workbook Lesson 2.5 ⬇ Differentiated worksheet 2A, B & C **Digital Classroom:** video – Be a sports commentator; activity – Football words
6 Project challenge	1.0–1.5	Project A: Make a poster about a type of sport. Project B: Create a description of a sports event	6Wca.03 6Wc.01 6Wca.04 6Ug.09 6Ug.12 6Sc.02 6Sc.05	Learner's Book Lesson 2.6 Workbook Lesson 2.6 ⬇ Unit 2 project checklists

(continued)

Cross-unit resources

⬇ Unit 2 Audioscripts
⬇ End of Unit 2 test
⬇ Unit 2 Progress report
⬇ Unit 2 Wordlist

BACKGROUND KNOWLEDGE

In Unit 2, learners explore the topic of sport. They look at different types of sport, how food can help with sport, and they give instructions for exercises using modal verbs. They read a biography of a gymnast and a story about a football match.

In Lesson 2.1, there is a link to maths when learners are asked to look at a bar chart and then create their own. Bar charts are also known as bar graphs or column charts.

In Lesson 2.4, learners read a biography about the American gymnast Simone Biles, who is one of the most successful gymnasts of all time. Simone has won more World Championship medals than any other man or woman in the history of gymnastics,

and four gold medals and one bronze medal at the Rio Olympics. The title of the biography in Lesson 2.4, 'High flyer!', can have two meanings: the literal meaning and someone who is extremely skilled at something (and has ambition).

Learners read a story about a football match in Lesson 2.5. The author, Tom Palmer, is a football fan – and reading about football changed his life. He wasn't keen on reading as a child. His mum encouraged him to read about football in newspapers, magazines and books, and he grew to enjoy reading – and, subsequently, writing. He is now a successful writer and has won awards for his books and services to literacy.

TEACHING SKILLS FOCUS

Cross-curricular learning and Global English

Cross-curricular learning or interdisciplinary learning allows learners to apply, combine or contrast knowledge from two or more subject areas. Each unit has at least one cross-curricular feature, which is connected to an activity in the Learner's Book.

For example, in Lesson 2.2, learners read in English about food for sports and in Lesson 2.3 they read about how to warm up for sports. The expectation is that they will be covering, or will have covered, these topics in their own language in another subject, such as Health Education. So the lesson content should be revision/consolidation of something they have already studied.

This is just one example of the cross-curricular links you will find throughout this Teacher's Resource. Each unit has a link with another subject. Here are the links:

- Unit 1: Geography
- Unit 2: Health education
- Unit 3: Natural science
- Unit 4: Design technology
- Unit 5: Mathematics
- Unit 6: Art and design
- Unit 7: Physical science
- Unit 8: History
- Unit 9: Music education

Cross-curricular learning has several advantages. For example, learners can practise using their English language skills and consolidate their knowledge of another subject simultaneously. Cross-curricular learning helps learners become independent, critical thinkers.

Your challenge

Before starting a unit, find out what learners already know about the focus subject, for example health education for Unit 2. Use this information to make a quiz or ask learners to share what they know. You could also find background information in (simple) English for learners to read.

2.1 Think about it: What can we get from sport?

LEARNING PLAN

Learning objectives	Learning intentions	Success criteria
6Lm.01 6Sc.03	• **Listening:** Understand, with support, most of the main points of short and extended talk. • **Speaking:** Ask questions to find out information and to clarify meaning on a range of topics and respond accordingly. • **Vocabulary:** *football, judo, gymnastics, basketball, tennis, swimming, badminton, volleyball, athletics, hockey, shuttlecock, swimming costume, goalposts, net, shin pads, racquet, hockey stick, goggles*	• Learners can listen to comments about favourite sports and understand the reasons for taking part. • Learners can interview classmates about their favourite sports.

21st-century skills

Critical thinking opportunity: Describe why we engage with different sports.

Materials: Learner's Book pages 27–29; Workbook pages 20–21; coloured pens (Activity 10)

Starter ideas

Have you ever played...? (5–10 minutes)

- Elicit the names of different sports and practise using the present perfect (and past simple) to talk about them.

- Write the prompt *Have you ever...?* on the board and elicit the past participle of verbs that are used to talk about sports, for example *(play) played tennis, (do) done judo, (go) been horse riding/(ride) ridden a horse, (try) tried*, etc.

- Ask learners questions about sports using the present perfect, for example *Have you ever tried karate? / played basketball?*

- Circulate and support learners while they ask and answer questions about the sports in pairs.

Getting started (10 minutes)

- For Part a, look together at the photos and ask learners if they do any of the sports. Elicit words for the equipment, in particular words they will hear on the audio: *pitch, space, goalposts, shin pads, court.* Elicit *hockey stick, racquets, shuttlecocks, swimming costume* and *goggles*, which are not in the photos but are on the recording.

- For Part b, support learners by writing prompts on the board, for example *You need to be good at ...ing. I learn and practice this/these by ...*

- Build up a list of vocabulary on the board (see box above), which will come in useful for the speaking activities later on in the lesson.

- For Part c, have a class discussion about the benefits of sport.

Answers
Learner's own answers.

> **Digital Classroom:** Use the video 'Sports' to introduce the theme and vocabulary of the unit.
The i button will explain how to use the video.

Main teaching ideas

1 Which sports do you do? (5–10 minutes)

- Demonstrate the activity by asking learners which sports they do and identifying the reasons why. For example: *It's good fun. / To keep fit. / I like playing with my friends/team. / There's a great team spirit.*

- Ask *where* and *when* learners do sport.

- Add words to the list of useful vocabulary that you started in the previous activity.

- Circulate and offer support while learners ask and answer the questions in pairs.

Answers
Learner's own answers.

2 Match a photo in Activity 1 with the words in the box. (5 minutes)

- Demonstrate the activity by matching the first photo with *athletics*.
- Circulate and offer support while learners match the words to the photos in pairs.
- Give class feedback on the correct answers.

Answers

a	athletics	d	volleyball
b	gymnastics	e	hockey
c	badminton	f	judo

3 Which sports in the box are the children talking about? (5–10 minutes)

- Tell the class they are going to listen to four children talking about the sports they like and the reasons why.
- Before listening, encourage learners to make predictions about what they might hear.
- Make it clear that learners are only listening for the main ideas and that they will get to listen again, later.

> **Differentiation ideas:** If learners need more support with this task, provide them with the four correct activities and ask them to match each one to the correct speaker.

- After listening to the recording, give class feedback on the correct answers and ask learners which words helped them.

Audioscript: Track 11

See Learner's Book page 28

1 I love it because you can play it anywhere – on the beach, on a playing field, in the park – you just need a ball! You don't even need a proper pitch, as long as there's enough space. You can make goalposts out of anything – we use our jackets or sweatshirts.

2 Last year I really hurt my leg playing in a match against another school. Someone hit me really hard with their stick, while we were trying to get the ball. I was wearing old shin pads and they didn't protect me very well. It can get really rough on the pitch, but I still love playing. I love being in a team because you work together and help each other to play a good game.

3 I really like it because you exercise all of your body and you feel really energetic afterwards. You don't need to buy much equipment, just trunks to wear in the water and goggles to protect your eyes from the chlorine.

4 I like it because you can play with one other person or in a group of four. There's a court in the sports centre near our house and my mum books it so I can play with my friends. We have to take our own racquets, but we can borrow the shuttlecocks from the sports centre.

Answers

1	football	3	swimming
2	hockey	4	badminton

4 Listen again and decide if these sentences are true or false. Correct the false sentences. (5–10 minutes)

- Before listening, read the sentences together and ask learners if they have any ideas about the answers. If they think they do, they can listen to check.
- Replay the audio. Then learners work in pairs to complete the activity.

> **Differentiation ideas:** If learners need support with this task, ask them to just focus on deciding if the sentences are true or false.

- When you are giving class feedback, play the audio again if necessary. Stop after each comment and highlight the parts of each comment needed for the answer.

Answers

a   True.

b   False. She likes being in a team because they work together and help each other play a good game.

c   True.

d   False. She likes it because she can play with just one other person or a group of four.

5   Talk about the reasons why the children like their sports. What other reasons are there? (5–10 minutes)

- Demonstrate the activity by eliciting the reasons why the first speaker likes playing football.

- Circulate and offer support while learners talk in pairs about the reasons the children like their sports.

- Then come together as a class and discuss other reasons for liking a sport.

Answers

Reasons:

1   Football – can play anywhere (as long as there's enough space); don't need a proper pitch; can make goalposts out of anything.

2   Hockey – loves playing in a team because they work together and help each other play a good game.

3   Swimming – exercises the whole body and makes you feel energetic afterwards; don't need much equipment (just trunks and goggles).

4   Badminton – can play with just one other person or a group of four; likes playing in the court in the sports centre near home.

Plus learner's own answers.

6   Match the pictures to words in the box. Then match the equipment to the sports in Activity 2. (10–15 minutes)

- Ask learners if they can remember any items of equipment mentioned by the four speakers. Then focus them on the pictures. In pairs, ask them to match the pictures to a word in the box.

- Give class feedback on the answers and the correct pronunciation, checking that everyone

understands the meaning of the words, so they can do the next part of the activity.

- Then ask learners to work in pairs to match the equipment to the sports in Activity 2.

> **Differentiation ideas:** Extend the activity by asking learners to write three sentences, each using an item of equipment and related sport from the word boxes.

Answers

a   shuttlecock – badminton

b   hockey stick – hockey

c   goalposts – hockey / football

d   goggles – swimming

e   racquet – badminton / tennis

f   shin pads – hockey / football

g   black bet – judo

h   net – volleyball / badminton / tennis

> **Digital Classroom:** Use the activity 'Sports and sports equipment' to revise sports and sports equipment vocabulary and reinforce pronunciation. The i button will explain how to use the activity.

7   What equipment do we need for the sports? Talk to your partner. (5 minutes)

- Focus on the example sentence in the Learner's Book. Explain to learners that they are going to talk about the four sports from the audioscript.

- Check learners understand the activity by eliciting more examples. Refer back to the Starter activity to look at the verbs that go with each sport.

- Circulate and monitor while learners talk to a partner about the equipment needed for the sports.

- Give class feedback on common errors at the end of the activity. Do this sensitively.

Answers

You need goalposts to play football / you need shin pads and a hockey stick to play hockey / you need trunks and goggles to go swimming / you need a shuttlecock and racquet to play badminton.

8 What about you? Ask and answer in pairs. (5–10 minutes)

- Invite two learners to demonstrate asking and answering the first question.

- Learners ask and answer the questions in pairs. Circulate and offer support with pronunciation and vocabulary.

- Give class feedback on common errors and write useful vocabulary on the board.

Answers
Learner's own answers.

9 Look at Shireen's bar chart. Which question in Activity 8 did she ask her classmates? (10 minutes)

- Ask learners to look at the bar chart and identify which question from Activity 8 Shireen asked her classmates.

- Draw learner's attention to features of the bar chart by asking questions like: *How many children did Shireen interview?* (20) *Which was the most popular answer?* (Meeting new friends), etc.

> **Critical thinking opportunity:** This is a good opportunity for learners to draw on their responses from Activity 8 and consider why we like different sports. Once you have established that the bar chart answers question 2, ask learners whether these responses match the types of things they talked about. Did they come up with any other responses in their discussions?

Answers
b   What is the best thing about your favourite sport?

10 Draw a bar chart (10 minutes)

- Tell learners that they are going to conduct their own survey and create a bar chart to show the results.

- Put them in groups of four. First, brainstorm possible answers for each Activity 8 question as a class and write them on the board. Classmates then choose from the options when doing the survey. Include the option 'other' in case learners don't want to choose one of the existing options. Then learners choose a question from Activity 8.

- If interviewing 20 classmates is appropriate, tell learners that each group of four will interview five classmates from another group (vary this according to your class size).

- Learners interview their classmates then come back to their original groups to combine the results and create the bar chart, either as a group or individually.

CROSS-CURRICULAR LINKS

Maths: Learners practise conducting a survey and use the results to create a bar graph.

Answers
Learner's own answers.

Plenary ideas

Reflection (5–10 minutes)

- In groups, learners reflect on what they have learned in the lesson. What did they enjoy and what did they find challenging? Ask them to share their ideas.

Homework ideas

- Learners write a paragraph (up to 100 words) about their favourite sport.

Workbook
Learners do Activities 1–3 on pages 20–21.

> **Assessment ideas:** Write a short checklist as a class so that learners can self-assess their work before handing it in. For example: *Have I used the new vocabulary from the lesson? Have I used punctuation correctly?*

2.2 Health education: Eat for strength and energy!

LEARNING PLAN

Learning objectives	Learning intentions	Success criteria
6Rd.01 6Ug.09	• **Reading:** Understand, with support, most of the main points of short and extended text. • **Use of English:** Begin to use *if* clauses in first conditionals. • **Vocabulary:** *carbohydrate, nutrients, oxygen, digest, protein, nutrition*	• Learners can find specific information in a text about the links between food and exercise. • Learners can recognise and use first conditional sentences.
21st-century skills		
Cross-curricular link: Health education: Learn about foods that help our bodies to be better at sport.		

Materials: Learner's Book pages 30–31; Workbook pages 22–23; card for the energy tips poster (Activity 7); **Photocopiable 4**

LANGUAGE BACKGROUND

The first conditional

We use the first conditional to talk about the likely outcome of a present or future situation. To form the first conditional, use *if + present simple* to describe the situation or condition and the future simple (*will/won't*) to describe the likely result.

For example: *If you have a lot of food before exercise, you'll probably get a stomach ache!*

And we can invert the clauses.

For example: *You'll probably get a stomach ache if you have a lot of food before exercise!*

We also use *unless* to mean *if you don't* or *if you aren't*.

For example: *You **won't get fitter unless** you train more. **Unless** you train more, you **won't get fitter**. **Unless** you get plenty of protein, your body **won't grow** well.*

Common misconceptions

Misconception	How to identify	How to overcome
Some learners think it is correct to use *will* in the *if* clause, for example: *I think if you ~~**will join**~~ the sports club, you will make friends too.*	Underline the two examples of the first conditional in a sentence. Explain that the *if* clause requires a present simple verb to describe the situation and the future simple to describe the result. For example: *If you drink plenty of water, you will stay hydrated when you do sport.*	Practise using the activities in the Workbook and **Photocopiable 4**.

Starter ideas

Types of food (10 minutes)

- Explain that this lesson is about how food helps us to do sport.

- Do a fun sorting activity to revise and pre-teach different types of nutrients.

- On the board, write: *bread, butter, chicken, eggs, fish, milk, pasta, oil, rice, sugar*.

- Then ask learners to create a three-columned table with the column headings *Carbohydrates*, *Proteins*, *Fats*. In groups of four, learners sort the foods into one of the three categories.

Answers
Carbohydrates: bread, pasta, rice, sugar
Proteins: chicken, eggs, fish, milk
Fats: butter, oil

Main teaching ideas

1 What do you know about food and exercise? (5–10 minutes)

- As a class, discuss the questions and write useful vocabulary and phrases on the board.

CROSS-CURRICULAR LINKS

Health education: This is a good opportunity for learners to find out more about how eating particular foods can help them do sport, and to share their knowledge.

Answers
Learner's own answers.

2 Improve your energy! Are the statements true or false? (5–10 minutes)

- Allow learners time to read the quiz questions. Check they understand what each statement means.

- Ask them to work in pairs to complete the quiz. Then share the answers as a class.

Answers
a True
b False
c False
d True

Reading tip – Finding specific information (5 minutes)

- Tell learners they are going to check the quiz answers by reading a short text.

- Look at the Reading tip together. Encourage learners to listen and look out for the specific information from the quiz.

3 Read and listen to the text and check your answers to the quiz in Activity 2. (5 minutes)

- Learners read and listen out for the specific information from the quiz.

- Give class feedback and ask learners if anything surprised them.

> **Differentiation ideas:** Extend the activity by asking learners to explain why the statements are false.

Audioscript: Track 12

See Learner's Book page 30

Answers
1 True
2 False. You'll get a quick energy lift then feel tired more quickly.
3 False. If you have a lot of food before exercise, it can give you a stomach ache.
4 True

4 Which tips in the text do you follow? What other tips do you know? (10 minutes)

- Circulate and offer support while learners ask and answer the questions.

- Share feedback and tips as a class. Ask learners to make a note of the tips, so they can draw on them for Activity 7, when they make an energy tips poster.

Answers
Learner's own answers.

> **Digital Classroom:** Use the slideshow 'Thinking drinks!' to extend the discussion about tips for health and energy. The i button will explain how to use the slideshow.

Key words: Nutrition (5 minutes)

- Write the four key words on the board and ask learners to explain what they mean (without looking at the definitions in the Learner's Book).

- Read the definitions together and check understanding.

Use of English – 1st conditional with *if/ unless* (15 minutes)

- Read the sentences about the 1st conditional. Elicit that they refer to a likely outcome of a present or future situation/action.

- Ask concept check questions to elicit the form *if + present simple* for the situation/condition and *will/won't* for a likely outcome.

- Check learners know that *unless* has the same meaning as *if you do not* or *if you are not*.

- You could complete **Photocopiable 4** to practise using the first conditional.

Workbook
Learners do Activities 1–3 on pages 22–23.

> **Digital Classroom:** Use the grammar presentation 'Conditional 1' to practise using *if* clauses in 1st conditionals. The i button will explain how to use the presentation.

5 Read the Use of English box and match the sentence halves. (5 minutes)

- Demonstrate the activity. Focus on the example, 1c.

- Circulate and offer support while learners match the sentence halves in pairs.

- Then give class feedback on the answers.

Answers
1c (Example), **2a, 3b, 4e, 5d**

6 Find more examples of the 1st conditional. (5 minutes)

- Support learners as they reread the statements and the text.

- Ask them to underline examples of the 1st conditional.

- Give class feedback.

Answers
Activity 2:
2 If you eat sugary food, you'll have energy for a long time.
4 If you drink plenty of water, it'll stop you from feeling thirsty.
Activity 3 text:
- If you eat these foods, you'll get a quick energy lift, but later you'll feel tired more quickly.
- If you have a lot of food before exercise, you'll probably get a stomach ache!
- If you drink plenty of water, you'll stay cool and hydrated when you do sport.

7 Make an energy tips poster, using 1st conditional sentences. (20 minutes)

- Explain to learners that they are going to make their own energy tips poster. Encourage them to use the tips from Activity 5 but also to include any ideas of their own.

- Start by looking at the example. Remind learners to use 1st conditional sentences in their posters.

- Learners work on the poster individually or in pairs.

- Circulate and offer support, making sure learners are using the first conditional.

- When the posters are finished, display them in the classroom.

> **Assessment ideas:** Give written feedback on the posters, focusing on the use of the first conditional and new vocabulary.

Answers
Learner's own answers.

Plenary ideas

What can you remember? (10 minutes)

- Learners discuss with a partner what they have learned in the lesson. Ask learners what they have enjoyed about the lesson and what they have found challenging. Have they enjoyed talking about their energy tips and making a poster? Is there anything else they would like to know about nutrition for sport?

Homework ideas

- Ask learners to find out energy and nutrition tips from a sportsperson who is popular in their country. They should report back to the class in the next lesson.

> **Workbook**
> Learners do Activities 1–3 on pages 22–23.

2.3 Talk about it: Ready to go!

LEARNING PLAN

Learning objectives	Learning intentions	Success criteria
6Sc.04 6Ug.12	• **Speaking/Use of English:** Give a sequence of instructions. Use an increasing range of modal forms (e.g. needn't (lack of necessity), should (advice), ought to (advice/obligation).	• Learners can prepare and give instructions for sports exercises, using modal verbs. • Learners can listen to someone giving instructions, noting specific language and vocabulary.
6Ld.01	• **Listening:** Understand a range of instructions.	
6Wc.01	• **Writing:** Write a sequence of instructions. • **Vocabulary:** *ankle, shoulder, thighs, heart, hamstrings, hip, bottom, toes, knees*	• Learners write a sequence of instructions for warm-up exercises.

21st-century skills

Communication: Give instructions for sports exercises.

Materials: Learner's Book pages 32–33; Workbook pages 24–25; **Photocopiable 5**

Common misconceptions

Misconception	How to elicit	How to overcome
Learners use the wrong form after modals or forget to add **be** after *must* and *should*. For example: We need ~~doing~~ **to do** sports to keep fit. You need ~~join~~ **to join** the sports club. You should **be** happy because you will make friends. You must **be** very healthy.	Look at example sentences and ask learners which form is used after the modal. For example: We need **to do** (to + verb) sports to keep fit. You should **be** (base form) happy because you will make friends. You must **be** (base form) very healthy.	Practise using: • pages 24–25 in the Workbook • **Photocopiable 5**

Starter ideas

Warm up! (10 minutes)

- To introduce the lesson theme, ask learners to do some warm-up exercises. Ask everyone to stand up, put their chairs under the desks and move away from their desks. Make sure there is sufficient space for learners to do the exercises safely, without knocking into classroom furniture or each other.

- Ask everyone to stand up straight with arms at their sides and do some slow knee-squats; then stand up straight again with hands on hips and turn to each side, twisting from the waist. Finally, ask learners to stand up straight with arms above their head, lean forward and touch their toes. Add any other exercises that you know can be done safely in the classroom but avoid jumping jacks, running on the spot and arm rotations, as these come up in the listening task.

- Try to use the words *muscles*, *bend* and *rotate* in your instructions to introduce/review these words in preparation for the listening activity.

Main teaching ideas

1 What are warm-up exercises? What parts of the body should you warm up and how? (5–10 minutes)

- Have a general class discussion about what warm-up exercises are and what parts of the body you should warm up. Draw on the Starter activity. Write any useful vocabulary on the board.

- Learners work in pairs to ask and answer the questions.

> **Differentiation ideas:** If learners need support with this task, give them a prompt sheet with some useful sentence starters, or write the sentence starters on a mini whiteboard. For example: *Warm-up exercises usually take … minutes. You should warm up your … before you …*

Answers
Learner's own answers.
Warm-up exercises prepare your body for longer periods of exercise by warming up the muscles beforehand. They usually last 10–20 minutes. You should warm up any parts of your body that you are going to use in the longer period of exercise. You can warm up with stretches of short periods of gentle exercise such as running on the spot, skipping, jumping, rotating parts of the body (e.g. wrists, ankles).

2 Match the words in the box with the labels on the picture in your notebook. (5 minutes)

- Focus learners on the words in the word box. Go through each one together and check learners know how to pronounce the words.

- Demonstrate the activity by matching ankle to b in the picture.

- Allow learners time to match the words in pairs before giving class feedback.

Answers
ankle – h, shoulder – e, thighs – c, hamstrings – g, hip – a, bottom – b, toes – d, knees – i, heart – f

> **Digital Classroom:** Use the activity 'Parts of the body' to revise body part vocabulary. The i button will explain how to use the activity

3 Listen to Sam giving instructions for warm-up exercises. (10 minutes)

- Tell learners they are going to listen to Sam giving instructions for warm-up exercises.

- Before listening, encourage learners to make predictions about what they are going to hear. Look at the pictures and elicit words for the movements that the people are doing.

- Learners listen to the recording and work in pairs to put the pictures in order. Play the recording again if necessary.

- Give class feedback on the order of the pictures and which parts of the body are mentioned.

Audioscript: Track 13

See Learner's Book page 32

1 First, we need to get your heart pumping ready for action with some high-powered jumping jacks! Ok, so first stand with your feet together, then jump so your feet are apart. Bring your hands up above your head, keeping your arms straight. Do 20 without stopping and finally relax!

2 You mustn't start running without warming up your leg muscles. First, run on the spot and warm up your legs and ankles. Second, place your feet wider apart and run to loosen up your hips too. Remember, you should warm up your hips too. At the same time bend your arms and move them backwards and forwards.

3 Now you need to warm up your upper body. Stand still and put your left arm in the air, right arm by your side. Your arms should be straight. Rotate your left arm at the shoulder, forward and backwards. Do the same with your right arm. You need to do about 15 turns. Then rotate both arms together, forwards and backwards! You should rotate your shoulders quite slowly. You mustn't rotate them too fast or you'll hurt your muscles.

Answers
Picture order: c, a, b
Parts of body mentioned: heart (feet, hands, head, arms); leg (muscles), ankles, hips; shoulder. (Parts of the body in brackets are not listed in Activity 2.)

4 Now stand up. Listen again and do the warm-up exercises. (5 minutes)

- As for the Starter activity, make sure learners have room to do the warm-up exercises before replaying the audio.

- Play the audio and pause between each activity, so learners can finish doing each one (e.g. 20 jumping jacks), or do enough to get the idea.

- When they have finished, ask learners to tell you how they feel. Elicit or suggest interesting adjectives, such as *energised*, *energetic*.

- Ask learners which parts of their bodies they exercised to help them remember the vocabulary from Activity 2. Also ask questions like: *Can you feel your heart pumping? Do your muscles feel stretched?*

› **Digital Classroom:** Use the animation 'Warm-up exercises' to reinforce vocabulary learned in the lesson. The i button will explain how to use the activity.

› **Digital Classroom:** Use the activity 'Should, need or mustn't?' to reinforce the use of *need, mustn't* and *should*. The i button will explain how to use the activity.

Use of English – *need/should/mustn't* for advice and instructions (20 minutes)

- Check learners understand the meaning of *advice* and *instructions*.

- Write *need / should / mustn't* on the board.

- Elicit example sentences and the difference in meaning between the verbs.

- Read the Use of English box. Check learners know the correct form: *need* is followed by *to*; *should* or *must(n't)* are not.

- Then write the following sentences on the board:

  1 After *should* and *mustn't* we use the *verb / to + verb*.

  2 After *need*, we use the *verb / to + verb*.

  Ask learners to choose the correct option to complete the rules.

- Learners write the correct rules in their notebooks.

Workbook

Learners do Activities 1–3 on pages 24–25.

Answers
1 After **should** and **mustn't** we use the *verb*.
2 After **need**, we use the *to + verb*.

---

5 Listen to the last warm-up exercise again. Complete the advice and instructions. (5–10 minutes)

- Before listening again, read the sentences in the Learner's Book together. Ask learners what kind of words they expect to hear to fill the gaps.

- Learners listen to the recording and complete the activity individually.

- Give class feedback on the answers.

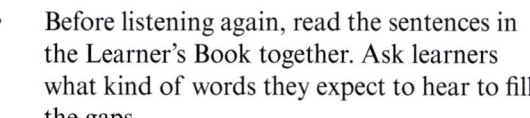

Answers

1	need to	3	need to
2	should	4	mustn't

---

6 Give instructions. Do you know any other warm-up exercises? (20 minutes)

- Explain to learners that now they are going to give a partner instructions for warm-up exercises. Start by brainstorming other warm-up exercises that your learners know and building up suggestions on the board.

- Tell learners that they should write the instructions first, then use their notes to tell a classmate what to do. They can use the pictures in the activity for help, or make up their own exercise.

- If possible, take learners outside to do this activity.

- Before learners write the instructions, download the audioscript, or part of it, so that they can use it as a model. Draw their attention to the types of sentences (with modals and imperatives) and ask them to highlight them. Also encourage them to use sequencing words and phrases (e.g. *first, then, finally*) in their instructions.

- Circulate and offer support while learners make notes to prepare them for giving instructions to a partner. Don't spend too long on this part of the activity as the priority should be on the speaking element.

> **Differentiation ideas:** Extend the activity by challenging learners to complete instructions for two activities.

- **Communication:** Circulate and offer support while learners tell a partner how to do a warm-up exercise. Check for pronunciation, the use of modals and imperatives, and sequencing instructions.

- At the end of the activity, sensitively give class feedback on common errors, including the pronunciation of parts of the body.

Answers

Learner's own answers.

Plenary ideas

Consolidation (15 minutes)

- Learners make a poster about a warm-up activity.

- To practise vocabulary from Lessons 2.2 and 2.3, use **Photocopiable 5**.

> **Assessment ideas:** Circulate, providing verbal feedback to learners on their use of vocabulary from the lesson and their use of modal verbs, imperatives and sequencing words to explain their warm-up exercise.

Homework ideas

- Ask learners to listen to part of an exercise video in English.

Workbook

Learners do Activities 1–3 on pages 24–25.

2.4 Write about it: Our favourite sports stars

LEARNING PLAN

Learning objective	Learning intentions	Success criteria
6Wc.02	• Write, with support, short texts which describe people, places and objects, and routine past and present actions and events. • **Vocabulary:** *talent, give up, foster care, improve, coach, tease*	• Learners can write a biography of a sports person, describing past and present actions and events.

21st-century skills

Creative thinking: Explore why a sports personality is inspirational.

Materials: Learner's Book pages 34–35; Workbook pages 26–27; access to the internet or information about sportspeople from magazines (for Activity 6); **Photocopiable 6**; Unit 2 sample answer

Starter ideas

What is a biography? (10 minutes)

* Introduce learners to the theme of the lesson: explain that they are going to read a biography about a sports star and then write one of their own.

* See if learners know what a biography is. Make sure they understand that it is an account of someone's life written by someone else. Ask learners if they have read the biographies of any famous people, including sports stars.

* During your discussions, try to introduce/revise words from the reading in the Learner's Book, such as *most successful… of all time, championship, bronze, gold, setbacks, stardom.*

Main teaching ideas

1 Who are your favourite sports stars? Why? (10 minutes)

* Have a class discussion about learner's favourite sports stars. Encourage learners to share why they admire these sports stars and interesting facts about their lives.

* Build up a list of useful facts and vocabulary that will help in the reading and writing activities.

Answers
Learner's own answers.

2 Read the biography of Simone Biles, the world-famous gymnast. (5–10 minutes)

* Before reading, look at the title and the photos of Simone Biles. Ask learners if they have heard of her and know anything about her.

* Don't worry if Simone isn't well-known in your learner's country(ies). Encourage learners to make predictions about what they will read by looking at the photos and asking questions to guide them. For example: *What's she doing in the pictures? Why do you think she is famous? How many gold medals do you think she has won?*

* Learners skim the text and look for the number of gold medals Simone has won. Before reading, make clear that learners don't need to understand every word, as they will reread the text in the next three activities.

Answers
Simone has won eight gold medals: four at the 2014 World Championships and four at the 2016 Olympic Games.

3 Read the text again and match the headings 1–4 to the paragraphs A–D. (5–10 minutes)

* Read the four headings together and check learners understand the meaning.

- Demonstrate the activity by reading paragraph A and eliciting that heading 2 matches with it. Make sure learners know they don't need to understand every word to complete the activity.

- Circulate and offer support while learners match the rest of the titles in pairs.

- Give class feedback on the correct answers.

Answers
1B, 2A, 3D, 4C

4 Find these words in the biography. (10 minutes)

- Read the words and then scan the text together. Find and underline the words.

- Focus on the first word, *talent*, and read the relevant sentence from the text. Encourage speculation about what it means, then write an appropriate definition on the board.

- Circulate and offer support while learners discuss the other words with a partner and note down possible meanings.

> **Differentiation ideas:** Learners could work in pairs so that more confident readers can provide language support.

- Share ideas and write the words and definitions on the board. Ask learners to copy them in their notebooks.

Answers
Suggested answers:
Talent: a special skill.
Give up: to stop doing something.
Foster care: caring for a child when you are not their parent.
Improve: to get better at something.
Coach: someone who trains sports people.
Tease: to joke about someone in an unkind way.

Reading tip and 5 Why are these dates and numbers important to Simone's story? (10 minutes)

- Look at the Reading tip and ask learners if they remember any dates or numbers from the text.

- Look at the dates and numbers in Activity 4 and elicit why they are important to Simone's story.

- Scan the text and check.

Answers
a   Simone won five medals in her first Olympics.
b   In third grade, she was teased by her classmates about her muscly legs.
c   In 2011, she just missed being selected for the National team (but this setback gave her the determination to improve).
d   In 2014, she won four gold medals at the World Championships – the first woman in 40 years to achieve this.

> **Digital Classroom:** Use the activity 'High flyer!' to reinforce comprehension of the text from the Learner's Book. The i button will explain how to use the activity.

Writing tip and 6 Talk to your partner about Simone's story and answer the questions. (15 minutes)

- Read the Writing tip together and check learners know what a *quote* (quotation) is.

- Learners find the quote from Simone's story. Then, in pairs, they discuss what it says about the way Simone sees her success, and share what they feel is the most interesting or surprising fact about her life.

- Circulate and offer support as learners talk to their partner.

- Then come together as a class and talk through the answers.

Answers
a   Quote: '*My first Olympics and I've walked away with five medals … It shows dreams can come true. I'm not the next Usain Bolt or Michael Phelps: I'm the first Simone Biles.*'
Sample answer: The quote tells us that Simone is very proud of her success and recognises how great her achievement is. She feels she is unique and isn't going to compare herself to any other athlete.
b   Learner's own answers.

7 Write a biography about an interesting sports person. (30–40 minutes)

- First, have a short class discussion about who learners could write about. Draw on learner's ideas from Activity 1 and suggest four or five sports stars that learners could choose from, if they're not sure who to write about.

- Then write the four headings from Activity 3 on the board: *Early life; Present day success; Journey to stardom; Some information about their childhood.* Elicit the kind of information learners could write under each heading.

- Circulate and offer support while learners search the internet and/or look at magazines and make notes under the headings. You may want to provide a choice of texts or websites to support learners in their research. Make sure learners look for important dates and numbers, and an interesting quote.

- Circulate and support learners as they organise their notes and plan their biographies.

⟩ **Assessment ideas:** Before beginning Step 3, show learners the sample answer for Unit 2 without the mark scheme comments. As a class, evaluate its strengths and weaknesses. Ask learners to look at the checklist on page 35 of the Learner's Book and **Photocopiable 6** too, so that they know exactly what they are aiming for with their biography including the vocabulary used, how well the writer uses the past simple and present perfect, and the use of headings, dates and numbers.

- Learners use their headings, dates and numbers to build their biographies. Circulate and make sure learners use the past simple and present perfect in their writing. If necessary, point out how the past simple and present perfect are used in Simone's story.

⟩ **Assessment ideas:** Once learners have finished writing their biographies, ask them to work through the checklist again to self-assess their work. When they have made any updates, ask them to swap their biography with a partner and check for any errors. Tell learners to give their feedback sensitively and to include at least one compliment.

Plenary ideas

Reflection (10 minutes)

- Have a class discussion about writing the biographies. What did learners enjoy about it? What were the challenges?

What can you remember? (5–10 minutes)

- To practise speaking about various aspects of sport (food, warming up, etc.) covered in Lessons 2.2, 2.3 and 2.4, use **Photocopiable 5**.

Homework ideas

- Under parental supervision, learners watch a video clip with an English commentary about a sports person they like.

2.5 Read and respond: An extract from *Off Side*

LEARNING PLAN

Learning objectives	Learning intentions	Success criteria
6Rm.02 6Sc.05	• **Reading:** Read independently a range of short, simple fiction and non-fiction texts with confidence and enjoyment. • **Speaking:** Pronounce familiar words and phrases clearly; begin to use intonation and place stress at word, phrase and sentence level. • **Vocabulary:** *strikers, defenders, (goal) keeper, midfield, goal (area), struggled, bounced, blasted, awesome, fired, strike, exploded*	• Learners can read and understand an extract from a novel about football. • Learners can understand meaning from intonation and word stress; they can practise reading with emphasis to express emotions and actions.
21st-century skills		
Social responsibilities: Identify roles and responsibilities within a team		

Materials: Learner's Book pages 36–39; Workbook pages 28–29; audio of sports events commentary or visuals of sports events (for Starter activity); **Differentiated worksheets 2A, B and C**

The Off Side text used in this lesson is very challenging and extends beyond the level of the Cambridge Primary English as a Second Language curriculum framework.

Starter ideas

Guess the sports event! (10 minutes)

- Explain to learners that in this lesson they are going to read a story about a boy and his dad at a football match.

- Introduce the lesson by playing several extracts of sport commentary. See if learners can guess the event or type of sport. Alternatively, show learners images of sports events, whether local, national or international, and ask them to identify the event.

Main teaching ideas

1 Have you ever been to a live sports event? What was it like? How did you feel? (10 minutes)

- Have a quick class survey about which sporting events learners have been to see.

- Then ask learners to discuss the three questions in pairs. Point out that the live sports event could be anything from a national event to a local match or school sports day.

  > **Differentiation ideas:** If learners need more support with this task, give them a prompt sheet with some sentence starters, or write prompts on a mini whiteboard. For example: *I've been to see…, Last year I went…, I felt…* .

- As a class, learners share their experiences of going to a live sports event. Use this time as an opportunity to revise/introduce useful vocabulary for the rest of the lesson, such as *commentator, score, cheer*, etc. Keep useful words and phrases on the board to refer to during the lesson.

Answers
Learner's own answers.

Listening tip – Listening for expression and emphasis (5 minutes)

- Read the tip about listening for expression and emphasis. Explain that learners need to listen out

for how the narrator reads the story and for the different expressions in their voice.

- Elicit that the expression in the narrator's voice can let us know if someone is excited, happy, sad, frightened, etc. Ask learners to predict how/why/when the commentator's voice might change during a football match.

2 Read and listen to Part 1. (5 minutes)

- Look at the pictures and title. Explain that Danny and his dad are at a live football game and that Danny is helping his dad. Encourage speculation about how and why.

- Learners read the text while they listen to the audio.

- Learners answer the questions individually and then check their answers with a partner.

- As a class, share feedback.

> **Audioscript:** Track 14
> See Learner's Book page 36

Answers
Danny helps his dad by telling him what's happening in the game/acting as commentator. He does this because his father is blind.

3 Read and listen to Part 1 again. (5–10 minutes)

- Read the questions together, checking learners understand *home city or away.*

- Learners reread and listen to Part 1 again and answer the questions at the end of the extract, following the same procedure as for Activity 2.

Answers
a Danny's football team is called City.
b They watch the team in their home city (near where they live).

4 Read and listen to the description of the live football match. (10–15 minutes)

- Tell learners that they are going to read and listen to the rest of the story, and then read it again and answer the questions after each part. Explain that the rest of the story describes the live football match in the stadium.

- After learners have listened to and read the rest of the story once, read the questions after each part together.

- Then circulate and offer support while learners read Parts 2, 3 and 4 again, and answer the questions after each section in pairs. The text is quite challenging, particularly in terms of vocabulary. Encourage learners to deduce meaning from context to avoid them having to look up words in the dictionary.

- After learners have completed the activity, put them in groups of 3 or 4 to check their answers together, before you come together as a class and discuss the answers. Where possible, use the pictures in the Learner's Book to illustrate the answers.

Audioscript: Track 15

See Learner's Book pages 36–38

Answers
a 1, b 2, c 1, d 2, e 2, f 2, g 3

5 Football. Use the words in the box to label the diagram. (5 minutes)

- Ask learners to look at the diagram and label it in pairs, using the words in the box.

- Go through the answers as a class.

Answers
1	(goal) keeper	4	defenders
2	goal (area)	5	midfield
3	strikers		

6 Word study: Descriptive words (5–10 minutes)

- Focus on the first blue word on page 37, *struggled*. Read the whole sentence and, if necessary, the sentences before and after. Elicit the meaning from the context.

- Offer support while learners repeat the procedure in pairs for the rest of the blue words.

> **Differentiation ideas:** If learners need support with this task, mix up the words and their definitions and turn this into a matching exercise.

- Give class feedback on the correct answers.

Answers
Suggested answers:
Struggled: found it difficult
Bouncing: go up and down
Awesome strike: a very good hit or kick
Exploded: shouted and cheered loudly in excitement
Blasted: run very fast or kick very hard
Fired: kick very hard

7 Replace the underlined words in the text with words from the box. (5–10 minutes)

- Demonstrate the activity by looking at the example.

- This text will help learners with the writing task (Activity 9), so once they have worked in pairs to replace the underlined words with descriptive ones, ask them to copy the text out so they have a model text to refer to.

- To check the answers, read out the text, stop at an underlined phrase and invite learners to tell you the replacement word. Read the text with expression, to help prepare learners for Activities 8 and 9.

Answers
a	blasted [Example]	e	strike
b	struggled	f	(goal) keeper
c	fired	g	bounced
d	awesome	h	exploded

8 Read with expression by emphasising key words. (5–10 minutes)

- Tell learners that they are going to listen to the last part of the story again and repeat the sentences. Ask them to make a note of the key words that are emphasised.

- Play the audio. Pause after each sentence or clause so that learners can repeat it and make a note of the words that are emphasised. Make this fun by exaggerating the stress on the words and asking learners to do the same.

- Circulate and offer support while learners compare their answers with a partner.

- Play the extract all the way through so learners can hear all the emphasised words again. This activity will help prepare learners for Activity 9.

Audioscript: Track 16

See Learner's Book page 39

'City's amazing Ghanaian international has scored the goal of the season. Picking the ball up on the edge of the area, he took it on his knee, then fired an unstoppable volley past the paralysed United keeper. That's Owusu's twentieth goal of the season. And just goes to show that he deserved the African Player of the Year award he received only two weeks ago.'

Answers

Emphasised words: amazing, goal, season, fired, unstoppable, past, paralysed, twentieth

> **Digital Classroom:** Use the video 'Be a sports commentator' to practise sports commentating. The i button will explain how to use the activity.

9 **Now write a similar description of someone scoring a goal, winning a race or a competition. (20 minutes)**

- Explain to learners that they are now going to write their own commentary on a sports event.

- Encourage them to choose a sport and event they feel passionate about, and to imagine watching it live and communicating what's happening to someone who isn't there.

- Ask learners to think of a dramatic opening line for their description – look back at the text from Activities 7 and 8 for examples. Tell them to use descriptive words from the text and other words they know.

> **Differentiation ideas:** If learners need support with this task, you could give them an opening line to start them off. For example: *Italy's best striker has done it again!*, or: *She's blasting down the track … this must be a record!*

- Circulate and offer support while learners write their descriptions and underline the words they want to emphasise.

- As learners read their commentaries to a partner, circulate and offer support with pronunciation and expression.

Answers

Learner's own answers.

10 **Teamwork. Talk about these questions with your partner. (10 minutes)**

- **Social responsibilities:** Explain to learners that you're going to discuss teamwork. First, as a class, talk about the different teams that learners are involved in at school and elsewhere. Write down the answers on the board to emphasise the variety of teams the learners belong to.

- Then learners discuss the questions with a partner. Circulate and offer support. Throughout the activity, encourage learners to listen to their partner and try to make sure every learner has a chance to contribute.

- During class feedback, invite learners to share their thoughts on each question.

Answers

Learner's own answers.

> **Digital Classroom:** Use the activity 'Football words' to revise football vocabulary and descriptive language. The i button will explain how to use the activity.

Plenary ideas

Guess the sport or event! (5–10 minutes)

- Invite learners to read out the funniest or most dramatic sports commentaries in front of the class.

- The other learners have to guess which sport or event each commentary is about.

- Use **Differentiated worksheets 2A, B or C** to practise vocabulary for sports commentaries.

Homework ideas

Workbook

Learners do Activities 1–5 on pages 28–29.

2.6 Project challenge

LEARNING PLAN

Learning objectives	Learning intentions	Success criteria
6Wca.03, 6Wc.01, 6Wca.04 6Ug.09, 6Ug.12	• **Writing:** Write a sequence of instructions. • **Use of English:** Begin to use *if* clauses in first conditionals. Use an increasing range of modal forms e.g. *needn't* (lack of necessity), *should* (advice), *ought to* (advice/obligation).	• Learners can create posters about a sport or physical activity, including factual information and a list of instructional *dos* and *don'ts* (using modal verbs and the first conditional).
6Sc.02, 6Sc.05	• **Speaking:** Describe people, places and objects, and routine past and present actions and events. Pronounce familiar words and phrases clearly; begin to use intonation and place stress at word, phrase and sentence level appropriately.	• Learners can deliver a sports description.

21st-century skills

Collaboration: Take responsibility for your own contribution in a group project.

Materials: Learner's Book pages 40–41; Workbook page 30; access to the internet; access to books about sports; video clips of sports events; examples of other learner's work; poster card; Unit 2 project checklists; End of Unit 2 test

Starter ideas

Raise interest in the projects (10–15 minutes)

- Tell learners they are either going to make a poster about a type of sport (Project A) or write a description of a sports event (Project B).

- If possible, raise interest in the projects by presenting examples of learner's work on similar topics from other classes or the internet. For example, for Project A, you could show learners posters with *dos* and *don'ts* about a type of sport. For Project B, you could read or listen to other learner's descriptions.

- Revise new vocabulary from the unit that learners may need for the challenges, in a fun way. For example, you could create games like a word search or crossword. Alternatively, write some letters from the words on the board with spaces, or create anagrams and ask the class to guess the words.

Main teaching ideas

Introduce and complete projects (60 minutes)

Encourage learners to choose one of the projects and then follow the steps for their chosen project.

Project A: Make a poster about a type of sport

- Divide learners into groups of five. First, make sure all groups have chosen a sport or physical activity to write about. Support learners while they brainstorm what they know about the sport and write five questions about things they want to find out. Tell them they can use the topics in the Learner's Book or write questions on other aspects of the sport/activity.

- Circulate and support learners while they research their questions.

- **Collaboration:** Learners should listen to each other and work together when planning the poster. Make sure that each person in the group has a say on which facts to include from the learner's research.

- Learners work together in their groups and create their posters, including the list of *dos* and *don'ts*. Circulate and make sure learners use the modal verbs and the first conditional correctly.

- Learners read through the steps in the Learner's Book and check they have followed the instructions and included everything that was required. Then they add pictures to their posters.

⟩ **Assessment ideas:** Learners use the Unit 2 project checklist to evaluate other groups' posters. Encourage them to write at least one interesting fact that they learned from the poster.

Project B: Create a description of a sports event

- First, divide learners into groups of four. Make sure all groups have agreed on a real/imaginary sports event. If possible, show learners video clips of events to help inspire them. If learners decide to invent a sports event, support them while they discuss who is taking part, where the event is and what happens.

- **Collaboration:** Learners should work together to write their short descriptions. Remind them that they only need to focus on one part of their chosen sports event. Once they have a plan about what they're going to write, encourage them to each focus on a small part of the description. Circulate and remind learners to use descriptive words and to write in the past simple and past continuous.

⟩ **Assessment ideas:** When learners have finished their first draft, ask them to exchange it with another group and give feedback, including on the use of the past simple and continuous and descriptive words. Offer support during this process.

- Learners use the comments on the first draft to write their second draft. Learners read the draft through in their groups and check they are happy with it.

- **Collaboration:** Each member of the group takes it in turns to read the description. Encourage learners to support each other as they read out loud and give constructive feedback. Remind group members not to say the name of the sports event, so that the other groups can guess.

⟩ **Assessment ideas:** Learners use the Unit 2 project checklist to evaluate other groups' commentaries.

Plenary ideas

Consolidation and reflection (10–15 minutes)

- If learners enjoyed the guessing activity, play them video clips of other sporting events to guess what they are.

- As a class, learners discuss what they enjoyed about the projects and what they found most challenging. Is there anything they would do differently next time?

> **Workbook**
>
> Learners do Activities 1–3 on page 30.

2.7 What do you know now?

What can we learn from doing and watching sports?

- **Learning to learn:** Learners have the opportunity to reflect and evaluate their own learning success.

- Reintroduce the question from the start of the unit: *What can we learn from doing and watching sports?* Discuss learner's responses to the question now and compare with their comments at the beginning of the unit. How much has changed?

- Ask learners to work on the questions in pairs.

- For questions 1 and 3–6, encourage learners to look back through the unit if they can't remember. Circulate and offer support while learners answer the questions.

- When learners have finished the questions, give class feedback on the answers.

Answers
1 Learner's own answers. Suggested answers:
- You wear these when you play hockey (shin pads).
- You wear these to protect your eyes (goggles).
- You use this to play badminton (racquet).
- You hit this with a racquet when you play badminton (shuttlecock).
- You hit the ball with this when you play hockey (hockey stick).
- You kick the ball into this when you play score a goal in football (goal posts).

- You hit the shuttlecock over this when you play badminton (net).

2 Learner's own answers.

3 Suggested answers (two of):
  - Healthy carbohydrates, e.g. wholemeal bread, pasta, brown rice, vegetables and beans (give your body energy for exercise and fill you up).
  - Protein, e.g. chicken, fish, eggs, milk, green vegetables and lentils (repair your muscles after exercise and help your blood cells carry nutrients and oxygen to your muscles).
  - Foods with calcium, e.g. milk and yoghurt (for strong bones).
  - Bananas or fruit (easy to digest, so good to eat before exercise).
  - Lots of water (your body needs water to stay healthy and to stay cool and hydrated when you do sport).

4 Learner's own answers.

5 Suggested answers (two of):
  - Simone has won more World Championship medals than any other man or woman in the history of gymnastics.
  - When she was 19, she won four gold and one bronze Olympic medal.
  - When she was six, on a school trip to a gymnastics centre, a coach noticed her natural talent and invited her to join a class.
  - In third grade, she was teased by her classmates about her muscly legs, but she didn't get upset because she knew she was stronger than most of the other children.
  - In 2014, she became the first woman in 40 years to win four gold medals at the World Championships.

6 Danny tells his dad what's happening in the football match. He needs to help him because he is blind.

7 Learner's own answers.

Look what I can do!

- There are six 'can do' statements. Learners read through the statements and tick the things they can do. Encourage them to reflect on how well they can do these things. Also invite them to think of ways they can improve further, for example what strategies they can use or learn to use.

- If learners find it challenging to read the statements, look through the unit with them and support them to find the relevant information.

- Finally, ask learners to work through the questions on page 31 of the Workbook. Encourage them to talk about what they enjoyed and also about any further support they might need.

> 3 Living things

Unit plan

Lesson	Approximate number of learning hours	Outline of learning content	Learning objectives	Resources
1 Strategies for survival	2.0–2.5	Discover how penguins survive in the extreme cold.	6Ld.04 6Ug.03	Learner's Book Lesson 3.1 Workbook Lesson 3.1 **Digital Classroom:** video – Survival; activity – Polar bears
2 Nature's food chains	2.0–2.5	Learn how living things survive through food chains. Present information about animal habits using relative clauses.	6Rd.01 6Us.05 1Bp.02	Learner's Book Lesson 3.2 Workbook Lessons 3.2 and 3.3 ⬇ Photocopiable 7 **Digital Classroom:** activity – Food chain; grammar presentation – Defining relative clauses
3 The strange world of carnivorous plants	2.0–2.5	Explain key facts about carnivorous plants using *wh-* questions.	6Sc.02 6Sc.06 6Ld.05 6Ug.01 1Bp.01	Learner's Book Lesson 3.3 Workbook Lesson 3.3 ⬇ Differentiated worksheets 3A, B, C **Digital Classroom:** activity – Questions
4 Animal types	1.5–2.0	Create an infographic text about a type of animal.	6Wor.03 6Wc.02	Learner's Book Lesson 3.4 Workbook Lesson 3.4 ⬇ Photocopiable 8 ⬇ Unit 3 sample answer **Digital Classroom:** activity – Which type of animal?
5 *Song for a Whale*	1.5–2	Read a story about a connection between a girl and a whale.	6Rm.01 6Rm.02 6Uv.06	Learner's Book Lesson 3.5 Workbook Lesson 3.5 ⬇ Photocopiable 9 **Digital Classroom:** activity – Collective nouns
6 Project challenge	1.0–1.5	Project A: A presentation about how an animal survives. Project B: Create a quiz about an animal.	6Sc.06 6Sc.02 6Wca.04 6Wca.01 6Ug.01 6Wca.03	Learner's Book Lesson 3.6 Workbook Lesson 3.6 ⬇ Unit 3 project checklists

(continued)

BACKGROUND KNOWLEDGE

Unit 3 focuses on living things and what they do to survive. Learners look at how penguins survive in the extreme cold and how living things survive through food chains. They find out about carnivorous plants, create an infographic text about an animal type and read a story about a connection between a girl and a whale.

In Lesson 3.1, the information in the audioscript is adapted from the penguin documentary in the *Dynasties* series. The 2018 documentary followed five endangered animals: chimpanzees, emperor penguins, lions, tigers and painted wolves. The series was produced by the BBC and narrated by David Attenborough.

Lesson 3.2 looks at food chains. The audioscript and text talk about herbivores, carnivores and omnivores. Herbivores eat only plants, carnivores eat other animals, and omnivores eat both plants and meat.

Learners create an infographic text in Lesson 3.4. Infographic is short for information graphic – in other words, a visual representation of information or data so it is easy to understand.

In Lesson 3.5, learners read an extract from a story called *Song for a Whale* (2019) by Lynne Kelly. Lynne is an American author who writes for children and young adults. Her first novel, *Chained*, won the South Asia Book Award in 2013. Lynne works as a sign language interpreter, which gave her the inspiration to write *Song for a Whale*. The novel tells the story of 12-year-old Iris, who is deaf. Iris has a connection to a whale whose song can't be heard by other whales, and she is determined to help him. In the English language, *whale* can refer to species of toothed and baleen whales.

TEACHING SKILLS FOCUS

Metacognition

What is metacognition? Encouraging learners to monitor their own progress and take control of their own learning.

Why use metacognition? To maximise the learning potential of each unit and each lesson.

How can I use it? You can apply metacognition to improve various skills, like listening, as well as learning factual information and new words more efficiently.

For more information, see *Getting started with Metacognition* on the Cambridge Assessment website.

Your challenge

Try these two strategies while you are delivering Unit 3.

1 Help learners start thinking about the learning process. Focus on the question at the beginning of the unit, look through the unit together and ask questions. For example:

- How cold is Antarctica and how do penguins survive these extreme temperatures?
- Have you ever heard of *primary*, *secondary* and *tertiary consumers* in the food chain?
- What do *carnivores*, *herbivores* and *omnivores* eat? Can you think of an example of each one?

CONTINUED

- Why and how do some plants eat meat?
- What do you know about amphibians?
- What is an *infographic*?
- What's the difference between a baleen whale and a toothed whale?
- What do you think you are going to learn about animals in this unit?
- What challenges do you think you might face with learning in this unit (for example, reading, listening, learning new vocabulary)?

2 Encourage learners to think of learning goals for the unit. For example:

- I want to know how penguins can survive in extreme temperatures.
- I want to understand more about the food chain.
- I want to use and understand defining relative clauses.
- I want to use and pronounce 10–20 new words correctly.

3.1 Think about it: Strategies for survival

LEARNING PLAN

Learning objectives	Learning intentions	Success criteria
6Ld.04 6Ug.03	• **Listening:** Understand, with support, most specific information and detail of short and extended talk. • **Use of English:** Use a range of present simple active forms and begin to use passive forms. • **Vocabulary:** *chick, breed, mate, hatch, huddle, colony*	• Learners can understand specific information in a documentary recording about Emperor penguins. • Learners can put factual sentences in the present simple about penguin chicks, in the correct order.

21st-century skills

Creative thinking: Explore how penguins survive in extreme temperatures.

Materials: Learner's Book pages 43–45; Workbook pages 32–33; information about the temperature in cold places (for example, the ten coldest places on Earth from the BBC Science Focus website); access to two audio devices for Activity 3; internet access for Activity 8

LANGUAGE BACKGROUND

Revising the present simple (active and passive)

- The present simple describes habits, routines and things that are always true. The present simple can be used in the active or the passive form.

  Active: *The sun doesn't rise for two months.*

  Passive: *Until the babies are a month old, they are fed by their mother.*

- The passive form is used when we can't, don't need to or don't want to say who does the action. We use the passive when we want to focus on the action, not the person/people/thing that does it. For example:

  Rice is grown in China. Here, the focus is on the fact that rice is grown.

  Mozzarella is produced in Italy.

Common misconceptions

Misconception	How to identify	How to overcome
Some learners find basic subject–verb agreement difficult. For example: *My brother* **watch watches** *TV.* This is especially common after irregular plural nouns; uncountable nouns, e.g. food; *everyone/ body, someone/body*; multiple singular subjects; parallel verb structures after *and;* and words between the subject and the verb *be* used to form the passive.	On the board, list some typical errors with subject–verb agreement. Include examples of *was/ were* used incorrectly with the passive. Identify the mistakes with the form.	Learners could practise using: • pages 34–35 in the Workbook

Starter ideas

Penguins (5–10 minutes)

- Explain to learners that over the next few weeks they are going to learn about living things, starting with penguins.

- Have a general class discussion about penguins. Encourage learners to share what they know about penguins. For example, has anyone seen a penguin or watched a documentary about one?

- Start building up some useful vocabulary for the first lesson, such as *huddle, colony, chick, breed*.

Getting started (5–10 minutes)

- Focus on the big question and look at the photos together. Then ask learners to answer the questions in pairs.

- As a class, work through the answers. Ask questions to ensure learners understand the meaning and pronunciation of the words in the boxes. Build up a list of words/expressions that will be useful for the unit.

> **Digital Classroom:** Use the video 'Survival' to introduce the topic of how living things survive. The i button will explain how to use the video.

Answers
a mammal – tiger; amphibian – (poison dart) frog; bird – geese; fish
b The tiger is moving/prowling/hunting; the frog is sitting in its habitat; the birds are flying in a group; the fish are swimming in a group (shoal).
c The tiger is hunting for food, looking for prey; the frog's bright colour warns other animals not to approach it (protecting it and them); the birds are migrating to a place where they can find a better climate and more food; the fish are swimming in large numbers for protection.

Main teaching ideas

1 What's the coldest place on Earth? (5–10 minutes)

- Have a brief class discussion about where learners think the coldest place on Earth might be. Also encourage them to predict the temperature. Then project a list of the top ten coldest places on Earth on the whiteboard (see Materials) and see if learners are correct.

- Explain that in Antarctica, the average winter temperature is –49 °C. Briefly talk about how cold that must feel! Then talk through how penguin families can survive at that temperature.

- **Creative thinking:** Encourage learners to explore different ideas about how penguins survive these extreme temperatures. Build up a list of problems caused by freezing temperatures and use the photos for clues about how penguin families survive. Encourage the use of modal verbs *could/might* from Unit 2.

Answers
Antarctica is the coldest place on Earth. Average temperatures in winter are about –49 °C.
Learner's own answers. Photo clues: 1 Emperor penguin fishing underwater; 2 A penguin chick balanced on its parent's feet for protection; 3 (Male) penguins huddle together in a large group for protection against the extreme cold.

2 What do you know about emperor penguins? (10 minutes)

- Use the quiz as an opportunity to raise interest in the subject in a fun way and help learners make predictions about what they will hear in Activity 3.

- Circulate and offer support with new vocabulary, but don't give the answers away at this stage.

Answers
See Activity 3 answers.

3 Listen to Part 1 of the documentary and check your answers. (5–10 minutes)

- Explain to learners that they are going to listen to an adapted recording from a documentary about penguins. They should be able to use the recording to check their quiz answers. The text is quite long and some of the vocabulary is challenging, so make it clear that it is not necessary to understand every word.

- In order to help with the length and detail of the recording, you could divide learners into two groups. Tell one group to listen to the first half of the recording and the other group to listen to the second half. Ideally, to do this you will need two audio devices, two recordings and two separate spaces. If this is not practical, you could play the recording to the whole class, but instruct each group to focus on one half of the recording.

- Give groups the chance to tell learners from the other group what they heard.

- If necessary, replay the audio, pausing when the answer to each question is covered.

- Go through the answers as a class and discuss any misunderstandings.

Audioscript: Track 17

See Learner's Book page 44

Every animal has a survival story. For emperor penguins in the Antarctic, the journey to raise their chicks is more dangerous than most.

In autumn time, thousands of emperor penguins meet together to breed and raise their babies – over the next nine months. They find a mate and then wait weeks for their eggs to develop. When their egg appears, they will keep it warm by balancing it on their feet and covering it with their lower body. While they are waiting, some even practise first with a snowball!

Winter arrives and the sun disappears. For two months, the freezing land is in darkness. The penguins protect their eggs under the bright moon until the chicks hatch.

The female lays the egg and protects it with her lower body. But she hasn't eaten for over a month and needs to return to the ocean to feed. She can't take the egg with her, so she leaves it with her mate to look after. She passes the egg from her feet to his feet. It's a delicate operation – if the egg touches the ice for too long, it will freeze.

The female goes out in the freezing blizzards and snowstorms to find food. Now it is all up to the male to protect and hatch the egg. Winter is getting colder and colder …

A giant group of thousands of male penguins huddle together to keep warm. The freezing winds can be 100 km per hour and the temperature, down to −60 °C. The blizzards rage for days on end.

Answers
1 b, 2 a, 3 b, 4 a, 5 a, 6 b, 7 b, 8 b

4 Listen to Part 2. Put the photos in order of the commentary. (10 minutes)

- First, look at the four photos together. Build up a list of useful vocabulary from the audio (such as *chicks, hatch, colony, balanced, protection*) by asking and answering questions about what the penguins are doing, why, and what the weather is like.

- Encourage learners to make predictions about the order of the photos in the commentary. Then play the audio so learners can check their predictions.

- Replay the audio if helpful.

- Give class feedback on the answers.

Audioscript: Track 18

See Learner's Book page 45

After two freezing months, daylight appears again and thousands of chicks hatch. The fathers only have enough food to keep the chicks alive for a few days. The mothers must return with more food. They find their mate and baby amongst the colony of thousands! …

Now the males must go and find food for the family. They haven't eaten for four months! They make the dangerous journey to the sea to find food. The temperatures are still freezing and the blizzards strong. The mothers move to safer places on the ice. The chicks stay balanced on their mother's feet.

The sun is getting higher every day and it warms the ice very slowly. The babies are a month old now. Mother and father work together to feed the babies. Soon they start to feed themselves. The parents go to the sea to fish. The babies gather together for protection. They can't be alone at this stage. The temperatures are still –25 °C.

Summer arrives, the ice melts and the storms disappear. All the penguins now leave the frozen land to go to the sea. The chicks are almost fully grown. Out of all the eggs that were laid, two-thirds of the chicks have survived. In the coldest place on Earth, that is an amazing achievement.

Answers

c, d, a, b

Language focus – The present simple (5 minutes)

- Read about the present simple together.

> **Differentiation ideas:** Invite more confident writers to write two or three more examples of the present simple, ideally about penguins, on the board.

> **Digital Classroom:** Use the activity 'Polar bears' to revise the present simple for things that are always true. The i button will explain how to use the activity.

5 **Put the sentences from Part 2 in order. Then match each sentence to a picture in Activity 4. (5–10 minutes)**

- Read the sentences from Part 2 together. Make sure learners understand the meaning of each sentence, for example words like *balanced, daylight appears, hatch* and *gather together*.

- In pairs, learners put the sentences in order and match each sentence to a picture.

- Circulate and offer support. Then give class feedback on the correct answers.

Answers

Order: 2 (c), 1 (d), 4 (a), 3 (b).

6 **Match a word from the documentary to the definitions. (5–10 minutes)**

- First, download the audioscript and distribute it to learners. Explain that to help learners complete this activity, they should first think about what kind of word it is. Then they should underline the sentences relating to each word in the audioscript so they can see the word in context.

- Demonstrate by looking together at the word *chick*. Elicit that it is a noun. For *chick*, there are multiple examples in the text, such as: *For emperor penguins in the Antarctic, the journey to raise their <u>chicks</u> is more dangerous than most …*; *Penguins protect their eggs under the bright moon until the <u>chicks</u> hatch.* Invite a learner to read the relevant sentences out loud.

- Read through the definitions and elicit that 1 and 2 refer to verbs and 3, 4, 5 and 6 refer to nouns.

- Learners look at definitions 3–6 and elicit which definition fits.

- Learners repeat this process in pairs for the remaining words.

> **Differentiation ideas:** If learners need more support with this task, work with them in a smaller group. Underline the sentences relating to each word as a group and invite learners to take it in

turns to read them out loud. Ask questions about each word, such as: *Is this word a noun? Is it a verb? How does this sentence help us know that definition x is correct?*

Answers

a	breed	d	mate
b	huddle	e	colony
c	chick	f	hatch

7 Tell your partner three new things you have learned about emperor penguins. (5–10 minutes)

> **Assessment ideas:** Circulate while learners tell their partners three new things they have learned about emperor penguins, checking for pronunciation and the use of new vocabulary.

- Come back together as a class and build up some facts which learners think are the most interesting or surprising.

Answers
Learner's own answers.

8 What would you like to know now? Choose one of these topics and write some questions. Research the answers, then share with your class. (25–30 minutes)

- Read through the choice of topics. For each one, create a mind map on the board with learner's ideas.

- Depending on time, ask pairs or small groups of learners to choose a topic, or allocate them one of the topics.

- Circulate and offer support while learners write three questions and then research the answers.

> **Differentiation ideas:** If learners need support with this task, ask them to focus on one or two questions and answers. Extend the activity by challenging learners to write five questions.

- Invite each pair/group to share their findings with the class.

Answers
Learner's own answers.

Plenary ideas

Reflection (5–10 minutes)

- Have a class discussion about the lesson. What aspects of it did learners find challenging (perhaps the listening text or specialist vocabulary)? What was the most fun part of the lesson? Has Activity 8 inspired them to find out anything else about their chosen topic (or another group's topic)?

Homework ideas

Learners practise their listening skills. Under adult supervision, they listen to a wildlife video clip in English, for example one by the British naturalist Sir David Attenborough.

Workbook

Learners do Activities 1–4 on pages 32–33.

3.2 Natural science: Nature's food chains

LEARNING PLAN

Learning objectives	Learning intentions	Success criteria
6Rd.01 6Us.05 1Bp.02	• **Reading:** Understand, with support, most specific information and detail in short and extended texts. • **Use of English:** Use an increasing range of defining relative clauses (e.g. with *whose* and *whom*) and begin to use non-defining relative clauses. • **Biology:** Know that animals, including humans, need air, water and suitable food to survive. • **Vocabulary:** *producer, primary consumer, secondary consumer, tertiary consumer, herbivore, carnivore, omnivore, top predator*	• Learners can understand, with support, specific information in a text about food chains. • Learners can recognise and use defining relative clauses to describe food chains. • Learners can understand that animals, including humans, need air, water and suitable food to survive.
21st-century skills		
Cross-curricular links: Natural science: Learners identify and define what a *food chain* is.		

Materials: Learner's Book pages 46–47; Workbook pages 34–37; **Photocopiable 7**; for Activity 6, internet access or library books about food chains

LANGUAGE BACKGROUND

Defining relative clauses

Relative clauses provide more information about nouns. They begin with a relative pronoun: *who(m), whose, when, where* or *which.*

In some relative clauses the information tells us which person or thing is being referred to.

These types of relative clauses are said to be *defining.* Defining relative clauses are also called *identifying or restrictive relative clauses.* In defining relative clauses, *that* is also commonly used as a pronoun to refer to people or things.

Common misconceptions

Misconception	How to identify	How to overcome
Learners sometimes forget to add the relative pronoun to a defining relative clause. For example: *There are so many TV programmes (**which**) are interesting.* *Some new friends (**who**) were sitting around there were very friendly.*	Write sentences on the board – one where the pronoun can't be omitted and one where it can. For example: 1 *The information **which** was most useful to me is that … . (The information was useful to me.)* 2 *The information (**which**) you gave me was useful.* Elicit that in sentence 1, *the information* is the subject of the sentence, so the pronoun is needed. In sentence 2, *you* is the subject, so the pronoun can be omitted.	Learners could practise by doing the activities on pages 36–37 of the Workbook and by completing **Photocopiable 7**.

Starter ideas

Matching game (10 minutes)

- Explain to learners that in this lesson they are going to look at food chains. Briefly define what a food chain is – the relationship between living things and their sources of food.

- Tell learners that to introduce them to this topic, they're going to play a matching game.

- Write *herbivore*, *carnivore* and *omnivore* on the board and elicit what they mean.

- Then write the names of the animals from the lesson on the board, or put them on a worksheet and distribute it to learners: *crocodiles, eagles, fish, frogs, insects, grasshoppers, lions, lizards, mice, rabbits, reptiles, sharks, small birds, spiders, tigers.*

- Check learners understand what each animal is. Then ask them to work in pairs to match each animal to one of the three groups.

Answers
Herbivores: rabbits, mice, insects, grasshoppers, (some) fish
Omnivores: lizards, small birds, (some) reptiles, (some) fish, (some) frogs
Carnivores: lions, tigers, crocodiles, sharks, eagles, spiders, (most) frogs, (most) reptiles, (some) fish

Main teaching ideas

1 Look at the photos. What do you think is the connection between these living things? (10 minutes)

- Look at the photos together. Ask learners to identify what is in each picture, including the names *eagle, mouse* and *snake.*

- As a class, spend a few minutes discussing the connection between each photo. Ensure that you include the expression *food chain.*

CROSS-CURRICULAR LINK

Natural science: Learners identify and define what a food chain is.

Answers
Learner's own answers.

2 Read and listen to the text and check your ideas for Activity 1. (10 minutes)

- Explain to learners that they are now going to read and listen to a text about food chains. Reassure them that they don't need to understand every word, particularly as there is some scientific vocabulary in the text.

- Briefly look at the key words together and ask learners to listen out for them. Also explain that they will hear some of the words from the Starter activity.

- Play the audio. Ask learners to read the text as they listen.

- Come together as a class to check learner's ideas from Activity 1. Next, read the question at the end together. Check learners understand what a *top predator* is then invite learners to think of another one.

Audioscript: Track 19
See Learner's Book page 46

Answers
The connection between the living things in the photos is that they are part of a food chain. Each depends upon the other for its food source, starting with the plant. For example, the mouse eats the grass; the snake eats the mouse; the eagle eats the snake.
Suggested answer: Human beings are also an example of a top predator.

3 Read the text again and order the pictures to show a food chain. (10 minutes)

- Before reading the text again, ask learners for their initial ideas.

- Learners then reread the text, order the pictures and do the matching activity in pairs.

> **Differentiation ideas:** Learners could just focus on rereading the text and ordering the pictures.

- Circulate and offer general support, particularly with vocabulary.

- Give the class feedback on the answers.

Answers

Order: **c.** Algae – producer; **a.** Krill – primary consumer; **e.** Squid – secondary consumer; **b.** Seal – tertiary consumer; **d.** Polar bear – top predator.

› **Digital Classroom:** Use the activity 'Food chain' to reinforce the concept of food chains. The i button will explain how to use the activity.

4 What is the habitat of the living things in Activities 1 and 3? What other animal habitats do you know? (5–10 minutes)

- First, make sure learners understand what *habitat* means. Ask them to give a couple of examples of different habitats.

- Then work together as a class to answer the questions. Invite learners to tell you the names of the living things from the two activities. Then encourage discussion about possible *habitats* for them.

- Build up a list of other animal habitats on the board.

Answers

Activity 1: forests, fields (grassland), desert.
Activity 3: the ocean, coastal areas (seals), sea ice in Arctic region (polar bears and seals).
Other animal habitats: Learner's own answers.

Use of English – Relative clauses (15 minutes)

- Ask learners to tell you what they can remember about relative clauses.

- Then read the information in the Use of English box together. Make sure learners are clear what relative pronouns are.

- Invite learners to share a couple of examples of sentences that use defining relative clauses, if possible on the theme of living things/food chains.

- Learners could complete **Photocopiable 7**, where the clues to the crossword use relative clauses.

> **Workbook**
>
> Learners do Activities 1–3 on pages 36–37.

› **Digital Classroom:** Use the grammar presentation 'Defining relative clauses' to revise defining relative clauses. The i button will explain how to use the activity.

5 Find all the sentences with relative clauses in the text. (5–10 minutes)

- Ask learners to work in pairs to do this activity. They should start by underlining all the sentences with relative clauses, then circling the relative pronouns.

- Before they complete the explanation, come together as a class and check their answers. Respond to any misunderstandings.

- Then ask learners to complete the explanation with each of the relative pronouns.

Answers

Sentences with relative clauses in the text (relative pronouns in bold):
- *… these are creatures **who** only eat plants.*
- *They are carnivores **whose** main diet is meat.*
- *Next, there are tertiary consumers **who** are usually larger animals like reptiles, birds or fish.*
- *There are also consumers **whose** food comes from plants and meat.*
- *The top predators **who** are at the top of the food chain are …*
1 that, 2 who, 3 whose

6 Work in a small group. Research and present a food chain. (40 minutes)

- Start by looking back at Activity 3 to see the kind of food chain that learners need to create. Also encourage learners to write down the words in blue and other words that might be useful, so they have them to hand when they are drawing their food chains.

- Circulate and offer support, particularly with vocabulary and pronunciation, while learners create and research their food chains using the internet or library books, and explain them to each other.

› **Assessment ideas:** Once learners have drafted their food chains, make a checklist together, to help learners evaluate them. For example: *Did we use the words in blue? Did we use relative clauses to describe the animals? Did we mention their habitat? Did we say what type of animals they are?* Ask learners to exchange their diagrams with another group and provide constructive and sensitive feedback on the drafts. They should include at least one compliment. Based on the feedback, learners update their drafts.

> **Assessment ideas:** While learners are presenting their diagrams, check in particular for their use of new vocabulary, their pronunciation and the use of relative clauses.

Plenary ideas

What can you remember? (10 minutes)

• Learners discuss with a partner what they have learned in the lesson. Ask them what they have enjoyed about the lesson and what they have found challenging. Did they enjoy creating and presenting the food chains? Is there anything else they would like to know about food chains?

• Learners could complete **Photocopiable 7** to help them learn new unit vocabulary and practise the present simple.

Homework ideas

To save time in class, learners can research the food chain for homework and present the information in the next lesson.

Workbook
Learners do Activities 1–3 on pages 36–37.

3.3 Think about it: The strange world of carnivorous plants

LEARNING PLAN		
Learning objectives	**Learning intentions**	**Success criteria**
6Sc.02, 6Sc.06	• **Speaking:** Describe people, places and objects, and routine past and present actions and events. Begin to produce and maintain stretches of language comprehensibly, allowing for hesitation and reformulation, especially in longer stretches of free production.	• Learners can deliver a presentation explaining the habits of a carnivorous plant.
6Ld.05	• **Listening:** Understand, with support, most of the detail of an argument in short and extended talk.	• Learners can understand specific details in a presentation about carnivorous plants.
6Ug.01	• **Use of English:** Use a limited range of verb forms to ask questions to develop ideas and extend understanding.	• Learners can make questions to find out information about carnivorous plants.
1Bp.01	• **Biology:** Identify living things and things that have never been alive. • **Vocabulary:** *leaves, hair, sticky, liquid, trap, crush, juices, dissolve, digest*	• Learners can identify living things and things that have never been alive.
21st-century skills		
Critical thinking opportunity: Explain the survival habits of carnivorous plants.		

Materials: Learner's Book pages 48–49; Workbook pages 36–37; **Differentiated worksheets 3A, B and C**; for Activity 10, access to the internet and/or library, or information photocopied on the plants in Activity 1

Starter ideas

What does carnivorous mean? (5 minutes)

- Explain to learners that in this lesson they are going to look at *carnivorous* plants.

- Ask learners if they can remember what *carnivore* means from Lesson 2. As a class, talk through what *carnivorous* might mean.

- Briefly ask learners if they have heard of carnivorous plants and, if so, if they know the names of any.

Main teaching ideas

1 Look at the photos. What are carnivorous plants? (5–10 minutes)

- First, look at the photos together and see if learners recognise any of them.

> **Critical thinking opportunity:** To help answer the two questions in this activity, encourage learners to look closely at the plants' features and consider how they might be different from other plants. Ask learners what most plants need to survive (sun, water, air and soil). Then ask learners questions to establish how carnivorous plants have different needs. For example: *What does a carnivorous plant eat to survive? How does a carnivorous plant catch food? How does it trap the food?*

Answers
Suggested answer: Carnivorous plants eat meat. They are different from other plants because they eat other living things to survive, whereas other plants get their energy from the sun.

2 Listen to Part 1. (5–10 minutes)

- Play the recording of Minh explaining key facts about carnivorous plants for learners to check their ideas from Activity 1.

- Ask questions to check learners understand the answers, for example *Do carnivorous plants survive on sunlight, water air and soil? What then? Why?*

- If necessary, replay the recording so that learners can listen to Minh explaining the key facts again.

Audioscript: Track 20

See Learner's Book page 48

Hi everyone. Today I want to talk about my favourite type of plants, called carnivorous plants. Most plants survive on four basic things: sunlight, water, air and soil. But carnivorous plants are different because they need something more, so they eat other living things.

I love these plants, but I didn't know much about them. So I wrote down four questions that I wanted to find out:

1 Where do carnivorous plants grow?

2 Why do these plants eat other living things?

3 What animals do they eat?

4 How does a carnivorous plant catch its prey?

Answers
See Activity 1 answers.

Use of English – *Wh-* questions review, and 3 Read the Use of English box and sort the words to make Minh's questions (5–10 minutes)

- To demonstrate the activity, write the question from the Use of English box on the board, but not in the correct order.

- Invite learners to tell you the correct order. Then look at the Use of English box together to check.

- Make sure learners know what the *Wh-* words are and how the questions are formed before they complete Activity 3 individually. Ask them to write each question in their notebook, as they will need them in the following activities.

- Explain to learners that they will find out the answers in the next activity.

> **Digital Classroom:** Use the activity 'Questions' to revise forming *Wh-* questions. The i button will explain how to use the activity.

Answers
a Where do carnivorous plants grow?
b Why do these plants eat other living things?
c What animals do they eat?
d How does a carnivorous plant catch its prey?

4 Intonation in question forms (5 minutes)

- Explain to learners that they are now going to find out the answers to Activity 3.

- Play the recording once so that learners can check their answers.

- Then replay the recording, several times if necessary, focusing on the intonation. Stop the recording after each question. Learners listen and repeat the questions with the correct intonation.

Audioscript: Track 21

See Learner's Book page 48

Narrator:	1
Girl:	Where do carnivorous plants grow?
Narrator:	2
Girl:	Why do these plants eat other living things?
Narrator:	3
Girl:	What animals do they eat?
Narrator:	4
Girl:	How does a carnivorous plant catch its prey?

---

5 Read the listening tip box. In pairs, make predictions about the answers to Minh's questions. (10 minutes)

- Read the Listening tip together. Briefly talk through how making predictions before listening can help with understanding and prepare you for what you are going to hear.

- Encourage learners to work in pairs to make predictions about the answers to Minh's questions.

Answers
Learner's own predictions.

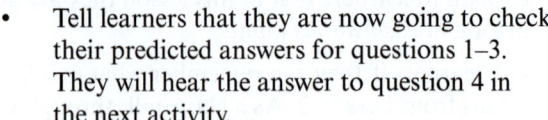

6 Listen to Part 2 and check your predictions for questions 1–3. (5 minutes)

- Tell learners that they are now going to check their predicted answers for questions 1–3. They will hear the answer to question 4 in the next activity.

- Play the recording all the way through. If helpful, replay the recording and pause after each sentence.

- Give class feedback on the correct answers. Ask learners: *Were your predictions correct?*

- To practice Wh-questions, use **Differentiated worksheets 3A, B and C**.

Audioscript: Track 22

See Learner's Book page 48

So where do carnivorous plants grow and why do they eat other living things? Carnivorous plants grow in places where the soil is low in nutrients, so they have to find other ways to feed themselves. They grow in wet places, where other plants can't grow very well – wet fields, sand, rocky places and even in ponds.

And what animals do they eat? Usually insects, such as ants and flies, but they can also eat spiders, small mammals and reptiles, such as frogs, lizards and mice. They have even been known to eat birds and rats!

Answers
1 Carnivorous plants grow in wet places, where other plants can't grow very well – wet fields, sand, rocky places and even in ponds.
2 They grow in places where the soil is low in nutrients, so they have to find other ways to feed themselves.
3 Usually insects, such as ants and flies, but they can also eat spiders, small mammals and reptiles, such as frogs, lizards and mice. They have even been known to eat birds and rats!

---

7 Listen to Part 3 about the Sundew plant. Check your predictions for question 4. Then match the sentences to the pictures. (5–10 minutes)

- Ask learners to look again at question 4 and their predicted answers.

- Remind them that they don't need to understand every word of the recording – just enough to check their predictions and match the sentences to the pictures. Then listen to Part 3 of the recording all the way through. Replay the recording, pausing after each sentence to give learners a chance to process the information.

- Ask learners whether their predictions were correct. Then, in pairs, learners match the sentences to the pictures.

> **Differentiation ideas:** If learners need support with this task, download the audioscript and give them a hard copy so they can see the sentences in context.

Audioscript: Track 23

See Learner's Book page 49

To answer my favourite question … How does a carnivorous plant catch its prey? I'm going to explain with the Sundew plant, which grows mainly in Australia and South Africa. Take a look at these pictures … The Sundew plant has long thin leaves covered in tiny hairs. At the end of each hair is a sticky drop of liquid. The insect is attracted to the sweet smell of the liquid on the leaves. But when it crawls onto the leaves, it is trapped by the thick sticky liquid. Then, the leaf curls around the insect and crushes it. Then the leaf produces juices which dissolve the insect's body, so the plant can digest it.

Then the leaves uncurl to wait for the next victim!

Answers
Sample answer: The Sundew plant has long thin leaves with tiny hairs. The hairs have a sticky liquid at the end. When an insect lands on the leaves, the liquid traps it. The leaf curls around the insect and crushes it. The juices in the leaf dissolve the insect's body, so the plant can digest it.
Picture 1 – sentence c
Picture 2 – sentence b
Picture 3 – sentence a

---

8 Work in pairs. Describe to each other how the Sundew plant catches its prey. (5–10 minutes)

- Explain to learners that they are going to describe to each other how the Sundew plant catches its prey, drawing on what they have heard. First, focus on the words in the word box and check learners understand their meaning. Tell learners to use the words in their descriptions. Make sure learners cover up the sentences a–c from Activity 7 so they're not tempted just to read them out.

> **Assessment ideas:** While learners are talking, circulate and give verbal feedback on their use of vocabulary from the word box and pronunciation.

- Ask learners to uncover the sentences from Activity 7. Ask: *Were these sentences close to your description?* Listen again to Part 3 of the recording and then share feedback as a class.

Speaking tip – Use visuals, and 9 Read the Speaking tip box. How could Minh use these ideas for visuals in her presentation? (5–10 minutes)

- Before reading the Speaking tip, ask learners to imagine that Minh is delivering a presentation about carnivorous plants. Check that learners understand what visuals are. Invite learners to give a few examples.

- Read the Speaking tip together. Then, as a class, elicit ideas about how Minh could use the ideas for visuals in her presentation.

- Ask learners which idea they like best and how they would use it.

Answers
Diagrams, photos and videos to show what the plants look like and how they trap prey; useful for close-ups of specific features. A 3D model could show the actions the plant takes to trap its prey. If available, real plants could be brought in to demonstrate the plants in action.
Learner's own answers.

---

10 Explain the habits of a carnivorous plant. (30 minutes + time for presentations)

- Learners work in small groups to explain the habits of a carnivorous plant and present their findings to the class.

- Make sure each learner has chosen a carnivorous plant from Activity 1.

- Learners research the answers to Minh's questions for their plant You may want to provide a choice of texts or websites to support learners in their research. You could put learners into groups of four and ask each learner to answer one question.

- Circulate and support learners while they plan and write their presentations, ideally using presentation software if this is practical. Make sure learners use the sentences and words in Activities 7 and 8.

- Allow learners time to create their own visuals, such as drawings/diagrams to show how their plant traps its prey.

- Learners use the visuals to present their findings to the class.

Plenary ideas

Consolidation (5–10 minutes)

- As a class, discuss what learners found most interesting about the carnivorous plants. Encourage learners to ask at least one follow-up question for each presentation.

Homework ideas

- Learners find out about one other carnivorous plant and report back at the start of the next lesson.

- Learners could complete **Differentiated worksheet 3A, B or C** to practise using defining relative clauses.

> **Workbook**
>
> Learners do Activities 1–3 on pages 36–37.

3.4 Write about it: Animal types

LEARNING PLAN

Learning objectives	Learning intentions	Success criteria
6Wor.03, 6Wc.02	• **Writing:** Use appropriate layout for a limited range of genres. Write, with support, short texts which describe people, places and objects, and routine past and present actions around events. • **Vocabulary:** *birds, reptiles, mammals, insects, amphibians, fish, breathe, fur, gills, lungs, scales, skin, fins, shell, feathers, egg*	• Learners can create an infographic text about a type of animal, using appropriate layout.
21st-century skills		
Learning to learn: Research information about a specific animal or group of animals.		

Materials: Learner's Book pages 50–51; Workbook pages 38–39; access to the internet and/or library books about animals or photocopied information learners can use for their research; magazines (Activity 6); Sample Answer for Unit 3; **Photocopiable 8**

Starter activity

What's an infographic text? (10 minutes)

- Tell learners that in this lesson they are going to read an infographic text about a type of animal, and then create one of their own.

- Ask learners if they know what an infographic is. Look back at the world map in Lesson 1.2 and review the characteristics of an infographic text (information graphic), i.e. written in a short, simple style because the visuals show a lot of the information.

- Show learners the infographic example on page 50 of the Learner's Book. Elicit that the information is far more digestible in this format than if the information was all text. If you have time, look at some of the design features of the infographic and talk about what makes the text easy to read (for example, clear headings, callouts, etc.).

Main teaching ideas

1 Listen to the animal sounds. Can you identify the animals? (10 minutes)

- Read the animal types together. Make sure learners understand what they are by asking them to share a couple of examples from each type. Learners should create a table with five columns in their notebooks and write each type of animal as a column heading.

- Listen to the sounds all the way through. Then replay, pausing after each sound, and identify the animals together. Write the name of each animal on the board.

- Ask learners, in pairs, to classify each animal by writing it under the correct column head in the table.

- When learners have completed the activity, invite a pair of learners to tell you which animal type is missing.

Audioscript: Track 24

See Learner's Book page 51

1 [whale song]

2 [Asiatic painted bullfrogs croaking loudly]

3 [a rattlesnake's rattle]

4 [crickets chirping]

5 [ducks quacking]

6 [a lion's roar]

7 [a toucan's screech]

8 [a snake's hiss]

Answers

1 Whale, 2 bullfrogs, 3 rattlesnake, 4 crickets, 5 ducks, 6 lion, 7 toucan, 8 snake
Mammals: whale, lion
Amphibian: bullfrog
Reptiles: rattlesnakes, snake
Insect: crickets
Birds: ducks, toucan
Type missing: fish

2 Match the words below with types of animals in Activity 1. Which features can you see in the photos? (10 minutes)

- Read the words and check learners understand their meaning and how to pronounce them. Use the photos to help explain some of the vocabulary. Invite learners to name the animals and point out the features in each image using the words in the word box.

- Learners create a new table in their notebooks with the six column headings from Activity 1.

- Circulate and offer support while groups of 3–4 learners match each word with a type of animal by writing the word in the appropriate columns.

- Then give class feedback on the answers.

Answers

Breathe: mammals, amphibians, reptiles, birds
Fur: mammals
Gills: fish, amphibians (most)
Lungs: mammals, birds, reptiles, amphibians (most)
Scales: fish, reptiles
Skin: mammals, amphibians
Fins: fish, young amphibians
Shell: some insects, some reptiles
Feathers: birds
Egg: birds (hard shell), reptiles (hard shell), fish, amphibians (soft gel layer).
Features seen in photos:
a   Duck, chicks and egg; feathers, egg, shell (of egg).
b   Whale: fins, gills (not really visible), skin.
c   Chameleon: scales.

> **Digital Classroom:** Use the activity 'Which type of animal?' to revise animal vocabulary and practise classifying animals into types. The i button will explain how to use the activity.

3   **What type of animals can you see in the photos? What are the similarities and differences between them? (10 minutes)**

- First, as a class identify the type of animal in each photo (*bird, mammal, reptile*). Read the example together. Point out that scales and skin are words from the word box and encourage learners to use these words in their discussions.

- Ask two learners to demonstrate this activity by sharing one similarity and one difference between the animals.

- Circulate and offer support with vocabulary and pronunciation while learners discuss the similarities and differences in pairs.

- As a class, share feedback and write useful vocabulary on the board.

Answers
a Duck – bird. b Whale – mammal. c Chameleon – reptile.
Learner's own answers.

4   **Read the infographic text about amphibians. Which of your points from Activity 3 are mentioned? (10 minutes)**

- Explain to learners that they are now going to read the infographic text on page 50.

- Ask learners what they already know about amphibians and encourage predictions about what they will read by asking questions. For example: *Do amphibians live in water and on land? Are their habitats wet/dry? Are they vertebrates or invertebrates? What is their skin like? Do they have lungs/gills? How many species are there? Where do amphibians lay their eggs?*

- Learners read the text and say which of the features of animals from Activity 3 are mentioned.

Answers
Learner's own answers.
Sample answer: Amphibians **breathe** in water and on land. Their **skin** is smooth. Most amphibians have **lungs** and **gills**; they can also **breathe** through their **skin**. They lay **eggs** in water. Their eggs don't have a hard **shell** (they are covered in a gel). Young amphibians are born (hatch) in the water; they live on the land when they get older.

5   **Find the key words underlined in the text and read the information. Which information is new for you? Which is the most interesting? (10 minutes)**

- Ask learners to scan the text and find the underlined words (*habitats, skin, species, young*).

- Check that learners understand what each key word means and what it tells you about amphibians, for example what it is, where it lives, its characteristics, etc. Then invite different learners to read the sentence relating to each key word.

- Next, as a class, discuss which information is new for learners and which is the most interesting. For example, ask: *Did you know that there are over 8000 species of amphibians?*

- Have a class vote on which fact is the most interesting.

Answers
Learner's own answers.

6   **Create an infographic text about a type of animal. Work in pairs. (20–30 minutes)**

- Learners work in pairs to create an infographic text.

> **Differentiation ideas:** Learners could work in pairs so that more confident writers can provide language support.

- For Step 1, brainstorm animals or groups of animals that learners could write about. Make sure each pair chooses an animal/group of animals, or, if research options are limited, allocate animals to each pair.

- **Learning to learn:** In Step 2, learners research information about their chosen animal/group of animals. Ask them to draw on the infographic on page 50 of the Learner's Book to do their research. For example, encourage them to use the key words to describe the animal, its habitat and its young, and to find out how many species there are, etc. Encourage learners to divide the research between them, for example by each taking three key words to research.

- For Step 3, support learners while they use their notes to create the text, by writing sentences. Make sure the sentences are concise and only include the most important information. For example, a learner's notes may say: *Habitat – near water, wet places.* A suitable sentence might be: *Their habitats are near water or in wet places.*

› **Assessment ideas:** Before beginning Step 3, show learners the sample answer for Unit 3 without the mark scheme comments. As a class, evaluate its strengths and weaknesses and also look at the list of steps on page 51 of the Learner's Book, so that learners are clear about what they are aiming to achieve in their infographic text.

› **Assessment ideas:** When learners have finished their infographic, ask them to work through **Photocopiable 8** to self-assess their work. When they have made any updates, learners could swap their infographic texts with another pair of learners and check for any errors (Step 4). Encourage them to give feedback sensitively and to include at least one compliment.

- Finally, for Step 5, learners find or create their own images to show the key points. They can either do this on a computer or cut and paste images from magazines. Learners add the text to complete their infographic.

7 **Present, display or publish your work. (5 minutes per pair)**

- If learners present their work to the class, remember to allow extra class time. Display the infographics in the classroom or on the school blog.

Plenary ideas

Reflection (10 minutes)

- Have a brief discussion about the advantages and disadvantages of infographics. Do learners think they are an effective way to present information on a topic?

Homework ideas

Learners write a paragraph about an animals from one of the other presentations.

> **Workbook**
>
> Learners do Activities 1–5 on pages 38–39.

3.5 Read and respond: *Song for a Whale*

LEARNING PLAN

Learning objectives	Learning intentions	Success criteria
6Rm.01, 6Rm.02	• **Reading:** Understand, with support, most of the main points of short and extended texts. Read independently a range of short simple fiction and non-fiction texts with confidence and enjoyment.	• Learners can read and enjoy a story about a girl who makes a connection with a whale, understanding the main points.
6Uv.06	• **Use of English:** Use collective nouns.	
	• **Vocabulary:** *plankton, marine biologist, migration, pod, ocean, sanctuary, species, hybrid*	• Learners can use collective nouns.

21st-century skills
Emotional development: Develop empathy towards other children.

Materials: Learner's Book pages 52–55; Workbook pages 40–41; short video clip introduction to sign language (Starter activity); **Photocopiable 9**

Starter ideas

Sign language (10 minutes)

- Explain to learners that the story in this lesson is about a girl called Iris, who is deaf. Check that learners understand what *deaf* means. Tell learners that Iris uses sign language to communicate.

- Ask learners what they know about sign language. Has anyone used it? If possible, show a short introductory video clip on sign language.

Main teaching ideas

1 What do you know about whales? How do you think they communicate? (5–10 minutes)

- Tell learners that the story they are going to read is about a connection between Iris and a whale. Explain that before they read the story, it is useful to share what learners know about whales. Elicit and write down some key whale facts on the board; for example they are the largest animals that live in the ocean; they are mammals; they live in groups; and a baby whale is called a calf.

- Discuss how whales might communicate. First, elicit different ways we communicate, like waving, sign language, whistling, etc. Learners say/guess which ways whales might communicate.

- Use **Photocopiable 9** about baleen whales as an introduction to the type of whale in the story. Remember to allow an extra **20 minutes** for this.

Answers

Learner's own answers.

Whales communicate with each other through sounds, including clicks, whistles and low frequency calling. Whale sounds are commonly called 'whale songs'.

---

2 Read and listen to the whole extract once. (10 minutes)

- Before reading and listening to the whole extract once, tell learners that they are going to read an extract from a story called *Song for a Whale*. Make it clear that it is not necessary to understand every word: they just need to identify how Iris, the young girl, finds out about the whale's story and what problem the whale has.

- Look at the pictures and elicit suggestions about the answers to the two questions. Elicit the word *sounds*.

- Play the recording without pausing and ask learners to follow the text as they listen.

- Then, as a class, talk through the answers to the two questions.

> **Audioscript:** Track 25
> See Learner's Book pages 52–54

Answers

The narrator, Iris, finds out about the whale's story by watching a documentary in one of her school lessons.

The whale has a problem because he makes sounds that are different to the other whales' sounds (so they can't hear and don't understand him).

---

3 Read the extract again and decide if the sentences are true or false. (10 minutes)

- Read the glossary and sentences a–g together. Check learners understand the meaning of new words.

- Circulate and offer support while learners reread the extract and work in pairs to decide if the sentences are true or false. Encourage learners to focus on the part of the story where they find the information about the questions and discourage them from translating every word.

> **Differentiation ideas:** If learners need support with this task, give them an extra glossary list with vocabulary they might find challenging.

- Give class feedback on whether the sentences are true or false, but don't correct the false sentences at this stage.

Answers
a True. b False. c False. d True. e True. f False.
g True. h True. i False. j False.

---

4 Work in pairs and correct all the false sentences. (10 minutes)

- Circulate and offer support while learners work in the same pairs as for the previous activity. If learners need support with this task, elicit why each sentence is false and point to the part of the story where they can find the information.

- Give class feedback at the end of the activity.

Answers
b Iris read the captions on the screen.
c The whale swam around by himself.
f The other whales couldn't understand him (because the sounds of his song were at a higher frequency).
i She couldn't remember standing up when the teacher started talking.
j He continued calling but no one heard him.

---

5 Match the marine wildlife words in blue to a definition. (10 minutes)

- Focus on the first blue word, *pod*, and the other words around it: 'a whale … who swam around by himself and not in a pod, like other whales'. Elicit suggestions about the meaning of *pod*. Ask: *If you are in a pod, do you think you are alone?* Read the definitions and identify that the answer is definition d.

- Circulate and offer support while learners work in pairs and match the other marine wildlife words to the definitions.

Answers
a plankton, b marine biologist, c migration, d pod,
e ocean, f sanctuary, g species, h hybrid

Language focus and 6 Can you match the collective nouns to the correct animals? (10 minutes)

- Read the Language focus about collective nouns together. Brainstorm and build up a list of other collective nouns.

- Learners do the matching exercise in small groups. Then come together as a class to check the answers.

Answers
1 e, 2 c, 3 d, 4 a, 5 b

> **Digital Classroom:** Use the activity 'Collective nouns' to revise collective nouns. The i button will explain how to use the activity.

7 Use the words in Activity 5 to answer the questions. (10 minutes)

- Explain to learners that they are going to use some of the words in blue to answer three questions. Either write the words on the board or give learners a worksheet with the words on.

- Circulate and offer support while learners answer the questions in pairs.

- Give class feedback on the correct answers.

Answers
a Blue 55's parents were different species: his mother was a blue whale and his father was a fin whale.
b They wanted to study his migration pattern, which was strange and not like other whales.
c Three of the following:
   - He didn't live in a pod (didn't live with a family or friends).
   - He was a hybrid.
   - He sang at a different frequency (so other whales couldn't understand him).
   - He had a different migration pattern.
Why he couldn't communicate: Blue 55 sang at a different (higher) frequency to the other whales and they couldn't hear him easily or understand him.

Reading tip – Look at writing style, and 8 Read the Reading tip. (5 minutes)

- Go over the Reading tip together. Then have a brief discussion about how the author's writing style makes learners feel about the whale.

- Encourage suggestions about why the author refers to Blue 55 as 'him' instead of 'it' and how she wants the reader to feel about Blue 55.

Answers

Suggested answer: The author refers to Blue 55 as 'he' to give him an identity, or a personality, so that the reader will feel closer to him and relate to him. The author wants the reader to feel close to Blue 55 and have feelings for his sad situation.

9 How did Iris feel when she was watching the video? (10 minutes)

- First, look at the picture of Iris and ask what she is doing. Then have a general discussion about how Iris was feeling when she was watching the video.

- Next, ask learners to scan the text to look for words that give clues about Iris's emotions, for example *my stomach tightened into a ball, my eyes were watery, I didn't remember standing up.*

- Elicit suggestions for why Iris felt like this.

Answers

Learner's own answers.

10 Feeling empathy. Discuss the questions in pairs or in a small group. (10 minutes)

- **Emotional development**: Use the questions to help learners begin to develop empathy towards other children. Circulate and offer support while learners discuss the questions in pairs or a small group.

- At the end of the activity, encourage learners to share three examples of when it can help to have empathy.

Answers

a   Learner's own answers.

b   1 – When you can understand someone's feelings because you can imagine their situation.

c   Learner's own answers.

Plenary ideas

Reflection (5–10 minutes)

As a class, discuss the story – what was challenging about it and what did learners enjoy? Would learners like to read the rest of the story?

Homework ideas

Learners write a paragraph about a time when they felt empathy for someone, or when someone else felt empathy for them.

> **Workbook**
>
> Learners do Activities 1–6 on pages 40–41.

3.6 Project challenge

LEARNING PLAN

Learning objectives	Learning intentions	Success criteria
6Sc.06, 6Sc.02	• **Speaking:** Begin to produce and maintain stretches of language comprehensibly, allowing for hesitation and reformulation, especially in longer stages of free production. Describe people, places and objects, and routine past and present actions and events	• Learners can deliver a presentation about how an animal survives.
6Wca.04, 6Wca.01, 6Ug.01	• **Writing /Use of English:** Use grammatical structures correctly, allowing for occasional mistakes. Use legible handwriting in written work with appropriate speed and fluency. Use a limited range of verb forms to ask questions to develop ideas and extend understanding.	• Learners can create a written quiz with questions about a specific animal. • Learners can edit and proofread the quiz, checking for errors in spelling and grammar.
6Wca.03	• **Writing:** Plan, write, edit and proofread short texts, with little or no support.	

21st-century skills

Collaboration: Take responsibility for your own contribution in a group project.

Materials: Learner's Book pages 56–57; Workbook page 42; access to the internet, library books, magazines or photocopied information about animal survival/animals' features, habitat, survival and diet; examples of other learner's work; Unit 3 project checklists; End of Unit 3 test; Progress test 1

Starter ideas

Raise interest in the projects (10–15 minutes)

- Tell learners they are either going to do a presentation about how an animal survives (Project A) or create a quiz about an animal (Project B).

- If possible, raise interest in the projects by presenting examples of learner's work on similar topics from other classes or the internet.

- Revise new vocabulary from the unit which learners may need for the challenges, in a fun way. For example, you could create games like a word search or crossword.

Main teaching ideas

Introduce and complete projects (60 minutes)

- Encourage learners to choose one of the projects and then follow the steps for their chosen project.

Project A: A presentation about how an animal survives

- Divide learners into groups of four. Look at the categories in the Learner's Book and give learners a few minutes to choose an animal and brainstorm what they already know about it. Circulate and support learners as they write four questions about it, focused on how it survives.

- **Collaboration:** Encourage each learner to make their own contribution to the project. For example, each group member should research one question and use the information to organise and write that part of the presentation, then present it.

- Support learners while they research their questions and then plan and write the presentation.

- Next, learners create visuals for their presentations. If each group has access to a computer, encourage them to use video clips and photos. If they don't have access to a computer, they should draw their own visuals.

- Learners read through the steps in the Learner's Book and check they have followed the instructions and included everything that was required before practising their presentations together.

- Allow time for learners to deliver their presentations to the class.

> **Assessment ideas:** Learners use the Unit 3 project checklist to evaluate other groups' presentations. Encourage them to write at least one interesting fact that they learned from the presentation.

Project B: Create a quiz about an animal

- Divide learners into pairs. Give learners a few minutes to decide on an animal to make a quiz about.

- **Collaboration:** Encourage learners to work together to research and create their quizzes. For example, each pair should divide the research task and question writing and check each other's quiz questions.

- Circulate and support learners as they write their quiz questions. Make sure they are writing down the answers on a separate piece of paper and that there is at least one question about each of the five topics in Step 1.

> **Assessment ideas:** When learners have finished drafting their quizzes, ask them to swap their questions with their partner, who can check the spelling and grammar and suggest improvements.

- Learners finalise their quizzes and add visual images.

- Learners swap their quiz with another pair. Allow time for learners to do the quizzes.

> **Assessment ideas:** Learners use the Unit 3 project checklist to evaluate another pair's quiz. Encourage them to write at least one interesting fact that they learned from the quiz.

- Finally, as a class, share new information that learners have gained from the quizzes. Make a classroom display of the quizzes.

Plenary ideas

Reflection (10 minutes)

As a class, learners discuss what they enjoyed about the projects and what they found most challenging. Is there anything that they would do differently next time?

Homework ideas

Learners follow the instructions to research and complete the project they didn't do in class.

Workbook

Learners do Activities 1–2 on page 42.

3.7 What do you know now?

What do living things do to survive?

- **Learning to learn:** Learners have the opportunity to reflect and evaluate their own learning success.

- Reintroduce the question from the start of the unit: *What do living things do to survive?* Discuss learner's responses to the question now and compare with their comments at the beginning of the unit. How much has changed?

- Ask learners to work on the questions in pairs.

- For questions 1–5, encourage learners to look back through the unit if they can't remember. Circulate and offer support while learners answer the questions.

- If learners find question 6 challenging, encourage them to think back to their discussions from Lesson 3.5.

- When learners have finished the questions, give class feedback on the answers.

Answers

1 Three of the following:
- Male and females work together to raise their young. One looks after the egg or chick, while the other goes to find food to bring back.
- They huddle together in big groups for warmth (adults and young).
- They keep their eggs and young chicks balanced on their feet, under their bodies, for warmth.
- The parents go to the sea to fish and work together to feed the babies.
- They move to different parts of the ice to survive against the extreme cold.

2 Learner's own answers.
Suggested answer: A food chain shows how living things get their food. Food chains begin with a plant, then animals that eat that plant, then it shows other animals that eat the first animals and so on.

3 Herbivores – animals that eat only plants. Carnivores – animals that eat meat (other animals). Omnivores – animals that eat meat and plants.

4 Carnivorous plants eat other living things because they grow in wet places where the soil is low in nutrients, so they have to find other ways to feed themselves.
Sample answers:
- Sundew plant: sticky hairs on the leaf trap the insect, then the leaf curls round so it can't escape. The plant's leaves produce juices to dissolve the insect's body, so the plant can digest it.
- Venus flytrap: nectar of the leaf attracts the insect, then the leaves close around it to trap and crush it.
- Pitcher plants: insects drop inside the plants, which are shaped like a thin cup.
- Butterworts: the leaves have a sticky surface that traps insects when they land.

5 (Three characteristics from the following):
- Amphibians can live on land and in the water.
- They live in wet places.
- They have back bones (they are vertebrates).
- Their skin is smooth, sticky, moist and thin.
- Most amphibians have lungs and gills.
- Some amphibians can breathe through their skin.
- They lay their eggs in water. The eggs are covered in gel, not a hard shell.
- The young develop on their own in the water.
Shared characteristics: amphibians breathe; they have lungs and gills; they live on land and water; they have smooth skin; they have back bones.

6 Iris has empathy with the whale because she is deaf and communicates in a different way to most other people. She lives in a silent world, like the whale.

Look what I can do!

- There are five 'can do' statements. Learners read through the statements and tick the things they can do. Encourage them to reflect on how well they can do these things. Also invite them to think of ways they can improve further, for example what strategies they can use or learn to use.

- If learners find it challenging to read the statements, look through the unit with them and support them to find the relevant information.

- Finally, ask learners to work through the questions on page 43 of the Workbook. Encourage them to talk about what they enjoyed and also about any further support they might need.

Check your progress 1

Learners answer the seven questions.

Answers

1 **a** nervous, **b** district, **c** pride, **d** goggles, **e** ankle,
   f goalkeeper, **g** chick, **h** gills, **i** flock
2 Suggested answers:
   b Words to describe locations (see Lesson 1.2)
   c Nouns to describe feelings and emotions
      (see Lesson 1.4)
   d Words to describe sports equipment
      (see Lesson 2.1)
   e Words to describe parts of the body
      (see Lesson 2.3)
   f Words to describe players' positions in a
      football match or general words about football
      (see Lesson 2.5)
   g Words to describe penguins (see Lesson 3.1) or
      young animals (general)
   h Words to describe parts of animals
      (see Lesson 3.4)
   i Collective nouns to describe groups of animals
      (see Lesson 3.5)
3 Learner's own answers.
4 1 *Have* you finished yet? 2 Is Ethiopia the hottest
   country *on* our planet? 3 Dad asked me *to* help him.
   4 The rollercoaster was *amazing*! 5 If you eat fruit,
   your body *will* get healthy vitamins. 6 You *should/
   need to* warm up before running. 7 In the Antarctic
   winter, the sun *doesn't* rise for two months.
   8 Herbivores are animals *that* only eat plants.
   9 What *does* a carnivore eat?
5 Learner's own answers.
6 Learner's own answers.
7 Learner's own answers.

> 4 Inventions

Unit plan

Lesson	Approximate number of learning hours	Outline of learning content	Learning objectives	Resources
1 Gadgets and us	1.5–2.0	Talk about our favourite gadgets and equipment.	6Ld.05	Learner's Book Lesson 4.1 Workbook Lesson 4.1 **Digital Classroom:** video – Incredible inventions; activity – Gadget and equipment sorting
2 Radical robotics	1.5–2.0	Discover more about robot technology. Give facts about robots using the past simple.	6Rd.01 6Ug.04	Learner's Book Lesson 4.2 Workbook Lesson 4.2 ⤓ Photocopiable 10 **Digital Classroom:** video – Here come the robots!; activity – Past simple
3 Bright ideas	2.0–2.5	Present an idea for a new invention using future tenses.	6Lm.01 6Sc.06 6Sc.07 6Ug.08	Learner's Book Lesson 4.3 Workbook Lesson 4.3 ⤓ Photocopiable 11 **Digital Classroom:** grammar presentation – *Will* for future predictions
4 Changing the world	2.0–2.5	Write about an important invention.	6Ro.01 6Rd.03 6Wc.03 6Wor.02	Learner's Book Lesson 4.4 Workbook Lesson 4.4 ⤓ Unit 4 sample answer ⤓ Photocopiable 12 **Digital Classroom:** activity – An important invention
5 *Start Small, Think Big*	1.0–1.5	Read a story about a young inventor.	6Rd.01 6Rm.02 6Rd.04 6Ug.10	Learner's Book Lesson 4.5 Workbook Lesson 4.5 ⤓ Differentiated worksheets 4A, B and C **Digital Classroom:** activity – Start small, think big
6 Project challenge	1.0–1.5	A presentation about the history of an invention **or** Create a quiz about inventions.	6Sc.06 6Sc.02 6Wc.02 6Wca.01	Learner's Book Lesson 4.6 Workbook Lesson 4.6 ⤓ Unit 4 project checklists

(continued)

Cross-unit resources
 Unit 4 Audioscripts
Unit 4 test
Unit 4 Progress report
Unit 4 Wordlist

BACKGROUND KNOWLEDGE

In Unit 4, learners explore the world of inventions.

In Lesson 4.1, learners discuss their favourite gadgets. The final activity involves a pyramid discussion. This is a speaking activity in which learners discuss a subject in progressively larger groups. Usually, each group has to reach agreement before joining another group. They then have to negotiate again to reach agreement in the bigger group.

This type of activity is particularly useful for:

* developing skills in putting opinions forward.
* persuading and considering different points of view.
* giving reasons to support your views.

Lesson 4.2 focuses on robot technology. Asimo (pronounced 'a-sh(e)-mo') is a humanoid robot

model that was created by Honda in 2000. ASIMO stands for Advanced Step in Innovative Mobility. Some of the models can walk, run, and go up and down stairs. In 2018, Honda stopped producing the robot.

In Lesson 4.3, learners plan and deliver an oral presentation to describe an invention that they have created, using appropriate language to predict the invention's use in the future.

Then, in Lesson 4.4, learners write a persuasive essay about an important invention, giving opinions and reasons.

Finally, learners read a story about the challenges of a young inventor and discuss the importance of self-belief.

TEACHING SKILLS FOCUS

Active learning – Think-Pair-Share (TPS)

Summary

* TPS is a collaborative learning strategy where learners work together to solve a problem or answer a question.
* The teacher presents learners with an issue or question to discuss/solve in pairs.
* TPS is very popular; you can download TPS apps.

Benefits of TPS

* Develops learner's knowledge of the given issue/problem.
* Helps learners develop their ability to think critically, by considering and evaluating other viewpoints.
* Provides you with an invaluable insight into learner's thought processes.

* Can be used to exploit each individual learner's level of motivation, confidence, interest or previous knowledge of the lesson content.

Your challenge

Try using TPS to help develop learner's critical thinking skills, build on their strengths, and identify and improve their weaknesses.

* Think of a task for learners to discuss in pairs (see below for a few examples).
* Circulate and listen to learner's ideas and thought processes. Encourage them to:
  * ask and answer questions
  * analyse evidence
  * connect evidence to knowledge of other subjects
  * draw conclusions.

CONTINUED

- When you have tried using TPS, write a list of ways the approach has benefited your learners.
- Are there any drawbacks?

A few suggestions about where to try TPS in Unit 4

- **Lesson 1:** Learners pool their knowledge in the Starter activity to come up with names of gadgets.

- **Lesson 2:** Learners work in pairs and pool their knowledge/ideas about what Asimo the robot (or robots in general) can and can't do. They make predictions about what they will hear before the listening activity.

- **Lesson 6:** Learners investigate the history of an invention together.

Ask learners to reflect regularly on their learning achievements, especially in Lesson 7.

4.1 Think about it: Gadgets and us

LEARNING PLAN

Learning objectives	Learning intentions	Success criteria
6Ld.05	• **Listening:** Understand, with support, most of the detail of an argument in short and extended talk. • **Vocabulary:** *gadget, hoverboard, zip, bicycle, compass, mobile phone, tablet*	• Learners can understand contrasting points in a discussion comparing favourite gadgets and equipment.

21st-century skills

Critical thinking: Evaluate and express own opinions comparing different inventions.

Materials: Learner's Book pages 61–63; Workbook pages 44–45

Starter ideas

Inventions (10 minutes)

- Explain to learners that this unit is going to be about inventions and gadgets.

- Introduce the unit objectives. Then ask learners to give you some general examples of a gadget (make sure learners understand that gadget means small mechanical or electronic piece of equipment).

- Next, put learners into pairs. Give each pair a different room of a house or school and ask them to think of gadgets or inventions you might find there.

- Elicit one or two ideas from each group and note them on the board.

Getting started (5–10 minutes)

- Focus on the Big Question (*How have important inventions changed our lives?*) and the photo on page 61 of the Learner's Book.

- Elicit the name of the gadget in the photo and possiblities for this invention. Encourage learners to think of both potential uses for leisure and for professional use.

- Elicit reasons why inventors create something new. Support learners by asking questions like *Why did we need …? Is it a completely new idea? Or is it a new idea to change/improve something old?*

Answers
a A virtual reality headset.
b Learner's own answers. Background: VR headsets simulate a 3D environment for the wearer. Curently they are mainly used in video

games to enhance the visual experience for the player, but are also used to simulate real environments for professional training.

c   Learner's own answers. Suggestions: inventors often create inventions to fill a need for something that is missing in existing things, for example to make something faster, more effective, more useful or more comfortable. They discover new ways of doing things and create something (such as a machine or device) that enables people to carry it out.

> **Digital Classroom:** Use the video 'Incredible inventions' to introduce the topic of inventions. The i button will explain how to use the video.

Main teaching ideas

1   What is your favourite gadget or piece of equipment? (10 minutes)

*   Write the expression *I can't live without …!* on the board. Then ask learners to name their favourite gadget/piece of equipment (such as a bike). Elicit and build up names of different gadgets/pieces of equipment on the board, when learners use them and why they are so important to learners.

*   Circulate and offer support while learners tell a partner about their favourite gadget/piece of equipment.

> **Critical thinking opportunity:** Learners identify their own preferences for gadgets/pieces of equipment, giving reasons why.

Answers
Learner's own answers.

2   Test yourself with this quiz! (10 minutes)

*   Before doing the quiz, look at the pictures and check learners know the correct pronunciation for each gadget.

*   Ask learners questions about *if/how often* and *why* learners use each gadget/piece of equipment.

*   Read the first question together and check learners understand the meaning of *kilometres per hour.*

*   Eliminate the other answers and focus on *bicycle* and *hoverboard.* Encourage speculation about how fast each one can go before confirming that *hoverboard* is the correct answer.

*   Read the other questions through together and check learners understand their meaning.

*   Offer support while learners discuss which picture goes with each question. Then give class feedback on the correct answers.

Answers
1 Hoverboard, **2** Zip, **3** Bicycle, **4** Compass, **5** Mobile phone, **6** Tablet

> **Digital Classroom:** Use the activity 'Gadget and equipment sorting' to revise gadgets and equipment vocabulary. The i button will explain how to use the activity.

Listening tip – Listening for specific information, and 3 Listen to the children talking about favourite gadgets and equipment. (10 minutes)

*   Tell learners they are going to listen to two children talking about their favourite gadgets and equipment.

*   Read the suggestion in the Listening tip then tell learners to read the two questions.

*   Ask learners to note down the gadgets the children talk about while they listen to the recording, and the advantages and disadvantages of each one after listening.

*   Play the recording. After learners have noted down their answers, ask them to compare them with a partner. If necessary, play the audio again to either check the answers or focus specifically on question b.

Audioscript: Track 26

See Learner's Book page 63

Ben:	What is your favourite gadget or piece of equipment? Choose one thing! What can't you live without?
Lucia:	It's got to be my tablet – I can't live without it! I can use it to go online, message my friends, look at YouTube, watch films and play games. If I could choose one thing, it would be my tablet. What about you?

> Ben: Hmmm. I like my tablet too but my favourite thing isn't a gadget, it's a piece of equipment. The most important thing for me is my mountain bike.
>
> Lucia: Really? Bikes are great but all you can do is ride around on them – that's just one thing. You can do lots of different things with a tablet. I think it's more interesting than a bike.
>
> Ben: It depends on the type of bike … With a tablet you have to stay inside. If you like being outside a lot, a mountain bike is better. Bikes are awesome … my mountain bike's got big tyres so I can race over grass and tracks. I can go fast, race my friends and see lots of places.
>
> Lucia: Yes, both things are great in different ways.

Answers

a   a tablet and a bike (bicycle)

b   Tablet: Advantages: lots of different uses: go online, message friends, look at YouTube, watch films, play games; Disadvantage: you can only use it inside.
(Mountain) bike: Advantages: good if you like being outside a lot; you can race over grass and tracks, go fast, race friends, see lots of places; Disadvantages: you can only ride it.

 4   Listen again and complete these sentences in your notebook. (10 minutes)

*   Ask learners to look at sentences a–e from the listening activity. Tell them that they all express preferences and compare the gadgets.

*   Before listening again, ask learners to predict what words might be missing.

*   Replay the audio. Then ask learners to complete the sentences and write down who says them

*   When you check the answers, do some pronunciation work on connected speech in preparation for Activity 6. For example: *It's got to be my tablet …*; *It depends on … .*

*   Challenge learners by expanding the points made in sentences a–e into a mini-debate. Ask learners if they agree with the points made by Ben and Lucia. If not, why not? Ask: *What other advantages and disadvantages are there to tablets and bikes?*

Answers

a   It's *got to be* my tablet – I can't live without it! (Lucia)

b   I can *use it to* go online and message my friends. (Lucia)

c   The *most important* thing for me is my mountain bike. (Ben)

d   I think it's *more interesting than* a bike. (Lucia)

e   It *depends* on the type of bike. (Ben)

5   What's the most important gadget or piece of equipment for you? (10 minutes)

*   The aim of this activity is to give learners time to articulate ideas and practise using the language from Activity 4, in preparation for the speaking activity in Activity 6.

> **Critical thinking opportunity:** Ask learners to work individually on this task. Give them a few minutes to think about the gadgets they use and which is the most important to them; then circulate and help with vocabulary as they complete the sentences.

*   Learners compare their ideas with a partner.

Answers

Learner's own answers.

6   Which 20th- and 21st-century inventions do you think are the most important? (30 minutes)

> **Critical thinking opportunity:** Learners practise evaluating and expressing their own opinions by having a pyramid discussion about which 20th- and 21st-century inventions are the most important.

*   Learners begin the discussion in pairs. Make sure they choose three important inventions (one of them can be from Activity 5). They should make notes on what they are used for and why they are important. Circulate and help, particularly with vocabulary.

- **Collaboration:** Each pair joins another pair to create a group of four. They compare notes and decide together on the three most important items from their lists. Learners should use their reasons to try and convince the other group why their ideas are best, using the phrases in Activity 4 to help. Each group then decides together on the three most important inventions.

- Finally, each group presents their ideas to the class. At the end, decide together as a class, through comparing and negotiating, which three inventions are the most important.

Answers

Learner's own answers.

Plenary idea

Be creative! (10 minutes)

Ask learners to look around the classroom and think of gadgets and inventions that are needed. Encourage them to give reasons.

Homework ideas

- Learners write a paragraph (up to 100 words) comparing their two favourite gadgets/pieces of equipment.

  > **Assessment ideas:** As a class, write a short checklist so that learners can self-assess their homework before handing it in. For example: *Have I used the new vocabulary? Have I used the new phrases from the lesson? Have I given reasons why I like the gadgets/pieces of equipment? Have I checked my spelling?*

> **Workbook**
>
> Learners do Activities 1–4 on pages 44–45.

4.2 Design technology: Radical robotics

LEARNING PLAN

Learning objectives	Learning intentions	Success criteria
6Rd.01 6Ug.04	• **Reading:** Understand, with support, most specific information and detail in short and extended texts. • **Listening:** Use a range of past simple active forms for habits and states and begin to use passive forms. • **Vocabulary:** *robot, humanoid, sensor, battery, upgrade*	• Learners can understand, with support, specific information in a text about the Asimo robot. • Learners can understand and give facts about robots using the past simple.

21st-century skills

Learning to learn: Research specific information about inventions from past and present times.

Critical thinking opportunity: Learners think about why a sentence is false and identify how to correct it.

Materials: Learner's Book pages 64–65; Workbook pages 46–47; access to the internet or photocopied information for Activity 7 (on Mars rover, snakebot, virtual assistant, robotic dog); **Photocopiable 10**

LANGUAGE BACKGROUND

The past simple

Most learners will already be familiar with the past simple. It is used to talk about actions in the past and is often used to write stories that happened in the past.

Be aware of learners switching from the past simple to the present simple to talk about past events; this can be to avoid problematic verb forms but also because there are many other things to think about when they are writing.

Problematic past simple verb forms include *chose, laughed, happened, swam, took, taught* and *told*.

Reinforce with learners that the past tense of *be* is *was/were*.

Look out for a common mistake which learners make – using *was/were* with the main verb, for example *It was rained; The band was played.*

Common misconceptions

Misconception	How to identify	How to overcome
Learners incorrectly add the auxiliary *be*, especially with certain verbs (such as *enjoy*) and where the subject and main verb are split by an adverb. For example: *I went to a concert last night and I* ~~was~~ *really* ~~enjoy~~ *enjoyed it.*	Write two sentences on the board, for example: *I **played** in a tennis match yesterday.* *Last week's match **was played** between Nadal and Federer.* Elicit that *was/were* is only used with a main verb (past participle) when forming the passive form and never for the past simple (or present perfect).	Practise using: • Activities 1–3 on pages 46–47 of the Workbook • **Photocopiable activity 10**.

Starter ideas

What can robots do? (10 minutes)

- Explain to learners that this lesson is looking at robot technology.
- As a class, brainstorm a list of things that robots can do.
- Try to elicit things that learners will come across in the reading text, e.g. *pour you a drink, work out distances, do tasks around the house, dance, play football.*
- Write the prompt *In the future, robots will…* and share ideas about things that robots will do in the future.

Main teaching ideas

› **Digital Classroom:** Use the video 'Here come the robots!' to introduce the subject of robots. The i button will explain how to use the activity.

1 Look at the pictures of Asimo, and Reading tip – Use your own knowledge. (5–10 minutes)

- First, look at the pictures of the famous robot together. On the board, make a list of things learners know about it. If learners don't know much/anything about Asimo, encourage them to make predictions from the pictures/your discussions from the Starter activity about what they think it can do.
- Then read the Reading tip together. Tell learners to look out for their predictions/ideas in the reading.

Answers
Learner's own answers.

2 Read and listen to the article. (10 minutes)

- Before learners listen to/read the text, read the Key words: design technology glossary together. Encourage learners to look out for the words as they read/listen.

- Play the recording all the way through. Ask learners to compare what they have heard/read with their ideas. The text is challenging so, if helpful, replay the audio, pausing after each paragraph.

- As a class, talk about the article. Learners write down the main things that Asimo can do.

Audioscript: Track 27

See Learner's Book page 64

Answers

Asimo is the most advanced humanoid robot in the world. It can play football, dance, hop, jump, pour a drink; walk on two legs, move by itself (using sensors inside its body); understand voice commands and human gestures; recognise moving objects and work out the distance and direction of those objects.

3 Work in pairs. What actions can Asimo do? Take it in turns to mime the actions. (10 minutes)

- Demonstrate the activity by miming one of Asimo's actions for learners to guess.

- Learners play the miming game, using the list of actions from Activity 2 to help them. Ensure that learners mix up the order in which they mime the actions, so their partner doesn't just read each action from their list.

- Circulate and offer support while learners mime and guess the actions in their pairs.

- Briefly come together as a class after the activity. Who mimed the most actions? How easy/difficult did learners find the activity?

Answers

(See answers for Activity 2.)

4 Decide if these sentences are true or false. Correct the false sentences. (10 minutes)

- Circulate and offer support while learners work individually on this task. Encourage learners to look back at the reading text and read the relevant parts of it again carefully.

> **Critical thinking opportunity:** Learners think about why a sentence is false and identify how to correct it.

> **Differentiation ideas:** Learners who don't feel confident about this task should focus on deciding whether each sentence is true or false.

- Give class feedback on the answers at the end of the activity.

Answers

a   False. Scientists presented Asimo to the world in 2000.
b   True
c   False. Since 2000, scientists have upgraded (improved) Asimo's technology (so it has more skills and abilities).
d   True
e   False. Honda stopped producing Asimo (in its current form) in 2018.

Use of English – Past simple review (5 minutes)

- Elicit examples of the past simple tense.

- Look at the examples in the Use of English box. Point out that the words highlighted in green are past simple verbs and the words highlighted in blue are time references.

- Then answer any questions learners have about the past simple; talk through any difficulties they have when using the past simple in their writing (see Language background).

- Use **Photocopiable 10** to practise past simple questions and answers.

> **Workbook**
>
> Learners do Activities 1–3 on pages 46–47.

5 How many past simple verbs can you find in the text? When did each action happen? Find the time references. (10 minutes)

- Briefly look back at the Use of English box. Ask learners to use the past simple verbs/time references in the examples as a model for this activity.

- Allow learners time to scan the text and look for past simple verbs. Tell them to highlight the past simple verbs in one colour and the time references in another (or underline the verbs and circle the time references).

- Give feedback by getting learners to point to each verb and asking *when* each action happened.

Answers
Past simple verbs (green) and time references (blue) appear in the text from Paragraph 2 onwards.
Scientists at Honda … started developing Asimo in the 1980s and presented it to the world in 2000. The company created Asimo to help people …
Asimo has become a worldwide celebrity … In 2005, Mickey Mouse welcomed Asimo at Disneyland.
In 2011, it appeared on a TV quiz show in the UK …; in 2014, it played football with the former US president, Barack Obama. …
In 2018, Honda stopped producing the robot in its current form …

〉 **Digital Classroom:** Use the activity 'Past simple' to practise using the past simple. The i button will explain how to use the activity.

6 What other jobs do you think robots can perform? (15 minutes)

- First, as a class, brainstorm other jobs that robots could perform.

- Then look at the pictures together. Invite learners to guess the jobs these robots perform.

- Ask learners to work in pairs to discuss the types of jobs it might be better for robots to do than humans. Tell them to think about jobs that humans might find boring/repetitive, dangerous tasks, or where human error might have negative consequences.

〉 **Assessment ideas:** Circulate and make notes while learners talk, focusing particularly on pronunciation and the use of new vocabulary. Wait until the end of the activity before giving feedback.

Answers
Learner's own ideas.

7 Work in small groups. Find out more about one of the robots in the photos. (20 minutes)

- Put learners in groups of 3–4. Allocate each group one of the robots from the photos to find out more about. Explain that learners need to find interesting facts about their chosen robot to share with the class.

- **Learning to learn:** Offer support while learners use the internet or pre-prepared photocopied material to find out about who invented the robot, why they invented it and what it does.

- **Collaboration:** Make sure learners are collaborating, so that each group member knows what to make notes on. Give the groups a few minutes to decide which two facts to share with the class.

- In their groups, learners read their two interesting facts to the class, who guess which robot they are talking about.

- Encourage learners to make notes of the interesting facts about the other robots – tell them they will need these for their homework task.

Answers
Learner's own answers.

Plenary ideas

Reflection (10 minutes)

Have a class discussion about the lesson. What aspects of it did learners find challenging (for example, the reading text or vocabulary)? What did they enjoy about it the most? Has it inspired them to find out about other robots? What's the most interesting thing they have learned today?

Homework ideas

Learners write a paragraph of up to 100 words about one of the robots from the lesson (a different one from the one they researched). It should answer the questions: *Who invented it? Why? What does it do?*

> **Workbook**
> Learners do Activities 1–3 on pages 46–47.

4.3 Talk about it: Bright ideas

LEARNING PLAN

Learning objectives	Learning intentions	Success criteria
6Lm.01	• **Listening:** Understand, with support, most of the main points of short and extended talk.	• Learners can understand the main points in a presentation explaining an idea for a new invention.
6Sc.06, 6Sc.07	• **Speaking:** Begin to produce and maintain stretches of language comprehensibly, allowing for hesitation and reformulation, especially in longer stretches of free production.	
6Ug.08	• **Use of English:** Use a range of future forms, including present continuous and present simple with future meaning.	• Learners can understand and use the future simple, *will*, when talking about an idea for a new invention.
	• **Vocabulary:** *communication, transport, food, comfort, convenience, entertainment*	

21st-century skills

Creative thinking: Design and present own idea for a new invention.

Materials: Learner's Book pages 66–67; Workbook pages 48–49; pictures of new inventions for the Starter activity (search *Inventions in transportation* on the internet); **Photocopiable 11**

LANGUAGE BACKGROUND

Will for future predictions

The auxiliary verb, *will*, is used to make the future simple tense. In Lesson 4.3, learners use the future simple to talk about an idea for a new invention. The main focus of Lesson 4.3 is *will* for future predictions (see Use of English box on page 67).

The future simple is also used to express certainty about future spontaneous decisions, requests and offers.

For example:

They will be here at 10am. (Certainty about the future)

I'll have a mineral water please. (Spontaneous decision/request)

Learners can practise *will* for future predictions using **Photocopiable 11**.

Common misconceptions

Misconception	How to identify	How to overcome
Learners incorrectly use other forms (such as *can, would, present simple*) instead of *will*. For example: *I'm sure I ~~can~~ will have a fantastic trip!* Hope you ~~would~~ **will** come to my party! *I want to invite you to another concert.* ~~It's~~ **It will be** *wonderful.*	Write sentences on the board and identify the difference in meaning. For example: *Next Saturday, I'm going to a picnic.* ~~Do~~ **Will** *you come with me?* (Future arrangement) **Does** *Sara come with you on Saturdays?* (= 'every Saturday' – therefore a habit is implied)	Practise using: • Activities 1–4 on pages 48–49 of the Workbook.

Starter ideas

Interesting inventions (10 minutes)

• On the board, project two or three inventions (e.g. a Segway, a Sinclair C5). Ask learners questions about them. For example: *What are they used for? Would you use one? Do you think the inventions have been successful? Why? Why not?*

Main teaching ideas

1 If you could invent something new, what would it be? (10–15 minutes)

• The idea of this activity is to generate interest in the topic and start to prepare learners for Activity 9, where they choose and present an idea for a new invention.

• First, look at the topic headings together. Ask learners to think about their own ideas for new inventions under any or all of the headings. The ideas can be as realistic or extravagant as they like.

• Then ask learners to work in pairs and choose one of the five topics. Give them a few minutes to talk to their partner about their ideas.

• As a class, spend a few minutes sharing some initial ideas.

Answers

Learner's own answers.

Speaking tip – Know your audience (5 minutes)

• Tell learners they are going to listen to a presentation by a girl called Kim, and then do a presentation of their own.

• Read the Speaking tip. Tell learners that they are going to listen to how Kim organises the information in her presentation in a logical order, so her audience can follow it clearly.

2 Listen to the teacher talking before Kim's presentation. Who is Kim presenting her idea to? Why? (5 minutes)

• Explain that Kim is listening to her teacher's advice before she gives her presentation.

• Ask learners to listen to find out who Kim is presenting her idea to, and why.

• Play the recording and check learner's ideas.

Audioscript: Track 28

See Learner's Book page 66

Teacher: Ok, Kim, are you ready? Remember … you are presenting your idea to a group of judges in a competition. They have a lot of money to give to someone with the best invention idea. If you win this money, you'll be able to make your invention and sell it. Convince them that it is a fantastic idea and deserves the prize! Now off you go …

Answers

Kim is presenting her idea to a group of judges in a competition. If she wins the competition, she'll win a prize of a lot of money. The money will enable her to make her invention idea and sell it.

 3 Listen to Kim's presentation about her idea for a new invention. Which picture describes her idea? (10 minutes)

- Look at the pictures together and identify the different inventions. Write useful words for the listening activity on the board, for example *jet boots, powerful, fly through the air,* etc.

- Before playing the recording, make it clear that learners don't need to understand every word; they just need to say which picture describes Kim's idea. They will have the chance to listen in more detail later.

- After listening, give learners a couple of minutes to discuss with a partner which picture Kim describes.

- Then give class feedback on the correct answer.

Answers

Picture c

Audioscript: Track 29

See Learner's Book page 66

Kim: OK. Good morning everyone. My name's Kim and today I'm going to describe an idea for a fantastic invention. Here is a picture of my idea. These are Uber Jet Boots. This invention will change the way people travel because it is much faster and safer than a car, and much cheaper than a plane.

As you can see, Uber Jet Boots let you fly through the air because they have these powerful jets on the bottom of the boot. You control these jets with buttons on the side of the boot. You put them on, press the buttons … and go! And the jets lift you high into the air.

Uber Jet Boots are a fast and easy way to travel. They will solve the traffic problems in our city because people won't need to travel by car anymore. Also, with Uber Jet Boots, people won't

have so many traffic accidents. There is plenty of space in the air for people to travel, so people won't crash into each other – and they'll be able to travel as fast as they like.

To sum up, Uber Jet Boots are a fast and safe way to travel because you can fly through the air instead of on the road. They are also environmentally friendly. If people travel by Uber Jet Boots, they won't need to use their cars.

Now that's the end of my presentation. Thank you for listening. Does anyone have any questions?

4 Listen again and put the headings in the order of the presentation. (10 minutes)

- Read the headings together. Then elicit predictions, such as: *I think the introduction will be first.*

- Play the recording, then learners discuss their ideas with a partner.

- Give class feedback on the correct order.

Answers

Order: d, c, a, b

5 Listen and complete the audience's questions. (5–10 minutes)

- Read the incomplete questions as a class.

- Then play the recording so that learners can complete the questions. If necessary, stop the audio after each question to give learners time to complete them.

- Check learner's understanding of each question. If learners aren't sure what *keep your balance* means, demonstrate by miming.

Audioscript: Track 30

See Learner's Book page 66

Judge 1:   Yes, thanks, Kim for your interesting idea. I've got a question … how do you keep your balance on the Uber Jet Boots?

Kim: Oh, that's not a problem! The jet will be so powerful that you can stand up straight.

Judge 2:	And where will you put the jet fuel to give the boots power?
Kim:	The power for the boots comes from electricity – so you won't need to put fuel into them. You will be able to plug them in and charge them up at home.
Teacher:	Ok, thanks very much, Kim, very interesting … but there are lots of good ideas in the competition. Which idea will the judges choose? We'll have to wait and see …

Answers

1 How do you _keep your balance_ on the Uber Jet Boots?

2 Where will you _put the jet fuel_ to give the boots power?

6 What do you think about Kim's idea? Write two more questions to ask her. (5–10 minutes)

> **Critical thinking opportunity:** Ask learners to discuss the question in pairs. Did they like Kim's idea? Why or why not? Then ask each pair to write two questions they would have asked Kim if they had been at her presentation.

> **Differentiation ideas:** Challenge more confident learners to write three or more questions to ask Kim.

- As a class, share some of the questions. Make a note of them on the board – they will be a useful reference point when learners ask each other questions in Activity 9. Then highlight a couple of questions and ask learners to imagine how Kim would respond. Again, this is good practice for Activity 9, when learners will need to spontaneously answer questions after their own presentations.

Answers

Learner's own answers.

Use of English – _will_ for future predictions, and 7 Read the Use of English box and choose the correct answers. (10–15 minutes)

- Write the three examples from the Use of English box on the board, leaving a space for _will_/_won't_ + verb. Ask learners if they remember the sentences from Kim's presentation.

- Ask learners to identify the missing components.

- Then ask learners some concept-check questions to establish when the future simple tense is used in this context. For example: _Are these sentences about the present or future time?_ (Future.) _Does Kim think these things will definitely happen or are very likely to happen?_ (She thinks there is a strong possibility – she is making a _prediction_.)

- Then highlight the form in the affirmative, negative and question forms. Write another example, such as _You will move house next year_. Change the pronoun (for example, change _you_ to _we_) and elicit that the form remains the same in all cases, even if the pronoun is changed. Then focus learners on the verb form that comes after _will_/_won't_ (base infinitive), so they can see how the whole structure is formed.

- After learners have had some practice, look at Activity 7 together and ask them to choose the correct option.

Workbook

Learners do Activities 1–4 on pages 48–49.

Answers

1 With pronouns (_I, you, he, she, it, we, they_), the form of _will_ / _won't_ **stays the same**.

2 We use the **verb** form **after** _will_ and _won't_.

> **Digital Classroom:** Use the grammar presentation '_Will_ for future predictions' to revise and practise using _will_ for predictions. The i button will explain how to use the grammar presentation.

8 Use the verbs in the box to complete the sentences. (5–10 minutes)

- Ask learners to complete these sentences in order to consolidate their understanding of the target language.

- They can either do the activity individually and compare their answers with a partner, or do the activity in pairs.

- Give class feedback on the answers.

Answers
1 You will *be able to* travel as fast as you like. [Example]
2 Will the boots *save* people money? Yes, they will!
3 Uber Jet Boots will *solve* the traffic problems in our city.
4 You won't *need to* travel by car any more.
5 You won't *have* so many traffic accidents.
6 The jet will *be* so powerful that you can stand up straight.

9 Present it! Choose and present a new invention. (25 minutes + time to present)

- **Creative thinking**: This is a great opportunity for learners to design and present their own idea for a new invention. Encourage learners to be creative and to have fun with their idea.

- First, go through the headings from Activity 4 – explain that this should form the structure for learner's presentations. Tell learners to draw a picture of their invention to engage their audience.

- Put learners into pairs or groups of three to prepare and deliver their presentations (either an idea from Activity 1 or a new idea). Ensure learners make notes under the headings from Activity 4.

- Learners write out their presentations from their notes. Remind them to make the purpose of their presentation clear from the start and add sequencing phrases, such as *Today we're going to talk about …; To sum up … .* Circulate and offer support as learners do this.

- Allow time for learners to practise their presentations before presenting their idea to the class. Each learner should deliver a part of the presentation. Circulate and offer help and support with pronunciation and delivery as learners practise.

- Learners deliver their presentations to the class. Generate a supportive atmosphere. Ask learners to applaud each pair after each presentation.

> **Differentiation ideas:** If less confident learners find presenting difficult, allow them to read from their notes.

- Appoint three or four learners as 'judges' for each presentation (have different 'judges' for each one). Ask them to think back to Activity 6 and the questions they asked Kim. Tell them to think of similar kinds of questions to ask the pair that are presenting.

- The presenting pair need to answer the questions. Again, ask learners to think back to Activity 6, where they practised answering some of the suggested questions for Kim.

> **Assessment ideas:** While learners are presenting, check their use of vocabulary and pronunciation, sequencing phrases, and use of the future simple form to make predictions. Note down any errors and positive points to go through in a correction session.

- At the end, learners vote for the best idea in the class.

Answers
Learner's own answers.

Plenary ideas

Presenting (10 minutes)

- Have a class discussion about presenting – in this lesson, what did learners enjoy about it and what did they find challenging?

- Invite learners to share any tips for presenting with the class.

- Also use this as an opportunity to give the learners positive feedback on their presentations.

Homework ideas

Learners write a paragraph describing the invention of one of their classmates.

> **Workbook**
> Learners do Activities 1–4 on pages 48–49.

4.4 Write about it: Changing the world

LEARNING PLAN

Learning objectives	Learning intentions		Success criteria
6Ro.01, 6Rd.03	•	**Reading:** Recognise, with support, the opinion of the writer(s) in short and extended texts. Understand, with support, most of the detail of an argument in short and extended texts.	• Learners can understand the viewpoint and opinions of the writer in a simple, persuasive essay discussing why an invention is so important.
6Wc.03, 6Wor.02	•	**Writing:** Express opinions and feelings. Link sentences using an increasing range of connectives to create a short text organised into paragraphs.	• Learners can express opinions in an essay discussing the most important inventions of all time, using connecting phrases to link ideas.
	•	**Vocabulary:** *the internet, satellites, smart phones, USB memory stick*	

21st-century skills

Cross-curricular link: Design technology: Learners explore important inventions in the history of design technology.

Materials: Learner's Book pages 68–69; Workbook pages 50–51; **Photocopiable 12**; internet access for Activity 7; Unit 4 sample answer

Starter ideas

Important inventions – which came first? (10–15 minutes)

- Write interesting inventions in random order on the board (without the dates) and ask learners which they think was invented first, for example the first air conditioner (1902), the first USB memory stick (2000), the first flight in a plane (1903), the first car (1769), the first internet satellite (1962), etc.

- Once learners have put the inventions in date order, ask: *Are you surprised by the order? Why or why not?*

- As a class, have a brief discussion about which of these inventions they think is the most important – and why, to prepare them for Activity 1.

CROSS-CURRICULAR LINK

Design technology: Interest learners in the subject of design technology by exploring important inventions through history.

Main teaching ideas

1 **What do you think are the most important inventions of all time? (10 minutes)**

- Write 'The most important inventions of all time' on the board. Allow pairs of learners one minute to write down all the inventions they can think of.

- Take suggestions for the most important invention and the reasons. Build up a list of them on the board.

- Help learners articulate their thoughts by reformulating awkward expressions and giving vocabulary support. The emphasis should be on generating ideas for the writing activity at the end of the lesson.

Answers
Learner's own answers.

2 Read Hassan's essay. Which invention does he discuss? (10 minutes)

- Tell learners they are going to read an essay about a very important invention. Look at the pictures and ask learners what they think the invention is going to be.

- Then look at the second question in the rubric (*What two things couldn't people do without this invention?*) and ask learners to look for this information as they read. Reassure learners that they don't need to understand every word at this stage; they will be reading the text again later in the lesson.

- After reading, give learners a couple of minutes to discuss answers to the questions with a partner.

- Then give class feedback on the correct answers.

Answers

The invention is the wheel.
According to Hassan, without it people wouldn't be able to travel easily or quickly, or work easily and efficiently.

Writing tip – Support your opinions, and 3 Read the essay again and answer these questions. (10 minutes)

- Focus learners on the Writing tip. Explain that when we give opinions in our written work, we should always explain the *reason* for that opinion.

- Tell learners that they are going to read the essay again and find the reasons for the two main points Hassan makes.

- Read questions a and b together; then allow learners time to reread the text and find the answers.

- Circulate and encourage learners to highlight the reasons in the text.

- Give class feedback on the correct answers.

› **Differentiation ideas:** Ask more confident learners to think of additional reasons for the points Hassan makes.

Answers

a   It is important for people to travel so that they can know/find out about other places. If they couldn't travel, their world would be very small or limited.

b   We need wheels to carry things and for parts for machines in factories and farms.

4 Giving opinions and reasons. (10 minutes)

- Tell learners that when they write an essay, it is important to give their personal opinion.

- Then ask learners to look at the phrases in blue in the text; explain that they are used to give a personal opinion. Read the phrases as a class and ask learners to work in pairs to match the phrases with a function.

- Ask learners to write the phrases in their notebooks, so they have a record and can refer to them in Activity 7.

- Give class feedback on the correct answers.

Answers

a   [Example] *In my opinion, I think that …*
b   *because / this means that / this is because / for these reasons*
c   *such as / for example …*

› **Digital Classroom:** Use the activity 'An important invention' to reinforce giving reasons, examples and opinions. The i button will explain how to use the activity.

5 How persuasive is Hassan's essay? What do you think is his strongest reason? Do you agree with his opinion? (20–30 minutes)

- First, check learners know the meaning of 'persuasive'.

- Then, as a class, answer the three questions in the rubric. Encourage learners to use the phrases from the previous activity in their responses.

Answers

Learner's own answers.

6 Describe one of these inventions to your partner, but don't say the name! (10 minutes)

- Demonstrate the activity by describing one of the inventions to the class without saying its name.

- Make sure you use phrases from Hassan's essay and Activity 4.

- Circulate and offer support with pronunciation, vocabulary and the new phrases, while learners complete the activity in pairs.

- As a class, briefly discuss how the activity went. Was it easy to describe and guess the inventions? Talk through some of the challenges.

Answers
Learner's own answers.

7 Write a persuasive essay about an important invention. (40–50 minutes)

> **Critical thinking opportunity:** Tell learners they are going to write their own opinion essay about an important invention. They need to explain why the invention is so important and give reasons and examples to support their opinion, using the language from the essay and Activity 4.

- Encourage learners to create a mind map for their invention to record their opinions.

- Learners could write about an invention they know, or you could provide them with photocopied material on a specific invention.

> **Assessment ideas:** Before learners start Steps 2 and 3 (Planning and Writing), show them the Unit 4 sample answer without the mark scheme comments. As a class, evaluate the sample answer's strengths and weaknesses, and look at the checklist together on page 69 of the Learner's Book, so that learners know what they are aiming to achieve.

- Offer support during the planning and writing stages. Remind learners to use Hassan's essay as a model. Encourage learners to start their essay by stating their opinion and to give reasons and examples. They should also use the phrases from Activity 4 and be as persuasive as possible in their writing.

> **Assessment ideas:** Once learners have finished their first draft, ask them to work through the checklist on **Photocopiable 12** to self-assess their work. Once they have made any updates, invite them to swap their draft with a partner, who will proofread it. Encourage learners to give feedback sensitively and to include at least one compliment.

Plenary ideas

Reflection (10 minutes)

- As a class, spend some time looking through the essays.

- Give everyone positive feedback on their work. Then take a class vote on the most persuasive essay. Ask learners to explain why they think it is the most persuasive.

Homework ideas

Workbook

Learners do Activities 1–5 on pages 50–51.

4.5 Read and respond: *Start Small, Think Big*

LEARNING PLAN

Learning objectives	Learning intentions	Success criteria
6Rd.01, 6Rm.02	• **Reading:** Understand, with support, most specific information and detail in short and extended texts. Read independently a range of short, simple fiction and non-fiction texts with confidence and enjoyment.	• Learners can read and enjoy a story about a young inventor, understanding specific details.
6Rd.04 6Ug.10	• **Reading / Use of English:** Deduce meaning from context, with support, in short and extended texts. Use common prepositional verbs (e.g. *walk away*). • **Vocabulary:** *run off, put together, run back, try out, hold up, pick up*	• Learners can deduce the meaning of multi-word verbs from context.

21st-century skills

Emotional development: Understand the importance and potential of creative thinking and self-belief.

Materials: Learner's Book pages: 70–73; Workbook pages 52–53; **Differentiated worksheets 4A, B and C**

Starter ideas

The inventing process (10 minutes)

- Tell learners they are going to read about a young inventor who creates an unusual invention. First, ask learners how the process of inventing something starts (i.e. an idea). Then talk about trial and error: you have an idea to do an experiment/make something, try it out, see what works and what doesn't.

- Ask learners if you think inventors should give up when something doesn't work; hopefully they'll agree that it's worth being persistent and determined.

- If you can, share a short anecdote about having a crazy idea, especially one that turned into something good. This would be a good springboard for the first activity.

Main teaching ideas

1 Have you ever had a crazy idea? (10 minutes)

- Learners work in small groups to answer the questions. Circulate and offer support with pronunciation and vocabulary while group members share their thoughts.

- Groups share their responses with the rest of the class.

Answers
Learner's own answers.

---

2 Read and listen to the first part of the story. What was Garth's crazy idea? (10 minutes)

- Tell learners they are going to read and listen to a story about a young inventor.

- Before reading and listening, encourage learners to describe what they see in the picture on page 70. Invite them to make predictions about what Garth's new invention is and its advantages over a traditional umbrella. Take the opportunity to elicit new words from the first part of the story by asking questions. For example: *What's Garth doing?* (Pre-teach *grinning from ear to ear.*) *What's the man doing?* (Pre-teach *wrestling with an umbrella, … dog on a lead.*)

- Read the question in the rubric together. Then learners read and listen to the text to check their predictions.

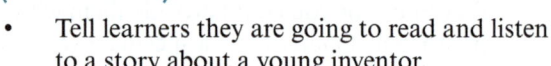

Audioscript: Track 31

See Learner's Book page 70

Answers

Garth's crazy idea was an invention for a 'Bodybrella' – a transparent umbrella that covers the body as well as the head.

---

 3 **Now read and listen to all the parts and answer the questions. (10–15 minutes)**

- Before learners read and listen to the rest of the story, look at the pictures and the words in the glossary (*humiliated, repugnant, sneer* and *jibes*). Elicit that the boys are *nasty* and *sneering* from their facial expressions in the picture. As a class, spend a few minutes talking about what is likely to happen in the rest of the story.

- Then listen to each part of the story; ask learners to read the text as you play each part of the recording. After each part, pause the recording and read the corresponding questions together.

- Once you have listened to all the parts, circulate and offer support while learners reread each part of the story and answer the questions in pairs.

> **Differentiation ideas:** If learners need more support with this task, organise them into pairs. More confident readers can provide language support and practise their speaking skills when sharing possible answers with their partner.

- Give class feedback on the correct answers.

Audioscript: Track 32

See Learner's Book pages 70–72

Answers

a   Garth was excited about his invention (because he believed it was very useful and everyone would want to own one).

b   In wet weather, it kept the whole body dry as well as the head, and the design left both hands free so you can carry things.

c   He went outside in the wind and rain to see if the invention protected him from the weather.

d   The Barker Boys were *hostile* towards Garth (unfriendly and aggressive).

e   Todd Barker pulled it off his head and threw it on the ground.

f   The boys laughed at it in a cruel way.

g   He thought it looked stupid ('dumb') and no one would want to wear it.

h   Garth felt very upset and shaken ('trembling'). The boys made him feel stupid ('humiliated').

i   He saw a lady standing and looking at him in a concerned way.

j   She was very interested in the invention and asked lots of questions.

k   Garth's mood changed and he felt much happier because the lady was interested in his invention (someone was positive about his creation).

l   The lady said that he shouldn't let stupid boys (like the Barker Boys) make him feel bad; that he should continue to invent things because one day he would make something really good.

m   She wanted to organise a competition to find the best young inventor in the town, to encourage children with creative ideas.

n   Garth felt much better and more enthusiastic (the implication is that the lady's interest made him believe in himself again). He started to think of lots of new ideas for inventions.

---

4 **Discuss these questions about the story. (10 minutes)**

- Circulate and offer support while learners work in pairs to answer the questions.

> **Differentiation ideas:** If learners need more support during the discussion, prepare and distribute a prompt sheet with sentence starters, or write them on a mini-whiteboard. For example: *I think my reaction would be …, The lady's reaction was …*

- As a class, share feedback on the answers. Help learners with the language they need to express their thoughts by reformulating sentences, where appropriate, and highlighting useful phrases on the board. Leave the phrases on the board – this will help learners with Activity 7.

Answers

a   Learner's own answers.

b   Suggested answer: The lady's reaction was completely the opposite to the boys' attitude. She thought the invention was interesting and a very good idea for a young boy to think of. She could see Garth's potential (good things he might do in the future) by looking at his invention.

c   Suggested answer: She told Garth not to let negative people (i.e. like the Barker Boys), who did not know anything about inventions, make him feel stupid. She also made the point that Garth should keep inventing because one day he might create something really great.

d   Suggested answer: He felt better because the lady had a positive, encouraging attitude and showed him that she believed in him and other children like him. Her comments and her competition idea showed this. Garth also felt better with the news of the competition and the chance to win a prize and to show his invention in the gadget shop (a place he knew and loved already).

> **Digital Classroom:** Use the activity 'Start small, think big' to reinforce comprehension of the story from the Learner's Book. The i button will explain how to use the activity.

Language focus – Multi-word verbs (5 minutes)

•   Before focusing on the Language focus, ask learners to give you examples of verbs, prepositions and adverbs.

•   Then read the Language focus box and look at the examples together. Answer any questions learners have on multi-word verbs.

5   Look at the multi-word verbs in blue in the story. Can you work out the meaning from the context of the story? (10 minutes)

•   Together, look at the multi-word verbs in blue.

•   Demonstrate how the meaning can be worked out from the context, for example *try it out*. Ask concept check questions, such as: *Is this a new invention? What do inventors do first when they have a new invention? Is it the first time Garth has used the Bodybrella?*

•   In small groups, learners work out the meanings of the other multi-word verbs together. Give class feedback before learners work on the sentences.

> **Differentiation ideas:** If learners need more support with this task, provide them with the five definitions and ask them to match each one to the correct multi-word verb.

•   Continue to offer support while learners work in pairs to choose the correct multi-word verbs to complete the sentences.

•   Give class feedback on the correct answers.

•   For extra practice of multi-word verbs, see **Differentiated worksheets 4A, B and C.**

Answers
Suggested definitions:
try it out – see if something works well.
run back – to turn around and run to the place you were at before.
ran off – run away or escape.
picked up – take something from off the floor.
held it up – hold something high up, so everyone can see it.
put it together – make something from different pieces or parts.
1   [Example] ran off
2   put (it) together
3   held up
4   run back
5   picked up
6   try (it) out

6   Listen and repeat the *a* sounds from the story. (5 minutes)

•   Ask learners to listen and repeat the words from the story, and identify the difference in the pronunciation of the 'a' sound in each group of words.

Audioscript: Track 33

See Learner's Book page 73

Answers
a   All contain a long 'a' sound eI.
b   All contain a short 'a' sound ae.

7 Believe in yourself. (10 minutes)

- First, ask learners what they think the heading means. If they are not sure, or find it hard to explain, tell them that it means that *you* believe that you can do things, even if someone else might tell you that you can't do something.

- Then read the sentences together and check learners know the meaning of *pointless* and *turn into something good*. Circulate and support learners as they work in small groups to discuss which sentence(s) they agree with.

- As a class, share feedback on the sentences. Accept all ideas and opinions.

- **Emotional development**: Use this activity to help learners understand the importance and potential of creative thinking and self-belief. Encourage them to talk about situations where they should try to believe in themselves more. This activity is a good opportunity for learners to empathise and find commonalities in challenging situations.

Answers
Learner's own answers.

Plenary ideas

Reflection (5–10 minutes)

Ask learners what they think might happen next in the story, in preparation for the homework activity.

Homework ideas

- Ask learners to write down what they think happened next in Garth's story (they should aim to write approximately 100 words). Encourage them to use the new vocabulary from the lesson and to try and include at least one multi-word verb.

  > **Assessment ideas:** Give written feedback on new vocabulary, how the writing is organised, the inclusion of multi-word verbs, and general use of grammar and pronunciation.

> **Workbook**
>
> Learners do Activities 1–4 on pages 52–53.

4.6 Project challenge

LEARNING PLAN		
Learning objectives	**Learning intentions**	**Success criteria**
6Sc.06, 6Sc.02	• **Speaking:** Begin to produce and maintain stretches of language comprehensibly, allowing for hesitation and reformulation, especially in longer stretches of free production. Describe people, places and objects, and routine past and present actions and events.	• Learners can deliver a presentation about the history of an invention.
6Wc.02, 6Wca.01	• **Writing:** Write, with support, short texts which describe people, places and objects, and routine past and present actions and events. Use legible handwriting in written work with appropriate speed and fluency.	• Learners can write a quiz with questions or clues about different categories of inventions, using clear handwriting.
21st-century skills		
Collaboration: Participate actively in group projects, creating a shared outcome.		

Materials: Learner's Book pages 74–75; Workbook page 54; access to the internet or to library books about the history of interesting inventions; poster card; large pieces of paper; examples of other learner's work; Unit 4 project checklists; End of Unit 4 test

Starter ideas

Raise interest in the projects (10–15 minutes)

- Tell learners they are either going to deliver a presentation about the history of an invention (Project A) or create a quiz about inventions (Project B).

- If possible, raise interest in the projects by presenting examples of learner's work on similar topics from other classes or the internet.

- Revise new vocabulary from the unit, which learners may need for the challenges, in a fun way. For example, create a word search or crossword for learners to complete, or put anagrams of the new vocabulary on the board.

Main teaching ideas

Introduce and complete projects (60 minutes)

Encourage learners to choose one of the projects and then follow the steps for their chosen project.

Project A: A presentation about the history of an invention

- Divide learners into groups of about four. First, make sure each group has chosen an invention to focus on. Support learners while they research their projects on the internet or at the library. If neither of these is practical in class, distribute photocopied information to each group.

- **Collaboration**: In Project A, learners need to participate actively in their group, creating a shared outcome. This starts with planning and note taking. Make sure learners work together and are clear about what part of the presentation they are planning and taking notes on.

- Circulate and offer support as the groups organise their notes into sections, using the Step 2 headings. Encourage learners to add other headings if that works for their presentation.

- Before learners finalise their presentations, ask them to review the sequencing words from Lesson 4.3 and remind learners to include them.

- Allow learners some time to practise their presentations and decide who is going to talk about each section. Also encourage learners to consider the kinds of questions they might be asked. This is a good time for learners to consider how to enhance and add interest to their presentation with photos, a video, etc.

- The groups deliver their presentation to the rest of the class and answer questions at the end.

> **Assessment ideas:** Learners use the project checklist to evaluate other groups' presentations. Encourage them to think of at least one question to ask at the end of the presentation.

- Finally, have a class discussion about how learners think the inventions will change in the future.

Project B: Create a quiz about inventions

- Support learners as they look for interesting information about inventions on the internet or at the library. If neither of these is practical in class, distribute photocopied information to each group.

- Before learners work on Step 2, remind them to look at the quiz questions in Lesson 4.1 for ideas of how to put their questions together. Also, if necessary, provide learners with examples of other styles of question, such as multiple choice and matching a question to a picture.

- **Collaboration**: In Project B, learners work in pairs and participate actively to create the quizzes. Encourage them to work together to decide how to formulate each question and to ensure there are questions on a range of inventions from different categories. Also make sure that learners have a clear record of each of the answers on a separate piece of paper.

> **Assessment ideas:** When learners have finished their rough drafts, ask them to swap their questions and answers with another pair to check. Encourage learners to give constructive feedback and at least one compliment.

- When learners have updated their drafts, ask them to use their best handwriting to write up the quiz questions, and to decorate their quizzes.

- Learners hand their quiz to another pair to complete (make sure this is a different pair of learners from the ones who checked their draft). When the pairs have finished the quiz, they swap back so the answers can be checked.

> **Assessment ideas:** Learners use the project checklist to evaluate another pair's quiz. Encourage them to write at least one interesting fact they learned from the quiz.

Plenary ideas

Reflection (10 minutes)

As a class, learners discuss what they enjoyed about the projects and what they found most challenging. Is there anything that they would do differently next time?

Homework ideas

Learners follow the steps in the Learner's Book to complete the project they didn't do in class.

Workbook

Learners do Activity 1 on page 54.

4.7 What do you know now?

How have important inventions changed our lives?

- **Learning to learn:** Learners have the opportunity to reflect and evaluate their own learning success.

- Reintroduce the question from the start of the unit: *How have important inventions changed our lives?* Discuss learner's responses to the question now and compare with their comments at the beginning of the unit. How much has changed?

- Ask learners to work on the tasks in pairs.

- For questions 1, 2, 4 and 6, encourage learners to look back through the unit. Circulate and offer support while learners answer the questions.

- When learners have finished the questions, give class feedback on the answers.

Answers

1 Five of: hoverboard; zip; bicycle; compass; mobile phone; tablet.
Learner's own answers.

2 Suggested answers (three of):
- In 2000, scientists presented Asimo to the world.
- In 2005, Mickey Mouse welcomed Asimo at Disneyland.
- In 2011, Asimo appeared on a TV quiz show in the UK.
- In 2014, it played football with the former US president, Barack Obama.
- Asimo has received royal welcomes in Dubai and the UK.
- Asimo has demonstrated its skills at science fairs and on TV shows all over the world.
- In 2018, Honda stopped producing the robot in its current form.

3 Learner's own answers.
4 Learner's own ideas.
Suggested answers (four of):
- Without the wheel, people could not travel anywhere easily or quickly.
- We depend on the wheel for all our transport, such as cars, trains and planes.
- It is very difficult to travel long distances without wheels.
- We couldn't visit other cities and countries easily.
- We couldn't find out about other places and our world would be very small.
- People wouldn't be able to work easily and efficiently.
- Wheels are also a very important part of machines in factories and on farms because they make the machines work.

5 Learner's own answers.
6 Garth invented (his version of) a full body umbrella – a 'Bodybrella'.
The Barker Boys sneered and laughed at his invention. Todd Barker threw it on the ground. The lady was impressed with the invention because she thought it was an interesting idea, and showed that Garth had a good creative mind.

Look what I can do!

- There are six 'can do' statements. Learners read through the statements and tick the things they can do. Encourage them to reflect on how well they can do these things. Also invite them to think of ways they can improve further, for example what strategies they can use or learn to use.

- If learners find it challenging to read the statements, look through the unit with them and support them to find the relevant information.

- Finally, ask learners to work through the questions on page 55 of the Workbook. Encourage them to talk about what they enjoyed and also about any further support they might need.

> 5 Money

Unit plan

Lesson	Approximate number of learning hours	Outline of learning content	Learning objectives	Resources
1 Spending a sum of money	1.5–2.0	Talk about different ways to spend money.	6Ld.05 6Uv.05	Learner's Book Lesson 5.1 Workbook Lessons 5.1 and 5.2 ⬇ Photocopiable 13 **Digital Classroom:** video – Money; grammar presentation – Comparative adverbs
2 Clever calculations	1.0–1.5	Practise being entrepreneurs.	6Rd.01 6Us.01	Learner's Book Lesson 5.2 Workbook Lesson 5.3 **Digital Classroom:** activity – Quantifiers
3 Spending plans	1.5–2.0	Compare ideas for spending a sum of money.	6Ld.05 6Lo.01 6So.01 6Ug.02	Learner's Book Lesson 5.3 Workbook Lesson 5.3 **Digital Classroom:** activity – Making suggestions
4 The question of pocket money	2.0–2.5	Discuss whether children should get pocket money.	6Ro.01 6Rd.03 6Wc.03 6Wor.02 6Wor.03 6Sor.01 6Us.03	Learner's Book Lesson 5.4 Workbook Lesson 5.4 ⬇ Photocopiable 14 ⬇ Photocopiable 15 ⬇ Differentiated worksheets 5A, B and C ⬇ Unit 5 sample answer **Digital Classroom:** activity – Connecting words; activity – Reflexive pronouns
5 *Billionaire Boy*	2.0–2.5	Read about a boy who wants a special present.	6Rd.01 6Rm.02 6Ro.01 6Rd.04 6Rd.05	Learner's Book Lesson 5.5 Workbook Lesson 5.5 **Digital Classroom:** activity – Billionaire boy!
6 Project challenge	1.0–1.5	Project A: Design a banknote. Project B: Making money grow for a good cause.	6Wc.02 6Sc.06 6Sc.02	Learner's Book Lesson 5.6 Workbook Lesson 5.6 ⬇ Unit 5 project checklists

(continued)

Cross-unit resources
- ↧ Unit 5 Audioscripts
- ↧ End of Unit 5 test
- ↧ Progress test 2
- ↧ Unit 5 Progress report
- ↧ Unit 5 Wordlist

BACKGROUND KNOWLEDGE

Unit 5 focuses on different aspects of money.

Pocket money (referred to in Lessons 5.1 and 5.4) is a small amount of money given to children by their parents, usually weekly, to help teach them how to manage money. They can usually choose to spend the money or save it. Some children, especially older ones, receive pocket money in return for carrying out household tasks.

You might want to discuss alternative ways of paying for things such as cryptocurrency and 'Bitcoin' (as seen in the background picture).

In Lesson 5.2, children raise money for charity. This is when events are organised and the profits are given to an organisation that helps people. An example is a 'fun run', a running event over a middle/long distance, where runners of different ages and abilities participate at their own pace. The emphasis is on having fun and raising money for a good cause.

In Lesson 5.5, learners read an extract from *Billionaire Boy*, a popular children's story. A *billionaire* is someone who has at least 1,000,000,000 in pounds, dollars, euros, etc. This is the third book written by David Walliams OBE, an English writer, comedian, actor and TV personality. *Billionaire Boy*, which has been translated into over 50 languages, tells the story of Joe Spud, a 12-year-old boy, and his father, Len. At the start of the book they have very little, but then Len invents a new toilet roll and Joe becomes the richest boy in England. This means he has everything he wants – except real friends. To help with this, he enrols at the local comprehensive school, where he finds out that you can't buy friends, and that family and friends are more important than possessions. Comprehensive schools, known colloquially as 'comps', are state run secondary schools in the UK.

TEACHING SKILLS FOCUS

Assessment for Learning: Peer assessment

Assessment for Learning is an approach to teaching and learning that creates feedback. This is then used to improve learner's performance. Learners become more involved in the learning process – they think more actively about where they are now, where they are going and how to get there.

There are a number of feedback strategies in assessment for learning. For example, in formative assessment: questioning, peer assessment, self-assessment, target setting, tests and exams. This section concentrates on peer assessment.

In the teacher's notes for Unit 5, there are suggestions for peer assessment in the *Assessment ideas*:

- Lesson 5.2: The class produce a checklist, so learners can give their peers feedback on their presentations.
- Lesson 5.4: Learners use the checklist for peer feedback.
- Lesson 5.6: Learners give each other feedback on the banknote design or presentation, using the checklist.

Your challenge

Before Lessons 5.2, 5.4 and 5.6, look at the *Assessment ideas* in the teaching notes. Use these ideas to help learners give peer feedback.

Encourage learners to give constructive peer feedback.

5.1 Think about it: Spending a sum of money

LEARNING PLAN

Learning objectives	Learning intentions	Success criteria
6Ld.05 6Uv.05	• **Listening:** Understand, with support, most of the detail of an argument in short and extended talk. • **Use of English:** Use comparative and superlative forms with regular and irregular adverbs. • **Vocabulary:** *a waste of money, afford (something), last* (v), *a charity, save money, a brand*	• Learners can understand contrasting points in a discussion about how to spend a sum of money. • Learners can use comparative adverbs to discuss spending habits.

21st-century skills
Critical thinking opportunity: Evaluate different opinions and attitudes to spending money.

Materials: Learner's Book pages 77–79; Workbook pages 56–59; **Photocopiable 13**

LANGUAGE BACKGROUND

Comparative adverbs

Comparative adverbs are used to show change or make comparisons. For example:

*She began to talk **more quickly**. These days, I grow out of things **less quickly**.*

We often use *than* with comparative adverbs.

For example:

*Sam usually works harder **than** Carly.*

Comparative adverbs are formed using the same rules as for comparative adjectives. For example:

fast	faster
quickly	more quickly
well	better
badly	worse

Common misconceptions

Misconception	How to identify	How to overcome
Learners use the simple adverb form instead of the comparative form. For example: *I'm sorry for not writing* ~~soon~~ **sooner**.	Write two sentences on the board – one with the simple adverb and one with the comparative form. Identify the difference in meaning/form. For example: *I'm sorry for not writing **sooner**.* *I'll write **soon**.*	Practise using: • Activities 1–4 on pages 58–59 of the Workbook • **Photocopiable 13.**

Starter ideas

What do you spend your pocket money on …? (5–10 minutes)

- Explain that in this lesson, you are going to talk about different ways to spend money.

- Then introduce pocket money. Write questions on the board. For example: *Do you get pocket money? What do you spend it on …? What do you do if you can't afford something? Do you save money? Do you think brands are a waste of money?*

- Check that learners understand the meaning of each question. Then circulate and offer support while, in pairs, learners ask and answer the questions.

Answers
Learner's own answers.

Main teaching ideas

Getting started (10 minutes)

- Look at the photos together. Use question a to stimulate discussion about the different ways there are to buy things, for example cheques, cash, credit cards, gift cards.

- Use questions b and c to start a brief class discussion about money and to start introducing money vocabulary.

Answers
a   Photos show: bank notes and coins ('cash'); credit and debit cards; a cheque; a gift card from a specific store or group of stores.
b   Cards are probably the method most often used; payment by cheque is probably used the least often. Learner's own answers.
c   Learner's own answers.

> **Digital Classroom:** Use the video 'Money' to introduce the theme of money and related vocabulary. The i button will explain how to use the video.

1   Imagine you have some money to spend! How would you spend it? (10 minutes)

- First, look at the photos together and identify what each one shows.

- Then circulate and offer support while learners ask and answer the questions with a partner.

> **Differentiation ideas:** If learners need support with this task, give them a worksheet with some prompts, or write the prompts on a mini-whiteboard. For example: *I would spend the money on …; No, I wouldn't buy/use … .*

- After a few minutes, work together as a class and share ideas. Write any useful vocabulary on the board.

Answers
Learner's own answers.

2   Try the Money Matters quiz! (10 minutes)

- First, read the quiz questions together and check that learners understand their meaning.

> **Critical thinking opportunity:** Doing the quiz should help learners evaluate different opinions and attitudes to spending money. Before learners complete the quiz individually, consider each question.

For question 1, ask: *Is it better to spend money doing something rather than having something? Are experiences and memories more valuable than having things?*

For questions 2 and 5, have a brief discussion about the consequences of each decision.

For question 3, make sure learners understand 'charity' by giving some well-known examples.

For question 4, ask: *Is it more justifiable to spend money on technology rather than things to wear? Should we always look for the cheaper options, whatever we are buying?*

- Circulate and offer support while learners complete the quiz. Remind them not to show anyone their answers.

Answers
Learner's own answers.

3   Work in pairs. Do the quiz again, but this time answer for your partner. Then compare answers. (10 minutes)

- Learners work with the same partner as for Activity 1.

- They complete the quiz again, but this time respond on behalf of their partner.

- Learners then compare their predictions with what their partners actually answered: one point for each correct guess.

- As a class, have a brief discussion about the scores – how well did learners know their partners?

Answers
Learner's own answers.

4 Listen to some friends discussing one of the quiz questions. (5–10 minutes)

- Tell learners they are going to hear friends discussing one of the quiz questions. Explain that it isn't necessary for them to understand every word of the recording – they need to focus on which question the children are talking about, and identify which speaker's opinion is most similar to theirs.

- Before you share feedback as a class, invite learners to discuss their ideas with a partner.

Audioscript: Track 34

See Learner's Book page 79

Boy 1: So, if you had some money to spend – let's say quite a lot – would you … a) buy expensive trainers, you know, really nice ones … an expensive brand? Or b) Would you buy cheap ones and maybe save the rest of the money for something else?

Boy 2: I'd buy expensive ones definitely, if I could afford them! The expensive ones are the best and what everyone wants. I'd buy ones like my favourite YouTuber wears … His trainers are awesome!

Boy 1: No one can afford those – they are super expensive!

Boy 2: OK, something similar. What about you two?

Girl: No way would I spend a lot of money just on trainers! I'd buy some cheaper ones and save the rest. It's a waste of money to buy expensive trainers. You are just paying for the brand name. You can get cheaper ones that are just as good. Then you have money left for something else.

Boy 2: I don't think cheaper trainers are just as good as the expensive ones. The expensive brands are designed better – so they last longer. They look better and last longer.

Boy 1: Yes, but what if your feet get bigger and you grow out of them quickly? Then it's a waste of money … My mum says that it's better to buy cheaper trainers because I grow out of shoes really fast … My brother gets more expensive ones because he grows out of them less quickly than me.

Girl: Yeah, better to spend your money on something that you can use for longer … And have money left for other things … *[fade out]*

Answers
The friends are talking about question 2 from the Money Matters quiz.
Learner's own answers.

5 Listen again. Write down two reasons for buying expensive trainers and two reasons against. (10 minutes)

- Learners listen again. This time, ask them to write down two reasons *for* buying expensive trainers and two reasons *against*.

> **Differentiation ideas:** If learners want an extra challenge in this task, tell them to write down all the examples they remember. If learners need support, download the audio script and ask them to underline the reasons for and against buying trainers.

- Then, as a class, think of any more reasons *for* and *against* buying expensive trainers.

- Finally, ask learners: *Is your opinion from the quiz still the same? Or have you changed your mind after listening to the discussion?* Have a brief discussion to see if anyone has changed their mind.

Answers
Reasons for (two of): Everyone wants expensive trainers. They are designed better and last longer.
Reasons against (two of): A waste of money – you pay for the brand name. Cheaper trainers are just as good. You grow out of trainers quickly so better to buy cheaper ones.
Other reasons: Learner's own answers.

6 Match the money words from the discussion to a definition. (10 minutes)

- Read the first money expression (*a waste of money*) and identify that it is a (compound) noun.

- Read through the definitions together and check that learners understand their meaning. Eliminate c, e and f as a match to *waste of money*, as they are definitions for verbs, not nouns.

- Reread a and b, and identify the correct match.

- Circulate and offer support while learners match the remaining expressions in pairs.

- Give class feedback on the correct answers.

Answers
1 b, 2 f, 3 e, 4 a, 5 c, 6 d

Use of English – Comparative adverbs, and 7 Read the Use of English box together and complete the sentences. (10 minutes)

- As a class, read the Use of English box on comparative adverbs. Talk through a couple of other examples (see Language background) and answer any questions that learners have on comparative adverbs.

- Then go through the first example (question 1) in Activity 7.

- Circulate and offer support while learners complete the remaining sentences in pairs.

› **Differentiation ideas:** Learners could work in pairs; less confident writers will benefit from language support and their partners will consolidate their understanding of comparative adverbs by explaining why an answer may be correct/incorrect.

- Give class feedback on the correct answers.

> **Workbook**
> Learners do Activities 1–4 on pages 58–59.

Answers
a more quickly (Example), b longer, c more easily, d more often, e more carefully
Learner's own answers.

> **Digital Classroom:** Use the grammar presentation 'Comparative adverbs' to revise and practise using comparative adverbs. The i button will explain how to use the grammar presentation.

8 Work in a small group. Choose another quiz question from Activity 2 and discuss it in your group. (25 minutes)

> **Differentiation ideas:** If learners want an extra challenge, ask them to write another quiz question about spending money. They should give it to another group to discuss.

- Circulate and offer support, making sure all learners have the chance to make a contribution and that they use vocabulary from Activity 6.

- Each group shares their opinions with the class. Try to make sure that each group member has a chance to share at least one point of feedback.

- Learners could complete **Photocopiable 13**.

Answers
Learner's own answers.

Plenary ideas

Reflection (5–10 minutes)

As a class, learners reflect on the lesson. Did any of their friends' opinions surprise them? Have they changed any of their opinions about spending money? Ask them to share their ideas.

Homework ideas

- Learners write a paragraph (up to 100 words) that gives possible reasons for and against options a) and b) for one of the quiz questions.

> **Assessment ideas:** As a class, write a short checklist so that learners can self-assess their homework before handing it in. For example: *Have I included reasons? Have I used comparative adverbs correctly? Have I used the new vocabulary from the lesson?*

> **Workbook**
>
> Learners do Activities 1–6 on pages 56–57.

5.2 Maths: Clever calculations

LEARNING PLAN

Learning objectives	Learning intentions	Success criteria
6Rd.01 6Us.01	• **Reading:** Understand, with support, most specific information and detail in short and extended texts. • **Use of English:** Use a wide range of quantifiers (e.g. *either, neither, both (of), several, plenty*). • **Vocabulary:** *kg (a kilogram), % (percent), cost, fraction, calculate, entrepreneur, profit, minus*	• Learners can understand, with support, specific information in a text showing calculations, numbers and amounts. • Learners can understand how quantifiers are used in a text describing calculations and amounts.

21st-century skills

Cross-curricular link: Mathematics: Working out percentages and fractions.

Materials: Learner's Book pages 80–81; Workbook pages 60–61; poster card and internet access for Activity 6

LANGUAGE BACKGROUND

Quantifiers

Quantifiers give information about the number of something – *how much* or *how many*.

Learners should already be familiar with quantifiers. This lesson introduces four more: *several, plenty* *of, either … or, both of*. These expressions are common with mother-tongue English speakers, so mastering their usage (e.g. *plenty of* instead of *many*, especially in positive sentences) can give your learner's English a more natural edge.

Common misconceptions

Misconception	How to identify	How to overcome
Learners often use *much/many* incorrectly in positive contexts. For example: *Bring ~~many~~ **plenty of** friends.* *Secondly, drink ~~much~~ **plenty of** water.*	Show examples like those from the Misconception column and elicit that they sound unnatural. Elicit alternatives, such as *plenty of.*	Discourage learners from using *many/much*, as this sounds unnatural. Encourage the use of *several/plenty of*, which sounds more natural. Practise using Activities 1–3 in the Workbook, pages 60–61.

Starter idea

Being an entrepreneur (5–10 minutes)

- Write the expression *entrepreneur* on the board and check learners know the meaning (someone who starts their own business, especially when this involves seeing a new opportunity).

- Have a class discussion about the kinds of characteristics you need to be an entrepreneur, for example, creative, daring, brave, likes maths.

- Identify some famous entrepreneurs, for example Henry Ford, Bill Gates, Steve Jobs, Walt Disney.

Main teaching ideas

1 Have you ever done activities to raise money? What did you do? How was the money spent? (5–10 minutes)

- Explain that this lesson is going to focus on two children, Ava and Alex, who are raising money at the community fair by making chocolate brownies.

- Ask learners to share their stories about raising money. Encourage them to explain what they did and how the money was spent. For example: *I did a … last year. The money was spent on gym equipment for the school.*

Answers
Learner's own answers.

Key words: Calculations (5 minutes)

- Write the symbols for the calculations (*kg, %)* on the board. Explain that they stand for *a kilogram* and *percent*. Remind learners what *cost* means.

2 Ava and Alex sold 95 chocolate brownies at the community fair and made a profit! Read the poster they made for their maths class. (10 minutes)

- First, ask learners if they have ever sold anything to raise money. Check they know the meaning of 'made a profit', 'costs' and 'minus'. Also make sure that learners understand what a *community fair* is – if necessary, give a few examples of the kinds of stalls and activities that there might be at a community fair.

- Look at the picture of the *chocolate brownies* together and make sure learners know what they are. Before you read the poster in detail, point out the ingredients used to make brownies.

- Then, in pairs, ask learners to read the poster and answer the two questions.

- Give class feedback on the correct answers.

Answers
a 100
b $15.00 ($13.00 for ingredients; $2.00 for paper bags)

---

3 Read the poster again. (10 minutes)

- Make sure learners understand what *50% of all money raised will go towards the charity* means.

- Learners reread the text and work out the answers in pairs. Give class feedback on the answers. Invite learners to explain how they reached their answers.

CROSS-CURRICULAR LINKS

Mathematics: Learners apply their mathematical knowledge to work out a percentage and fraction. Elicit the meaning of *percent*(age) and *fractions*. Write a few different corresponding fractions and percentages on the board (not 50%) and encourage learners to match them and identify which is which.

Answers
a   b $40.00   b   (a) $\frac{1}{2}$

---

4 Ava and Alex want to make 200 brownies for the next school fair. (15 minutes)

- First, read through the questions together and make sure learners understand their meaning.

- Then ask learners to work in pairs to answer the questions.

- Allow learners time to answer the questions. Then, as a class, work through the answers.

Answers

a 2200 g (2.2 kg) butter, 3000 g (3 kg) sugar, 32 eggs, 600 g cocoa powder, 800 g self-raising flour, 800 g chocolate chips

b

2200 g (2.2 kg)	butter	$10.00
3000 g (3 kg)	sugar	$ 2.00
32	eggs	$ 5.00
600g	cocoa powder	$ 2.00
800g	self-raising flour	$ 1.00
800g	chocolate chips	$ 6.00
TOTAL:		$26.00

c $4.00

d Total sales of brownies: 200 × $1.00 = $200.00
Total cost of ingredients + paper bags: $26.00 + $4.00 = $30.00
Total profit: $200.00 – $30.00 = $170.00

Use of English – Quantifiers, and 5 Read the Use of English box and find examples of the quantifiers in the poster. (10 minutes)

- Read the Use of English box together. Ask learners to give you an example of each quantifier in a sentence, to check their understanding.

- Then ask pairs of learners to write down the quantifiers from the poster text and where they found them.

- Finally, as a class, ask learners to tell you the correct option for each part of the explanation.

> **Differentiation ideas:** Learners could write down the explanation with the correct options and you could then share feedback as a class.

Workbook

Learners do Activities 1–3 on pages 60–61.

Answers

Paragraph 1: *several* – line 1; *plenty of* – line 2; Paragraph 2: *either … or* – lines 1 and 2; *both of* – line 2.

Plenty of means [1]**lots of**; *several* means [2]**a smaller amount** (e.g. 3 or 4).

> **Digital Classroom:** Use the activity 'Quantifers' to revise quantifiers. The i button will explain how to use the activity.

6 Work in a small group. Create an activity to raise money for charity at a community event. (30 minutes + presentation time)

- Before learners start working in their groups, brainstorm a list of local, national or international charities that they might want to raise money for.

- Circulate and support learners while they think of ideas for their product and calculate quantities, prices and costs. If you have internet access, encourage learners to check real-time prices; otherwise, ask learners to imagine how much ingredients/products cost. Try not to limit learner's creativity, but encourage them to be realistic about what is achievable.

- Make sure learners keep notes about how much things cost, how many of the product they want to sell, etc.

- When learners have completed their discussions, distribute poster card for them to make their poster.

> **Assessment ideas:** Before learners complete their posters, make a checklist as a class. For example: *Have we included the product name on the poster? Did we include the costs and profit? Do our calculations make sense? Did we use the vocabulary from the lesson in our presentation? Did we explain our calculations clearly?* The groups can use the list to check what they need to include on their posters and to give peer feedback on their presentations.

- Continue to offer support while learners create their posters. Encourage them to refer to Ava and Alex's poster to help them.

- Learners present their posters to the class. Remind them to talk about their calculations and to use relevant vocabulary from the lesson, for example *costs, profit*.

Answers
Learner's own answers.

Plenary ideas

Reflection (5–10 minutes)

Ask learners what they have enjoyed about the lesson and what they have found challenging. For example, did they enjoy the mathematical aspect? Was it fun being an entrepreneur in Activity 6? Why or why not?

Homework ideas

Ask learners to research and read about a local, national or international charity event, and share what they found out at the start of the next lesson.

> **Workbook**
>
> Learners do Activities 1–3 on pages 60–61.

5.3 Talk about it: Spending plans

LEARNING PLAN

Learning objectives	Learning intentions	Success criteria
6Ld.05 6Lo.01 6So.01 6Ug.02	• **Listening:** Understand, with support, most of the detail of an argument in short and extended talk. Recognise, with support, the opinions of the speaker(s) in short and extended talk. • **Speaking/Use of English:** Express opinions, feelings and reactions. Use *what/how about + noun/-ing* to make suggestions. • **Vocabulary:** *formal, informal, polite, rude, aggressive, friendly*	• Learners can recognise different opinions being put forward in a discussion comparing ideas about how to spend a sum of money. • Learners can make suggestions, give opinions and compare ideas about how a sum of money should be spent.

21st-century skills

Communication: Make suggestions, sharing ideas and responding appropriately in a discussion about a money question.

Materials: Learner's Book pages 82–83; Workbook pages 60–61

Starter ideas

How should you spend the money? (5 minutes)

- First, ask learners to share what they found out about a local, national or international charity event.

- Explain that there are lots of amazing causes and many different ways to raise money to help them. This lesson is going to compare ideas for how to spend a sum of money that a class has raised.

Briefly talk about how difficult it can be to decide what to spend money on when there are lots of different options.

Main teaching ideas

1 What ideas for raising money can you see in the photos? Which do you like best? (5–10 minutes)

- Invite learners to identify the activities in the photos. If learners are not familiar with the term 'fun run', explain that it's a fun running activity for people of different ages and abilities (see Background knowledge). Explain that families often do activities, like running, together to raise money for charity.

- Have a class vote on which activity learners like best. Then build up a list on the board of other ideas for raising money.

Answers

Photo images: a lemonade and cake stall; a fun run or sports day/event; face painting; a book fair/stall. Learner's own answers.

2 Listen to the class discussion and answer the questions. (10 minutes)

- Tell learners they are going to listen to a class discussion about what to do with the money a class has raised.

- Encourage predictions about the kinds of things the money might be spent on in a school.

- Read the questions together and check that learners understand what to listen for.

- Play the recording and give learners a few minutes to answer the questions. If necessary, play the recording again.

- Give class feedback on the correct answers.

Audioscript: Track 35

See Learner's Book page 82

Teacher: Hello everyone. Our class raised an amazing $825 through our Fun Run last month. Once again, a huge thanks to all of you. Now the question is: how do we spend the money? I want to hear your ideas and the reasons why. In your groups, you have five minutes to talk and come up with some ideas. Then we'll share our ideas as a class. Off you go … five minutes!

OK everyone, now you've had time to think, let's hear your ideas. I also want to know what you think of each other's ideas. Who's going first? Yes, Nacho?

Nacho: We think we should spend the money on some new laptops for the computer room. At the moment, we have to share the computers.

Teacher: Thanks, Nacho. $825 would probably buy about three new laptops. What does everyone else think?

Answers

a A fun run
b $825.00
c Nacho suggests buying new laptops for the computer room, because the students have to share them at the moment (there are not enough for each student to have their own laptop).

3 Listen to the next part of the discussion. (5–10 minutes)

- Before learners listen to the next part of the discussion, ask them what they think of Nacho's suggestion. Encourage agreement and disagreement.

- Play the next part of the recording so that learners can hear Marina's response to Nacho's idea. Ask learners just to focus on Marina's response for now and not to worry too much about what the other speakers are saying.

- Share class feedback about Marina's response. How does it compare to learner's opinions about Nacho's suggestion?

Audioscript: Track 36

See Learner's Book page 82

Teacher: So $825 would probably buy about three new laptops. What does everyone else think? Yes, Marina?

Marina: We think it is better to spend the money on some new equipment for the after-school table tennis club. Last week one of the tables broke. We could buy a lot for the club with $825. It would only buy three laptops for the computer room, which isn't many.

Teacher:	Good points, thanks for your comments. What do other people think?
Pablo:	We think it's a good idea to buy sports equipment but not for the table tennis club. Only five of the class are members and we should spend the money on something everyone likes doing.
Daniel:	We agree with that. How about spending it on our end-of-term celebration? Everyone in the class would like that!
Teacher:	(*laughing*) Thanks for your idea, Daniel, but I think it is too much money to spend on our end-of-term celebration! What about using a small amount of the money for the celebration and for something else as well? What do you all think?
Luisa:	Why don't we use the money for a school trip? We could go somewhere that would help us with one of next term's projects.

Answers
Marina makes another suggestion. She suggests buying equipment for the table tennis club.

4 Listen again. What other ideas do the classmates have? (10 minutes)

- Before listening again, ask learners if they can remember any of the other classmates' suggestions.

- Replay the recording so learners can hear the other classmates' ideas and their reasons. If helpful, play the recording again and pause after each speaker, to give learners time to process the information and make notes.

- Circulate and support learners while they discuss the questions in pairs.

> **Differentiation ideas:** If learners need support with this task, ask them to focus on answering the first and the third question.

- Give class feedback on the answers. Then do a quick survey to see which idea learners preferred.

Answers
Marina suggests equipment for the table tennis club because $825.00 could buy a lot of equipment (and one of the tables has broken). She says that the money would only buy a few (three) new laptops. Pablo thinks that they should spend the money on something that everyone likes doing; but not on the table tennis club, because only a few classmates are members.
Daniel thinks they should spend the money on the end-of-term celebration.
Luisa suggests spending the money on a school trip, to help with one of next term's projects.
Learner's own answers.

5 How much is $825 US in the currency of your country? (5 minutes)

- Check learners understand the difference between *money* and *currency*.

- Elicit guesses before confirming the actual value.

Answers
Learner's own answers.

Speaking tip – Negotiating, and 6 Read the Speaking tip. Match the phrases from the discussion with a function (1–4). (10 minutes)

- Read the Speaking tip together as a class. On the board, write down a few suggestions for introducing a point, making suggestions and responding to other people, for example *I like to make the point that …; Could I suggest that/ + ing?*

- Then look at the phrases a–d and allow learners time, in pairs, to match each one with a function.

- Give class feedback and elicit some more similar expressions.

Answers
1 b, 2 a, 3 d, 4 c

7 Listen and complete the phrases for making suggestions. Which phrases are followed by verb + -ing? (10 minutes)

- First, read the phrases 1–4 without saying the missing words.

- Then play the recording and ask learners to complete the phrases. If necessary, stop the recording after each phrase, to allow learners to write down the missing words.

- Invite learners to tell you which phrases are followed by verb + *ing*.

Answers

1 *Let's* hear your ideas.
2 *How about* spending it on our end-of-term celebration?
3 *What about* using a small amount of the money for …?
4 *Why don't we* use the money for a school trip?
Phrases 2 (*How about …?*) and 3 (*What about …?*) are followed by the verb + -*ing*.

> Audioscript: Track 37

See Learner's Book page 83

Narrator:	1
Boy:	Let's hear your ideas.
Narrator:	2
Girl:	How about spending it on our end-of-term celebration?
Narrator:	3
Boy:	What about using a small amount of the money for …?
Narrator:	4
Girl:	Why don't we use the money for a school trip?

> **Digital Classroom:** Use the activity 'Making suggestions' to reinforce the use of different verb patterns to make suggestions. The i button will explain how to use the activity.

8 What role does the teacher have in the discussion? (5–10 minutes)

- Read the adjectives in the box together and check that learners understand their meaning.

- Circulate and offer support while learners discuss their ideas about the teacher's role with a partner.

> **Differentiation ideas:** If more confident learners want an extra challenge in this task, download the audioscript and ask them to underline examples to support their adjective choices.

- As a class, share feedback on the teacher's role and identify the most appropriate adjectives from the box.

Answers

The role of the teacher is to moderate / manage / facilitate the discussion.
Adjectives to describe communication: informal, polite, friendly.

---

9 In small groups, discuss a 'money' question. (20 minutes)

- Tell learners that now it's their turn to discuss how to spend $825 on something for their class or school.

- First, give learners a few minutes to brainstorm possible spending ideas.

- Make sure each group has chosen a favourite idea. Then give learners some time to think of reasons to support it. They should practise explaining their ideas to their group, making sure they use the phrases from the Speaking tip and Activities 6 and 7.

> **Assessment ideas:** Circulate and offer support to learners, providing verbal feedback on their pronunciation, use of negotiating phrases, and how well their reasons support their idea.

- Finally, each group should share their ideas with the class.

- **Communication:** During the class discussion, encourage learners to make suggestions, listen to ideas and respond appropriately, for example by listening without interrupting and being polite, even when they don't agree with an idea.

- Guide the class discussion, making sure everyone has a chance to contribute. As a class, decide what to spend the $825 on.

Answers
Learner's own answers.

Plenary ideas

Reflection (5 minutes)

Learners share what they found easy/difficult about negotiating in the class discussion. Did they enjoy the discussion, or would they prefer to have time to think about their opinions and write them down?

Homework ideas

Learners write a paragraph summarising how they decided to spend the $825 during the discussion, giving reasons for their decision.

Workbook

Learners do Activities 1–3 on pages 60–61.

5.4 Write about it: The question of pocket money

LEARNING PLAN

Learning objectives	Learning intentions	Success criteria
6Ro.01, 6Rd.03	• **Reading:** Recognise, with support, the opinions of the writer(s) in short and extended texts.	• Learners can understand the points in a simple discursive essay discussing the issue of pocket money and recognise the opinions of the writer.
6Wc.03, 6Wor.02, 6Wor.03 6Sor.01	• **Writing:** Express opinions and feelings. Link sentences using an increasing range of connectives to create a short text organised into paragraphs. Use appropriate layout for a limited range of genres.	• Learners can express opinions in an essay discussing the issue of pocket money, using connectives, and use a layout with an introduction, comparative points and a simple conclusion.
6Us.03	• **Use of English:** Use reflexive pronouns. • **Vocabulary:** *pocket money, because, in my opinion, however, but, therefore, firstly, secondly, finally*	• Learners can link sentences using an increasing range of connectives. • Learners can use reflexive pronouns.

21st-century skills

Creative thinking: Compare ideas and form opinions about the issue of pocket money.

Materials: Learner's Book pages 84–85; Workbook pages 62–63; Unit 5 sample answer; **Photocopiable 14; Photocopiable 15; Differentiated worksheets 5A, B and C**

Starter ideas

What would you like to buy? (5–10 minutes)

• Ask learners to tell the class if they are saving up to buy anything at the moment. What are they hoping to get? Build up a list on the board.

• Play a game. Player 1 begins, for example *I'd like to buy some trainers.*

• Player 2 continues, for example *I'd like to buy some trainers and a computer game.*

• Keep going with more players, each time adding one object until a player can't remember all the objects.

• Ask learners if they know the price of some of the objects.

Main teaching ideas

1 What is pocket money? (5 minutes)

- Write *pocket money* on the board. If you did the Starter activity in Lesson 5.1, see if learners can remember what it means. Look at the photo and talk about its meaning.

- Circulate and offer support while learners tell a partner if they get any pocket money from their families and how they decide how much (for instance, do they get more money if they help their family with tasks around the house?). Make it clear to learners that they don't need to specify how much they receive, especially if this makes them feel uncomfortable.

Answers
Pocket money is a small allowance of money given to children by parents or other family members, usually weekly.
Learner's own answers.

2 Read 11-year-old Ismail's essay discussing children and pocket money. What is his opinion? (5 minutes)

- Give learners a few minutes to skim-read Ismail's essay so that they can answer the question. Tell them not to worry too much about the detail of the essay, as they will get a chance to read it again in the next activity. They should just focus on whether Ismail thinks that children should get pocket money.

- Give class feedback on the answer.

Answers
Ismail thinks that children should get pocket money.

3 Read Ismail's essay again. Find three reasons he gives to support his opinion. (10 minutes)

- Ask learners to read the essay again, this time in more detail. They should look out for three reasons Ismail gives to support his opinion, including one real-life example, and write them down.

- Before sharing class feedback, ask learners to compare their ideas with a partner. Did they identify the same reasons?

Answers
Reasons (three of):
- Pocket money teaches children useful things about money.
- Children learn to spend money in a good way. They have to make decisions about what to buy (and what isn't necessary or a good idea).
- Pocket money helps children learn how much things cost. Children learn how to compare prices and find things to buy more cheaply.
- It helps children learn how to save their money. / It teaches children to manage money themselves.

Real-life example: Ismail saved up and bought himself a video game last year.

4 Match the descriptions to paragraphs 1–4. (5 minutes)

- Read the descriptions together. Check learners understand where an introduction, conclusion and points for and against the main opinion would normally be in an essay.

- Ask learners, in pairs, to match each description to a paragraph.

- Give class feedback on the answers.

Answers
a 4 b 1 c 3 d 2 4 a

5 Do you agree with Ismail's opinion? (5–10 minutes)

- Circulate and offer support while learners think of two more reasons why children should or shouldn't have pocket money.

- **Creative thinking:** This is a good opportunity for learners to compare ideas and form their own opinions about why children should or shouldn't have pocket money, using Ismail's essay and their earlier discussions to help them.

> **Differentiation ideas:** If learners don't feel confident about this task, ask them to think of one more reason. If learners want a challenge, ask them to think of three more reasons.

Answers
Learner's own answers.

Language focus – Reflexive pronouns, and 6 Find more examples of reflexive pronouns in the essay. (15 minutes)

- Look at the Language focus box on reflexive pronouns together. Explain to learners that the other reflexive pronouns are *yourself*, *himself*, *herself*, *itself*, *yourselves* and *themselves*.

- To help learners practise using reflexive pronouns, ask them to ask/answer these questions with a partner. Write the questions on the board and ask learners to identify the reflexive pronoun in each question before they start talking.

  1 *Have you ever bought something expensive yourself? What was it?*

  2 *What jobs at home do you do yourself?*

  3 *Why can it be good for us to do things for ourselves? Think of some examples.*

- Circulate and offer support, encouraging learners to use reflexive pronouns in their answers (see suggested answer below).

- Then ask learners, in their pairs, to find and write down more examples of reflexive pronouns from the essay.

- Give class feedback.

Answers
Examples of reflexive pronouns: yourself, myself, ourselves.

> **Digital Classroom:** Use the activity 'Reflexive pronouns' to revise reflexive pronouns. The i button will explain how to use the activity.

> **Digital Classroom:** Use the activity 'Connecting words' to revise connecting words. The i button will explain how to use the activity.

7 Writing tip – Connecting words, and What do connecting words do in the essay? (10 minutes)

- Read the Writing tip together. Then invite learners to tell you some other connecting and sequencing words to check their understanding.

- Demonstrate the activity. Look at the phrase in the second callout (*In my opinion*) and match it with function number 2 (*introduces your opinion*).

- Circulate and offer support while learners work in pairs to match the words in bold with a function.

- Give class feedback on the correct answers.

Answers
Connecting words link ideas and points together in a logical order, so the reader can follow the points in the essay easily.
a 2 **b** 5 **c** 4 **d** 1 **e** 3

8 Write an opinion essay. (50 minutes)

- First, make sure each learner has chosen one of the titles – A: Should children do jobs to earn pocket money? or B: Should you get a lot more pocket money if you are older? Alternatively, you or the learners could choose another money-related title.

- Circulate and offer support while learners make notes. Check they have decided on a clear opinion and have clear points to support their view.

- Learners can practice useful expressions for their essays using **Differentiated worksheets 5A, B and C**.

> **Assessment ideas:** Before learners start Step 2, show them the Unit 5 sample answer without the mark scheme comments. As a class, evaluate the sample answer's strengths and weaknesses and also look at the checklist on page 85 of the Learner's Book, so that learners know what they are aiming to achieve in their opinion essay.

- Continue to offer support while learners use the headings in Activity 4 to organise their essay. Remind learners to use connecting words in their drafts.

> **Assessment ideas:** Once learners have finished their first draft, ask them to work through the checklist on **Photocopiable 14** to self-assess their work. Once they have made any updates, invite them to swap their draft with a partner, who will proofread it. Encourage learners to give feedback sensitively and to include at least one compliment.

- Share class feedback on writing the essay – what were the challenges for learners and what did they enjoy?

Answers

Ideas for points:

A: Should children do jobs to earn pocket money?

- Yes: *Gets them used to the idea that, if you want something, you have to work for it. Motivates them to work hard and help at home. Helps them appreciate the value of money because they have had to earn it.*

- No: *If children earn pocket money for helping at home, they will expect to be paid for every job. Children will have to work when they are adults – they shouldn't have to work when they are children!*

B: Should you get a lot more pocket money if you are older?

- Yes: *Things get more expensive as you get older. You are nearly grown-up so learning to manage money is more important. You are older and more responsible, so you can manage larger amounts of pocket money.*

- Yes, but: *You should do more jobs around the house to earn a higher amount of pocket money.*

Plus learner's own answers.

Plenary ideas

Consolidation (15 minutes)

This is a good opportunity for learners to complete **Photocopiable 15,** to consolidate the grammar points from Lessons 2 and 4.

Homework ideas

- Under parental supervision, learners do some research to find out how much pocket money children are given in different countries.

- Use **Differentiated worksheets 5A, B and C** for extra practice writing essays.

> **Workbook**
>
> Learners do Activities 1–5 on pages 62–63.

5.5 Read and respond: *Billionaire Boy*

LEARNING PLAN		
Learning objectives	**Learning intentions**	**Success criteria**
6Rd.01, 6Rm.02, 6Ro.01	• **Reading:** Read independently a range of short, simple fiction and non-fiction texts with confidence and enjoyment. Recognise, with support, the opinions of the writer(s) in short and extended texts.	• Learners can read and enjoy a story about a very wealthy young boy, understanding specific details and recognising the opinions of the author.
6Rd.04	• **Reading:** Deduce meaning from context, with support, in short and extended texts.	• Learners can deduce the meaning of descriptive vocabulary from context with the support of synonyms.
6Rd.05	• **Reading:** Explore common idiomatic phrases and their meanings.	
	• **Vocabulary:** *fake, pictured, forlorn, proper, milling, motor-up, frustration, chauffeured, posh*	• Learners can explore common idiomatic phrases and their meanings.
21st-century skills		
Emotional development: Consider the issues around having a lot of money, especially the negative aspects.		

Materials: Learner's Book pages 86–89; Workbook pages 64–65; internet access (for Activity 8)

Starter ideas

For my birthday, I want … (5–10 minutes)

- Tell learners to imagine that they have so much money they can have anything they want for their birthday.

- Brainstorm the presents that learners would like to receive. Encourage them to have fun with this activity.

Main teaching ideas

1 How rich is a billionaire? (5 minutes)

- Tell learners that in this lesson they are going to read and listen to a story about a boy who is a billionaire.

- Invite learners to tell you how rich they think a billionaire is. Before sharing the answer, you could ask a learner to come up to the board and write down how much money they think a billionaire has.

- Give learners a few minutes to discuss, in pairs, the advantages and disadvantages of having a lot of money.

- Build up a list on the board.

Answers
A billionaire is someone who has (at least) 1,000,000,000 in pounds, dollars, euros, etc.
Learner's own answers.

2 Read and listen to the first part of the story. (15–20 minutes)

- Tell learners that in this first part of the story, it is Joe Spud's birthday.

- Brainstorm learner's predictions about what special presents a billionaire boy might like. Try to elicit some of the vocabulary from the story, for example *cheque, loads of money, solid gold sunglasses, his own speedboat, vouchers,* etc.

- Before reading and listening, read the words and definitions in the glossary. Also make it clear that learners don't need to understand every word first time – initially they just need to work out the special present that Joe would like.

- Remind learners to read the story as they listen. Then ask learners to write down the special present.

- Give class feedback on the answer.

- Before learners reread the first part of the story, read questions a–i together and check that learners understand their meaning.

- Give learners time to read the story again and answer the questions. Then go through the answers as a class.

> **Differentiation ideas:** If learners need support with this task, ask them to focus on answering the first four questions.

Audioscript: Track 38

See Learner's Book pages 86–87.

Answers
Joe Spud would like a friend for his birthday present.
a   Because Joe's house is so big.
b   Joe only knows a quarter of his house, because it is so huge.
c   The taps are made of gold and the carpets are made of animal fur.
d   He already has lots of money.
e   Joe already has two speedboats.
f   They are boring.
g   'High-class problems' are problems that only extremely rich people might have. They are problems of a very different kind to the problems of most people.
h   A friend.

3 Before you read the next extract, think of ways Joe could make his wish happen. (15 minutes)

- As a class, discuss ways that Joe could make his wish to have a friend happen. Build up a list of ideas on the board.

- Look at the glossary definition. Then invite learners to read and listen to Part 2 of the story to see if Joe's ideas are the same as theirs.

- As a class, spend a few minutes comparing the ideas. Are learners surprised about what they have heard/read?

- Before answering questions a–f, read the questions together and check learners understand what they are asking. Tell learners not to worry about understanding every word of the story, as they will be looking at the new vocabulary later in the lesson.

- Learners listen to and read the text and answer the questions.

> **Differentiation ideas:** Learners work in pairs to answer the questions. Less confident readers and writers will benefit from language support, and their partners will consolidate their understanding of the story. Circulate and check that all learners are participating.

- Go through the answers as a class.

Audioscript: Track 39

See Learner's Book page 87

Answers
Learner's own answers
a Joe wants to go to the local state school. Joe's dad is very surprised; he can't believe it.
b Mr Spud offers to build him a school in the back garden.
c Joe thinks that it looks like fun and that he will make a friend there.
d Mr Spud thinks that the other children will bully Joe or will only want to be friends with him because he is rich.
e Joe won't tell the other children that he is a billionaire.
f Mr Spud says 'yes'; Joe can go to a normal school.

4 Match the words in blue with their synonyms, and Reading tip – Powerful words and idioms. (15–20 minutes)

- Demonstrate the activity. Focus on the first blue expression, *motor up*. Read the whole sentence (*It took five minutes just to motor up the drive.*) and ask learners what they think *motor up* might mean. Elicit that *motor up* is a verb and then look at the synonyms. Eliminate *false, sad, real, anger* and *high quality,* as they aren't verbs. Elicit that, in this context, the synonym must be *drive.*

- In pairs, learners match the remaining words in blue with their synonyms.

- Invite learners to consider why the author uses these words instead of the synonyms. After a class discussion, explain that the synonyms are more descriptive and help the reader imagine the story in more detail.

- Then look at the Reading tip, which explains this point in more detail. This is beyond the requirements of the Cambridge Primary English as a Second Language curriculum framework.

- Next, introduce idioms. Explain that in the example, being 'given the sack' means to lose your job, but 'the sack' individually has a different meaning (a container for something). Ask learners if they know any more idioms before continuing to the next activity.

Answers
1 fake, 2 pictured, 3 forlorn, 4 proper, 5 milling, 6 motor up, 7 frustration, 8 chauffeured, 9 poshest
The author uses these words because they are more descriptive and help the reader to imagine the story in more detail.

5 Read the sentences with idioms about money. Which ones describe Mr Spud? (10 minutes)

- Together, read the three sentences. Invite learners to identify the idiom in each sentence.

- Then give learners a few minutes to discuss the questions in pairs.

- As a class, share the answers and talk through possible meanings for the idioms.

Answers
Sentences 1 and 3 describe Mr Spud.
a 'He has more money than sense' – when someone has a lot of money but isn't clever enough to spend it wisely or responsibly.
b 'He has a job that pays peanuts' – a job that doesn't pay very much money (implying that it is less than the job is worth).
c 'He has money to burn' – when someone has more money than they need, or they spend their money on things that are unnecessary (in the opinion of the speaker).

> **Digital Classroom:** Use the activity 'Billionaire boy!' to reinforce comprehension of the story from the Learner's Book. The i button will explain how to use the activity.

6 Work in a small group. Read the story again and discuss the questions together. (10–15 minutes)

*   Before learners work in their groups, read through the questions together to check that learners understand what they mean.

*   Offer support while learners either take turns to read a paragraph of the story or read the story individually and then discuss the questions together.

*   **Emotional development:** This activity gives learners the opportunity to consider issues around having a lot of money, especially the negative aspects. Encourage learners to listen respectfully to each other and try to ensure that everyone has a chance to contribute.

> **Assessment ideas:** Circulate and offer support, checking for pronunciation and how effectively learners express their opinions.

*   As a class, summarise possible responses.

Answers

a   Learner's own answers.

b   Learner's own answers. Clues in the story: The author describes lots of outrageous and unnecessary things that the Spuds have, for example a house that is so big that Joe has only ever seen a quarter of it; more rooms than they would ever need to live in; so many facilities (ski slope, tennis courts, helipad) that they would never have time to use very much. This emphasises to the reader how unnecessary they are. The author also describes things that are expensive but don't function very well, such as gold sunglasses and the orangutan butler who was fired. The author also describes the silly suggestions Joe's dad makes for his birthday present. Some suggestions are things that Joe already has (and his father has forgotten); everything is outrageously extravagant, but nothing excites Joe's interest. He finds most of the suggestions boring or useless. Another negative point is that Joe doesn't have a friend. The details in the text infer that his outrageous lifestyle prevents him from having a more normal life where he might make friends with other children. As his father points out, his wealth means that he might be bullied by other children at a 'normal' school, who will get jealous or find it difficult to relate to him. Also, he can never know if any friends he makes are true ones.

c   Learner's own answers.

7 Pronunciation: 's' sounds (5 minutes)

*   Play the recording all the way through so that learners can hear the words from the story. Then play the track again. Pause after each word so that learners can repeat them and consider which words have a soft 's' sound and which ones have a hard sound.

*   Look at the first two words. Elicit that *visible* has the hard 's' sound, whereas /*house*/ has the soft 's' sound.

*   Circulate and offer support while learners put the words into two groups: /s/ and /z/.

*   As a class, go through the answers.

> **Audioscript:** Track 40
> See Learner's Book page 89

Answers

Soft 's' sound (/s/): *house, seven, solid, son.*
Hard 's' sound (/z/): *visible, mountains, handles, pounds, problems.*

8 Spending money wisely (10–15 minutes)

*   The idea of this activity is to get learners thinking about the value of items and to dispel the idea that things we want can instantly be supplied.

*   When learners are in their pairs, have a fun competition to see which pair can remember five things that the Spuds own most quickly, without looking at the story. If learners find it hard to remember, allow them to look back at the story.

*   On the board, build up a list of things the Spuds own. Learners, in their pairs, discuss which are *important to have* and which they think the Spuds *need*.

- After a few minutes, share ideas as a class.

- Invite learners to look at the items in question 2. If necessary, update the items so they are more relevant to your learners. Again, ask learners to discuss whether they are things that people *want* or *need.*

- Learners choose one of the items and find out how much it costs. Then ask them to calculate how long it would take them to save their pocket money to buy it. Learners can also include other money they receive, for example as gifts for their birthday or a festival.

- Circulate and offer support while learners tell their partner about something they/their family saved for. Ask them to explain how they felt when they finally bought it.

- As a class, discuss learner's responses to questions 2–4. Were learners surprised about how much the items cost and how long they would take to save for? Have a more general discussion about the differences between luxuries and necessities. Try to ensure learners understand that 'wants' are things to be saved for – and worth waiting for!

Answers
a (Five from): a huge house with lots of rooms; tennis courts; a boating lake; a helipad; a ski-slope; sold gold taps, door handles and toilet seats; fur carpets; medieval goblets. Joe himself has loads of money and two speedboats. Plus learner's own answers.
b–d Learner's own answers.

Plenary ideas

What happened next? (5–10 minutes)

Have a class discussion about what might happen next in the story.

Homework ideas

Learners look for a copy of *Billionaire Boy* and find out if their predictions are correct.

Workbook

Learners do Activities 1–6 on pages 64–65.

5.6 Project challenge

LEARNING PLAN

Learning objectives	Learning intentions	Success criteria
6Wc.02	• **Writing:** Write, with support, short texts which describe people, places and objects, and routine past and present actions and events.	• Learners can describe the details of their own design for a banknote.
6Sc.06, 6Sc.02	• **Speaking:** Begin to produce and maintain stretches of language comprehensibly, allowing for hesitation and reformulation, especially in longer stretches of free production. Describe people, places and objects, and routine past and present actions and events.	• Learners can deliver a presentation about an idea for making money.

21st-century skills

Learning to learn: Research information on a specific topic and reflect on progress made.

Materials: Learner's Book pages 90–91; Workbook page 66; internet access; pictures of different currencies; pictures, magazines and newspapers for learners to use for their banknote design; PCs and a screen to project learner's presentations; poster card; the current US exchange rate for learner's currencies; examples of other learner's work; Unit 5 project checklists; End of Unit 5 test

Starter ideas

Raise interest in the projects (10–15 minutes)

- Tell learners they are either going to design a banknote (Project A) or deliver a presentation about an idea for making money (Project B).

- If possible, raise interest in the projects by presenting examples of learner's work on similar topics from other classes or the internet.

- Revise new vocabulary from the unit, which learners may need for the challenges, in a fun way. For example, create a word search or crossword for learners to complete, or put anagrams of the new vocabulary on the board.

Main teaching ideas

Introduce and complete the projects (60 minutes)

Encourage learners to choose one of the projects and then follow the steps for their chosen project.

Project A: Design a banknote

- Divide learners into pairs. If possible, supply real cash currency in small denominations for learners to look at. Alternatively, project images of different currency on the whiteboard for the whole class to look at together. If you take this approach, make sure it's possible to see the details on the coins and notes for the discussion. Encourage discussion about what the notes and coins are made of and what the different images are on the currency.

- **Learning to learn:** This is a good opportunity for learners to research information on a specific topic together. Encourage them to question why the images of certain well-known people are on the notes and to find out why the notes and coins are made from particular materials. Is it easy to see what value is on each note/coin?

- Explain to learners that they are going to design a new banknote. Support pairs while they brainstorm

ideas and make notes on the questions. They will need these later in the project. Make sure they all decide on an amount for the note, who will feature on the note – and why, and other images and features they are going to include.

- Check learners understand what a *collage* is. Distribute magazines/newspapers and also encourage learners to draw their own features. Make it clear that they should have fun and be creative with their design.

- Learners work together to create their posters. Circulate and support learners while they draft the text to explain their design choices.

- Encourage learners to read through the steps in the Learner's Book and check they have followed the instructions and included everything that was required.

- Make a classroom display of the posters. Learners look at all the designs and note down their favourite, with the reason why.

> **Assessment ideas:** Learners use the Unit 5 project checklist to evaluate another pair's banknote design.

- As a class, learners share their favourite banknote designs and give reasons why they like it.

Project B: Making money grow for a good cause

- Divide learners into groups of around four. First, make sure learners understand what $50 (US) is worth in their currency.

- Make sure all groups have agreed on who to help and why. Give learners time to brainstorm ideas for making money, and then about how to make the idea happen.

- Circulate and help learners to estimate the costs involved in their project. This means using your own knowledge of the cost of items learners choose (such as food, clothing) to help them develop their ideas. Remember that costs need only be rough estimates; the important thing is for learners to experience the process of developing an idea to raise money. Encourage learners to look back at Lesson 5.2 to help them create a chart to show their calculations.

- Circulate and offer support to groups as they make notes/create an infographic or diagram about how their profits will help another person or people.

- Make sure that each group member is involved in creating and delivering part of the presentation. If using presentation software is not practical, distribute poster card so that learners can create a poster presentation.
- Learners deliver their presentation to the class.

⟩ **Assessment ideas:** Learners use the Unit 5 project checklist to evaluate another group's presentation.

- After each group has presented, learners refer to their checklists and, as a class, share which was their favourite idea and why. Have a class discussion about a possible project you could do as a class to raise money for a good cause.

Plenary ideas

Reflection (10 minutes)

As a class, learners discuss what they enjoyed about the projects and what they found most challenging. Is there anything that they would do differently next time?

Homework ideas

Learners follow the steps in the Learner's Book to complete the project that they didn't do in class.

> **Workbook**
>
> Learners do Activities 1–2 on page 66.

5.7 What do you know now?

How can we use money in a good way?

- **Learning to learn:** Learners have the opportunity to reflect and evaluate their own learning success. Reintroduce the question from the start of the unit: *How can we use money in a good way?* Discuss learner's responses to the question now and compare with their comments at the beginning of the unit. How much has changed?
- Ask learners to work on the tasks in pairs.
- For questions 3–6, encourage learners to look back through the unit if they can't remember. Circulate and offer support while learners answer the questions.
- When learners have finished the questions, give class feedback on the answers.

Answers
1 Learner's own answers.
2 Learner's own answers.
3 a $825.00, b $275.00, c $82.50
4 Reasons (two from):
   - Pocket money teaches children useful things about money.
   - Children learn to spend money in a good way. They have to make decisions about what to buy (and what isn't necessary or a good idea).
   - Pocket money helps children learn how much things cost. Children learn how to compare prices and find things to buy more cheaply.
   - It helps children learn how to save their money. / It teaches children to manage money themselves.
5 Joe wants to go to the local state school to make new friends. His dad thinks he will either get bullied or other children will only want to be his friend because he is rich.
6 Learner's own answers.

Look what I can do!

- There are seven 'can do' statements. Learners read through the statements and tick the things they can do. Encourage them to reflect on how well they can do these things. Also invite them to think of ways they can improve further, for example what strategies they can use or learn to use.
- If learners find it challenging to read the statements, look through the unit with them and support them to find the relevant information.
- Finally, ask learners to work through the questions on page 67 of the Workbook. Encourage them to talk about what they enjoyed and also about any further support they might need.

› 6 People and work

Unit plan

Lesson	Approximate number of learning hours	Outline of learning content	Learning objectives	Resources
1 How do you get a job?	1.5–2.0	Talk about why people do the jobs they do.	6Ld.04 6Uv.07 6Uv.01	Learner's Book Lesson 6.1 Workbook Lesson 6.1 ⬇ Photocopiable 16 **Digital Classroom:** video – Different jobs; activity – Compound nouns; activity – Adjectives + prepositions
2 Designs that work!	1.5–2.0	Design a uniform for a job.	6Rd.01	Learner's Book Lesson 6.2 Workbook Lesson 6.2 **Digital Classroom:** slideshow – Uniforms for jobs; activity – Uniforms
3 Working in space	2.0–2.5	Discover what it's like to be an astronaut. Use reported speech to describe someone's job.	6Ld.02 6Sor.02 6Sc.07 6Ug.11 6Us.06	Learner's Book Lesson 6.3 Workbook Lesson 6.3 ⬇ Photocopiable 17 ⬇ Differentiated worksheets 6A, B and C **Digital Classroom:** grammar presentation – Reported speech; activity – Personal qualities – opposites
4 Let's get a job!	1.5–2.0	Write a job advertisement.	6Ro.01 6Wor.03 6Wca.04 6Ug.05	Learner's Book Lesson 6.4 Workbook Lesson 6.4 ⬇ Unit 6 sample answer ⬇ Photocopiable 18 **Digital Classroom:** activity – Present continuous fun!
5 *You can be anything*	1.5–2.0	Read and enjoy a poem about jobs and work.	6Rd.01 6Rm.02 6Rm.01 6Ro.01	Learner's Book Lesson 6.5 Workbook Lesson 6.5 **Digital Classroom:** activity – Suffixes; activity – Rhyming words
6 Project challenge	1.0–1.5	Project A: A quiz about different jobs. Project B: A presentation about an inspiring job.	6Wca.02 6Wca.03 6Wca.04 6Sc.06 6Sc.02	Learner's Book Lesson 6.6 Workbook Lesson 6.6 ⬇ Unit 6 project checklists

(continued)

Cross-unit resources
- ⬇ Unit 6 Audioscripts
- ⬇ End of Unit 6 test
- ⬇ Unit 6 Progress report
- ⬇ Unit 6 Wordlist

BACKGROUND KNOWLEDGE

In Unit 6, learners explore jobs and work: how people choose the work they do, the skills and qualities needed to do certain jobs, and positive attitudes to work.

In Lesson 6.3, the interview with the astronaut 'Karina' is based on a real interview with Christina Koch, a US astronaut and NASA engineer. In 2019, Christina and her colleague, Jessica Meir, became the first women to participate in an all-female spacewalk. Koch has also broken the record for longest continuous time spent in space by a woman.

In Lesson 6.5, learners read a poem entitled 'You can be anything' by Teri Hopkins. Teri Hopkins is a British writer who is also known as Gaia Rose. The poem describes what a number of jobs involve. One of these jobs is a *blacksmith*. A blacksmith makes shoes for horses.

TEACHING SKILLS FOCUS

Skills for life

The *Cambridge Framework for Life Competencies* helps equip learners with the required competencies to meet the fast-changing demands of the 21st-century. Key areas of competency for this course are:

- Creative thinking
- Critical thinking
- Learning to learn
- Communication
- Collaboration
- Social responsibilities
- Emotional development.

Can do statements have been devised for each age and competency. They help you to assess your learner's grasp of each of the competencies. More information and a list of the *Can do* statements for each level are in the Cambridge Competency Booklets, which can be downloaded on the Cambridge University Press Language and Pedagogy Research for ELT website.

In each unit of the Learner's Book, opportunities to practise and develop these skills are highlighted. In Unit 6, five competencies are highlighted:

- 6.1 Critical thinking: Evaluate qualities and skills needed to do a range of different jobs.
- 6.3 Communication: Interview someone about their job and then describe the information learned to others.
- 6.4 Creative thinking: Imagine own professional future and explain reasons for choice.
- 6.5 Emotional development: Examine ideas around being ambitious, aiming high and setting goals.
- 6.6 Collaboration: Take responsibility for own contributions in a group task.

Your challenge

Tick off the *Can do* statements that apply to your learners at the end of each unit.

Look through Unit 6 and find opportunities to develop one of the *Learning to learn* and one of the *Social responsibilities* skills (or choose two other skills that you would like to practise).

6.1 Think about it: How do you get a job?

LEARNING PLAN

Learning objectives	Learning intentions	Success criteria
6Ld.04	• **Listening:** Understand, with support, most specific information and detail of short and extended talk.	• Learners can understand information and details in short explanations about how people have got the jobs they do.
6Uv.07, 6Uv.01	• **Use of English:** Use a limited range of abstract nouns and compound nouns. Use common dependent prepositions following adjectives.	
	• **Vocabulary:** *marine biologist, vet, science teacher, physiotherapist, computer programmer, engineer, computer software, marine, wildlife, TV documentary, conservation group, sports injury, work experience, voluntary work, a university degree*	• Learners can use compound nouns and adjectives followed by dependent prepositions (+ noun) to describe different details about specific jobs.

21st-century skills

Critical thinking: Evaluate qualities and skills needed to do a range of different jobs.

Materials: Learner's Book pages 93–95; Workbook pages 68–69; **Photocopiable 16**

LANGUAGE BACKGROUND

Common dependent prepositions following adjectives

A *dependent preposition* is a preposition that usually follows the same expression; for example, *pay* **for** to indicate the action of buying something and *pay* **at** to indicate where we can pay.

In some phrases, there are dependent prepositions after popular adjectives:

• good + at: *I was* **good at** *English and history.*
• keen + on: *I was always really* **keen on** *football.*
• happy + about: *I'm* **happy about** *your news.*
• important + to: *She is* **important to** *me.*
• angry + with: *I was so* **angry with** *her.*
• sorry + about: *I'm really* **sorry about** *this.*
• interested + in: *All the classmates were (very)* **interested in** *China.*

Common misconceptions

Misconception	How to identify	How to overcome
Learners forget that some adjectives can be used with more than one preposition and that this usually affects the meaning, or the agreement. For example: It is **important (to)/for** me to learn English. She is **important for to** me. I feel sorry **for** her. I'm sorry **about** this.	Write typical mistakes on the board and elicit why they are wrong. In cases where the choice of preposition affects meaning, write possible combinations on the board and elicit the implied difference in meaning. For example: I feel sorry **for** her / how she feels. I'm sorry **about** this / about something.	Learners practise writing sentences with common dependent prepositions following adjectives, and swap them with a partner to peer assess. Learners can use **Photocopiable 16** as a platform to practice these expressions.

Starter idea

Jobs (5–10 minutes)

- Start by telling learners that this unit is going to be about jobs and work – they will look at different qualities and skills needed for a particular job, and at what different jobs involve.

- Identify and build up a list of different jobs on the board.

- In pairs, learners practise using the question *Would you like to be …?*, to ask about jobs they would and wouldn't like to do.

Main teaching ideas

Getting started (10 minutes)

- Learners look at the pictures and say what the children are doing. Elicit words for the activities and objects in the pictures and, as a class, discuss which talents and skills are needed for the activities (see answers for some ideas).

- Discuss what kind of jobs these children might have when they are older. On the board, write down *electrician, electrical engineer, scientist, art and design, carpenter, joiner*, etc.

Answers

a   Main image: a girl is fixing something electrical. Other images: a boy is studying something through a microscope (could be a science task); a boy is drawing; a girl is making something out of wood.

b   Learner's own answers. Suggested answers:
- Fixing something electrical: basic knowledge of the way electricity operates; design technology; ability to focus and concentrate.
- Studying with a microscope: science, analytical skills, critical thinking (evaluating, categorising information/results).
- Drawing: art and design, creative thinking.
- Making something out of wood: woodwork, carpentry, mathematics (measurements); design technology.

c   Learner's own answers. Suggested answers:
- Fixing something electrical: electrician, electrical engineer, mechanical engineer.
- Studying with a microscope: scientist, lab technician.
- Drawing: art- and design-related careers.
- Making something out of wood: carpenter, joiner, furniture designer.

> **Digital Classroom:** Use the video 'Different jobs' to introduce the subject of jobs and work. The i button will explain how to use the video.

1   What kind of jobs do people in your family have? (10 minutes)

- Circulate and offer support while learners ask and answer the questions.

- Share feedback as a class. Pick up especially on any ideas that are similar to those in the listening text. Also discuss how it can be difficult to decide what job you want to do when you are young, unless there is something you are very good at or feel passionate about.

> **Critical thinking opportunity:** Learners express opinions about jobs that are familiar to them through the experience of family members.

Answers
Learner's own answers.

2 **Match the photos to the words in the box. Do you know anybody who has these jobs? (5–10 minutes)**

- Focus on the first photo and elicit what the worker is doing. Elicit useful words like *screen* and match the photo to the name of the job.

- Circulate and offer support while learners match the words in the box to the photos.

- When learners have finished matching, do some pronunciation work on difficult sounds, word stress and connected speech to prepare learners for the listening task.

- Give class feedback on the answers. Then do a quick class survey to see if learners know anyone who has these jobs.

Answers
a   computer programmer
b   marine biologist
c   physiotherapist
d   engineer
e   science teacher
f   vet
Learner's own answers.

3 **Listen to these people describing how they got their jobs. Which jobs are they talking about? (15 minutes)**

- Tell the class that they are going to listen to four people describing how they got their jobs.

- Before listening, make predictions about how people get jobs: for example, working hard at school/university; knowing someone with the same job; being keen on/getting interested in an activity; having an experience when they were young.

- Ask learners to listen and write down each job. Pause the audio after each speaker, to allow learners sufficient time to write the word. Then ask them to check their answers with a partner, before going through the answers as a class.

Audioscript: Track 41

See Learner's Book page 94

Narrator: 1

Female: I've been crazy about animals ever since I was a little girl. When I was about 12, I met a friend of my parents, who worked with animals. She said it wasn't enough just to love animals; I had to work really hard at maths and science at school, then go to university and study for a long time. So that's what I did! It helped that I was good at maths and science anyway. And I also did work experience at an animal hospital during my holidays. So, it's no surprise to anyone that I'm a vet!

Narrator: 2

Male: I've always loved computers and technology. I was really into gaming and Minecraft when I was younger. Then, as I got older, I became more interested in coding, which is when you write instructions that a computer can understand. The instructions tell the computer what you want it to do. Coding is used to create computer software, apps and websites. Now I'm a computer programmer and I use code to create computer software for companies all over the world.

Narrator: 3

Female: How did I get to do my job? Well, I was always really keen on sport at school but then I broke my leg when I was 13, playing football. In the hospital, the doctor gave me exercises to make my leg strong again. I was scared that I wouldn't be able to play again, so I worked hard and did all the exercises. And I became interested in how the exercises helped my muscles and bones to recover. Now I use this experience in my work as a sports physiotherapist. I help athletes with sports injuries to use exercises to make their bodies strong again.

Narrator: 4

Male: I was always fascinated by the ocean because my family lived by the sea. Then something happened when I was about 14, which kind of changed my life. We watched a TV documentary at school about how bad the pollution in the sea was, and it got me thinking … what can I do to help? So when I was 16, I started doing voluntary work for a conservation group with one of my friends. Then later, I did a university degree in marine biology – studying wildlife and plants that live in the ocean. Now I work for an organisation that finds out how our oceans are changing and what we can do to protect marine wildlife.

Answers
Speaker 1 – vet; Speaker 2 – computer programmer; Speaker 3 – physiotherapist; Speaker 4 – marine biologist

4 Which job do you think sounds the most interesting? (5–10 minutes)

- Check learners know what *skills* are. Gain interest by eliciting what learners find interesting and what they are *good at*.
- Circulate and offer support while learners answer the questions in pairs.
- Ask learners to share their thoughts with the whole class and vote for the *most interesting* job.

Answers
Learner's own answers.

Language focus – Compound nouns, and 5 Can you find five compound nouns in the word puzzle? (10 minutes)

- Read the Language focus. Explain that the first word of a compound noun is usually a noun or adjective. It describes the second word, which is a noun. As the examples show, the words can be joined together or separate. Build up other examples of compound nouns on the board, for example *bus stop*, *football*, *sunrise*.

- Look at the word puzzle together. Check learners know the meaning of words such as *conservation*.
- Demonstrate the activity by finding one of the compound nouns in the puzzle, for example *conservation group*.
- Offer support while learners look for the other four compound nouns.
- Give feedback on the answers. Check learners know the meaning of each compound noun.

Answers
computer software, marine wildlife, conservation group, TV documentary, sports injury

6 Can you complete the definition of a compound noun? (5 minutes)

- Give learners time to work with a partner to fill in the gaps.
- Then go through the answers as a class.

Answers
1 adjective (for example, 'marine' in Activity 5)
2 website (or any other one-word compound noun)
3 science teacher (or any other two-word compound noun)

7 Find out the meaning of these compound nouns. How do you think these things can help you get a job? (5–10 minutes)

- Focus learners on the compound nouns and read out the words. Ask the class if anyone knows what they mean. If not, explain the meanings, drawing on real-life examples and the examples in the audio extract (Speakers 1 and 4 for university degree and voluntary work respectively).

> **Critical thinking opportunity:** Ask learners to discuss in pairs how these things might help someone get a job. Then invite learners to share their thoughts as a class. Support their understanding by giving examples from your own experiences.

Answers

Learner's own answers.

Suggested answers:

Work experience – when you work for a company or organisation for a short time while you are still at school or university. This can give you useful experience in a job, before you do it for real. You can get an idea of what to expect and this can make you better prepared and trained for the future. People usually do work experience without being paid.

Voluntary work – when you work free of charge (or for a very small payment) for a charity or organisation that supports a good cause/does good work. Doing this can give you valuable work experience and knowledge of the type of work. It also shows that you are interested and enthusiastic because you are prepared to work free of charge.

A university degree – a qualification that you get after several years of study at a university. A degree gives a lot of knowledge of a subject that is important for many types of job. Sometimes university degrees give students opportunities for work experience too.

> **Digital Classroom:** Use the activity 'Compound nouns' to revise compound nouns. The i button will explain how to use the activity.

Use of English box – Adjectives + prepositions + nouns (10 minutes)

• Read the Use of English box together. Make sure learners understand what an adjective, preposition and noun are. Check they understand that a pronoun can replace a noun and elicit examples of words that can be used as pronouns, for example *her, me* and *this*. Identify and write on the board other examples of adjectives + prepositions + nouns (see Language background).

Workbook

Learners do Activities 1–4 on pages 70–71.

> **Digital Classroom:** Use the activity 'Adjectives + prepositions' to practise common dependent prepositions. The i button will explain how to use the activity.

8 **Look at the comments about interests and abilities. Can you match with a job from Activity 3? (10 minutes)**

• Before listening to the audio again, ask learners what they can remember, asking in particular about what interests and skills the speakers had that led to their choices of job.

• Focus learners on the comments. Ask learners to match each one with a job from Activity 3. If they can't remember, write the four jobs on the board and then ask learners to do the matching activity.

• Next, tell learners you are going to play the extract again and stop after each comment, so that they can complete the gaps.

• Challenge learners by asking them to shout *Stop!* after they hear each target sentence.

• Give class feedback on the correct answers. Focus learners on the structure of the target phrases. Ask them to identify the adjectives (for example, crazy) and then tell you what kind of words follow (prepositions and nouns).

Answers

1 crazy (vet)
2 at (vet)
3 in (computer programmer)
4 keen (physiotherapist)
5 by (marine biologist)

---

9 **What kind of job would you like to do? What interests and talents do you have now that might lead to a job in the future? (10 minutes)**

• Brainstorm ideas about interests and talents that learners could talk about using *adjective + preposition* structures, for example *I'm (really) good at …; Doing/Being/Having the chance to … is important to me; I'm interested in …* .

• Demonstrate the task by asking a confident speaker to tell you about a job that he or she is interested in and why. Either write the learner's response on the board as an example or elicit a sentence such as: *I'd like to be an astronaut because I'm interested in space. I'm also good at science and I know a lot about …*

- Offer support while learners ask and answer the questions with their partners, making sure they use the phrases in Activity 8.

⟩ **Critical thinking opportunity:** Learners evaluate the qualities and skills needed to do a range of different jobs and relate this to themselves.

Answers
Learner's own answers.

Plenary ideas

Consolidation (5–10 minutes)

Invite learners to tell the class about jobs that they had in common with their partner and ones that were very different.

Homework ideas

- Learners write a paragraph (up to 100 words) about a job they would like to do.

⟩ **Assessment ideas:** Write a short checklist as a class so that learners can self-assess their work before handing it in. For example: *Have I used the new vocabulary from the lesson? Have I included any compound nouns or dependent prepositions? Have I checked my grammar and punctuation?*

Workbook

Learners do Activities 1–7 on pages 68–69.

6.2 Art and design: Designs that work!

LEARNING PLAN

Learning objectives	Learning intentions	Success criteria
6Rd.01	• **Reading:** Understand, with support, most specific information and detail in short and extended texts. • **Vocabulary:** *a firefighter, a police officer, a nurse, a chef, a postman or woman, light, stripe, logo, zip, sleeve, zipped pocket, waterproof material, trainers, alarm, inside pocket*	• Learners can understand, with support, specific details in a text describing a design for a work uniform.

21st-century skills

Cross-curricular link: Art and design: Learners design and draw a new school uniform.

Materials: Learner's Book pages 96–97; Workbook pages 70–71; if learners don't wear a school uniform, pictures of learners in school uniforms; pictures of firefighters, police officers, nurses, chefs and postmen/women from your country (for Activity 1)

Starter idea

School uniforms (5–10 minutes)

- If your learners wear a school uniform, have a class discussion about it. What features does it have and why? Is there a different uniform for different seasons of the year?

- If learners don't wear a school uniform, show pictures of other learners in uniforms and discuss these.

Main teaching ideas

1 What do people wear for these jobs in your country? (5–10 minutes)

- Focus on the jobs in the word box. Read the job titles together and check learners know how to pronounce them.

- Show pictures of the people who do these jobs in their uniforms. Elicit descriptions of what they are wearing and the reasons why.

- Brainstorm a list of other jobs where people wear a uniform.

Answers

Learner's own answers.

> **Digital Classroom:** Use the slideshow 'Uniforms for jobs' to introduce the topic of uniforms. The i button will explain how to use the slideshow.

2 What things do designers think about when they design a uniform? (5–10 minutes)

- Focus on the example together and have a class discussion about other things designers think about.

> **Critical thinking opportunity:** Stimulate learner's thought processes by giving prompts to answer this question. For example: *Would a firefighter wear a t-shirt?* (No – he or she has to protect his arms.) *Would a postwoman's uniform include shoes with a heel?* (No – she has to walk a lot.)

- Build up a list of suggestions on the board (see Answers for ideas). Try to include words that learners will come across in the listening activity (for example, *tracksuit, reflective stripe, pockets, logo, waterproof material, comfortable trainers, a light, belt with pockets, an alarm*) and reasons for having these.

Answers

Learner's own answers. Suggested design considerations:
- The climate and weather in the country where they work.
- What a person has to do in their job, for example do they have to do a lot of physical activity such as walking, running, climbing, carrying, lifting, cleaning?
- Are there safety or security issues in the job?
- People's different shapes, sizes and ages.
- Whether men or women, or both, will wear the uniform.

- If the uniform needs to have distinctive colours or logos so it will be easily recognised by people in shops, in the street, from a distance, at night time, etc.
- The times when the person will be working, for example when it is dark.
- The cost of the uniform.

3 Read and listen to Seb's description of his design for a work uniform. (10 minutes)

- Tell learners that they are now going to read and listen to Seb presenting his idea for a work uniform. Make sure learners know that at this stage they should just focus on which job in Activity 1 the uniform is for and which of their ideas from Activity 2 are mentioned. They will have a chance to look at the description in more detail later in the lesson.

- Learners discuss their ideas in pairs. After a few minutes, give class feedback on the answers.

> **Differentiation ideas:** If learners need support with this task, ask them to focus on identifying which job the uniform is for.

Audioscript: Track 42

See Learner's Book page 96

Answers

Seb is presenting an idea for a postman/woman's uniform.
Possible ideas from Activity 2:
- Climate and weather.
- What a person has to do in their job; in this case, a lot of walking, carrying things.
- Working hours, especially when there is little or no natural daylight.
- People of all shapes and sizes will wear the uniform.
- Safety and security issues (for example, the need for an alarm or headlight).

4 Match the words in blue in the description with the letters, a–k, on the picture. (10 minutes)

- Demonstrate the activity. Look at the example and reread the first sentences of the text. Elicit what a *stripe* is.

- If necessary, do more examples together.

- Offer support while learners match the other blue words to the picture in pairs.

- Give class feedback on the correct answers.

Answers
a light, **b** stripe (Example), **c** logo, **d** sleeve, **e** zip, **f** zipped pocket, **g** inside pocket, **h** belt with pockets, **i** alarm, **j** waterproof material, **k** trainers

---

> **Digital Classroom:** Use the activity 'Uniforms' to revise uniform vocabulary. The i button will explain how to use the activity.

Key words: design, and 5 Read the description again. (10 minutes)

- Read the Key words box and the instructions for the task together and check learners understand what to do.

- Look at the issue *Climate and weather* together. Scan the text and elicit which part focuses on this and the features in Seb's design that help with this.

- Circulate and offer support while learners complete the activity in pairs.

- Give class feedback on the correct answers.

Answers
- *Climate and weather*: waterproof materials on the trousers; the jacket can be removed in warmer weather.
- *Safety*: the reflective stripe shows up in the dark; the light on the hat helps the person see clearly when natural light is low; the belt carries an alarm to sound if help is needed or there is any danger; zipped pockets help the person carry small things securely.
- *Carrying personal things*: the jacket and trousers have zipped pockets for carrying small personal possessions; the belt has pockets too.
- *Comfort*: the zipped pockets and belt with pockets leave the person's hands free to do the job; the tracksuit is loose-fitting and made of

stretchy material to fit all shapes and sizes; trainers are comfortable to wear when there is a lot of walking to do; zips make the jacket quick and easy to put on and take off; the waterproof material on the trousers keeps the person's legs and feet dry in wet weather.

---

6 What do you think of Seb's design? (10 minutes)

- Ask learners to discuss the questions in pairs.

> **Differentiation ideas:** If learners don't feel confident about this task, provide a worksheet with prompts or write them on a mini-whiteboard. For example: *In Seb's design … but in my country postmen/women (don't) wear/ have … .*

- Make time for class feedback to share ideas, as this will help stimulate ideas for learner's own presentations in the next activity.

Answers
Learner's own answers.

CROSS-CURRICULAR LINK

Art and design: Learners collaborate to draw, describe and explain their own new uniform.

---

7 Present it! In groups, think about a uniform in your country that you would like to change. (15–20 minutes + 5 minutes for each group presentation)

- Tell learners that they are going to prepare a presentation about their own idea for a uniform. Give the groups a few minutes to choose a uniform.

- Learners work together in their groups to draw a picture of their idea and label the features. Circulate and check learners are considering the issues from Activity 5 in their designs.

- Learners work together on their descriptions to present to the class. Remind learners to look back at Seb's description to help them.

- Before learners present their ideas to the class, ask them to reread their work and self-assess if they have completed all of the instructions.

- Learners present their idea to the class. Give them plenty of positive feedback on their presentations – focus on what they did well.

> **Assessment ideas:** As learners are delivering their presentations, note down the main errors. Write the errors on the board, without saying who made them. Encourage the class to correct the errors together.

___

Answers
Learner's own answers.

___

Homework ideas

Learners write a description of one of the uniforms designed by another group.

> **Workbook**
>
> Learners do Activities 1–4 on pages 70–71.

Plenary ideas

Class vote (10 minutes)

Have a class vote on the most interesting and practical design idea. If you have time, you could have several categories, for example most realistic idea, best artwork, etc.

6.3 Talk about it: Working in space

LEARNING PLAN

Learning objectives	Learning intentions	Success criteria
6Ld.02	• **Listening:** Understand a range of questions that ask for detailed information.	• Learners can understand a range of questions asking for information in an interview with an astronaut.
6Sor.02, 6Sc.07	• **Speaking:** Briefly summarise what others say, with support, in a range of exchanges in order to achieve a shared outcome	• Learners can use reported speech to summarise points from an interview about what a person does in their job.
6Ug.11, 6Us.06	• **Use of English:** Use subordinate clauses following *say* and *tell*. Begin to use simple forms of reported speech to report statements and commands.	• Learners can use subordinate clauses following *say* and *tell*.
	• **Vocabulary:** *a spacewalk, experiment, gravity, exploration, risky, confident, exciting, fit, enthusiastic, adventurous, hardworking, boring, unfit, unadventurous, lazy, shy, unenthusiastic*	

21st-century skills

Communication: Interview someone about their job and then describe the information learned to others.

Materials: Learner's Book pages 98–99; Workbook pages 72–73; **Photocopiable 17; Differentiated worksheets 6A, B and C**

LANGUAGE BACKGROUND

Reported speech and subordinate clauses with *say* and *tell*

Reported speech is when you tell someone what another person said:

Direct speech	Reported speech
*'I went **to** the supermarket yesterday,' said Jessica.*	*Jessica said she **had been** to the supermarket yesterday.*
*'I**'ll go to** the supermarket tomorrow,' said James.*	*James said he **would go** to the supermarket tomorrow.*

In reported speech, the tense is often 'further back' in the past than the tense originally used (in the example, *went* becomes *had been* and *'ll* becomes *would*). This is called backshift. You sometimes have to change other words, such as pronouns. *He/she* is often used in reported speech instead of *I*.

The verb can stay in the same tense if you refer to something that is still true. For example:

Direct speech	Reported speech
*'I **work** in Karachi,' Mo said.*	*Mo said he **works** in Karachi. (He still works there.)*

Two common reporting verbs for direct and reported speech are *say* and *tell*. In this lesson, learners start to use subordinate clauses after *say* and *tell*. A subordinate clause is a group of words with a subject and verb that cannot stand alone. For instance, in the reported speech example above, he **would go** to the supermarket tomorrow is a subordinate clause (the meaning isn't clear without the preceding clause, *James said*).

Common misconceptions

Misconception	How to identify	How to overcome
Learners use an incorrect reporting verb or omit the object after *tell*. For example: *We ~~talked~~ **told** a lot of stories about learning English.* *I told (**him**) my name and he told (**me**) his too.*	Identify common reporting verbs and give examples of when it's best to use them. Using a simple example, explain that *say* does not require an object, but *told* does: *She **told me** her name was Kay.* *She **said** her name was Kay.*	Practise using: • Activities 1–3 on pages 72–73 of the Workbook • **Differentiated worksheets 6A, B and C.**

Starter ideas

Would you like to go into space? (5 minutes)

• Write the question on the board. Ask learners if they would like to go into space. Why or why not?

• Offer support as learners share ideas by suggesting and writing words and expressions on the board.

Answers
Learner's own answers.

Main teaching ideas

1 Look at the photo of an astronaut doing a spacewalk. (10 minutes)

• Look at the photo and make sure learners understand what *spacewalk* means.

• Have a class discussion about what is happening in the photo. Make it clear to learners that, at this stage, they don't need to know the specific answers to the second question. However, encourage them to imagine what the challenges could be (see suggested answers). They will check their ideas when they listen to the interview in Activity 3.

- As well as words and expressions from the answers, try to elicit/pre-teach words that learners will come across in Activity 3, for example *floats, outer space, risky, space suit, protection, carry an oxygen backpack, there is no gravity,* etc.

Answers

Learner's own answers.

Suggested answers: The astronaut is outside the spacecraft. She is doing a *spacewalk* – this means that she goes out of the spacecraft while it is in space (but she is still attached to the spacecraft). Challenges – very risky: if the astronaut's space suit gets damaged during the spacewalk, then their life is at risk (for example, this can cause breathing difficulties, problems seeing). They also need to be physically strong to do the spacewalk.

2 What do these words mean? How do you think the words are connected with astronauts and their work? (10–15 minutes)

- As a class, look at the words and work out what they mean. Write the definitions on the board.

- In pairs, learners discuss how they think the words are connected with astronauts and their work. Ask them to think of a sentence for each word. Demonstrate the activity by referring to the example. Tell learners that they are not expected to know exact answers and encourage them to reason critically. The aim of this activity is to come up with some general ideas that they can check against when they listen to the interview in Activity 3.

- Circulate and offer support before giving class feedback at the end of the activity.

> **Differentiation ideas:** If pairs of learners feel confident about this task, they could write two or three example sentences for each word.

Answers

Suggested answers:

Spacewalk – when astronauts go out of the spacecraft while it is in space (but are still attached to the spacecraft).

Experiments – when tests are done to discover something new. Astronauts carry out scientific experiments in space (to discover new things about healthcare, medicine, climate change, the sun's energy, communications technology)

Gravity – the force or power that makes things fall to the ground. There is no gravity in space, so astronauts have to 'float' in their spacecrafts.

Exploration – to search and find out about something. Astronauts take journeys into space to explore and find out important new things.

Risky – if something is risky, then there is the possibility of something bad happening. Space travel is risky for astronauts because the conditions in space are very difficult to work with.

3 Listen to the interview with Karina, an American astronaut. (15 minutes)

- Explain to learners that they are going to listen to an interview with an American astronaut and check their ideas from Activities 1 and 2.

- Tell learners that rather than trying to understand every word, they should focus on how Karina describes the *spacewalk* and her reasons for doing it, and what she says about the other words from the word box, i.e. *experiments, gravity, exploration* and *risky.*

- After listening, learners make notes with a partner.

- Circulate and offer support, before sharing ideas as a class. What new information have learners discovered? Write the main points on the board.

Audioscript: Track 43

See Learner's Book page 98

Interviewer: Karina, going into space is a dream for a lot of people. Tell us … when did you know you wanted to be an astronaut?

Karina: I'm not sure because I don't remember a time when I didn't want to be an astronaut! When I was 11 or 12, I had posters of space on my bedroom wall, alongside my favourite boy bands. I've always been really interested in space exploration and science.

Interviewer: And what do you do in your job?

Karina:	One of the most important things astronauts do is research and also science experiments in space. We do experiments using the weightless atmosphere – in space there is no gravity and everything floats! These experiments give us important information about how the human body adapts to different situations. It helps us produce better medicines and healthcare. And there are also experiments to find out more about the sun's energy and climate change … And of course, we find out information about space travel that will help astronauts in the future go further and further into space.
Interviewer:	What is your favourite part of the space journey?
Karina:	The spacewalk! This is where you go out of the space station and you are outside in outer space! I have done three spacewalks in my career so far and it is the most amazing experience you can imagine. The views of planet Earth are incredible. It is also very risky: we have to wear a space suit for protection and carry an oxygen backpack. If the space suit or equipment gets damaged, then your life is at risk. Astronauts do spacewalks to do repairs and experiments on the outside of the space station, if it can't be done by a robot!
Interviewer:	What's the strangest thing you've learned about your job?
Karina:	While you're in space, you get taller! Your backbone stretches because there is no gravity. So when you land again on Earth, you are taller than before. But it doesn't last; soon your body goes back to the same height as you were before!

Answers

Spacewalk: Karina describes a spacewalk: 'This is where you go out of the space station and you are outside in outer space! I have done three spacewalks in

my career so far and it is the most amazing experience you can imagine.' She describes the reasons for doing a spacewalk: 'Astronauts do spacewalks to do repairs and experiments on the outside of the space station, if it can't be done by a robot!'

Experiments: 'One of the most important things astronauts do is research and also science experiments in space. We do experiments using the weightless atmosphere – in space there is no gravity and everything floats! These experiments give us important information about how the human body adapts to different situations. It helps us produce better medicines and healthcare. And there are also experiments to find out more about the sun's energy and climate change … And of course, we find out information about space travel that will help astronauts in the future go further and further into space'.

Gravity: 'We do experiments using the weightless atmosphere – in space there is no gravity and everything floats!'

Exploration: Karina mentions that she has always been interested in space exploration and goes on to describe the kind of information that astronauts search for and find out in space (see 'experiments' above).

Risky: Karina describes the risks of doing a spacewalk – 'It is also very risky: we have to wear a space suit for protection and carry an oxygen backpack. If the space suit or equipment get damaged, then your life is at risk.'

---

4   Listen again. Are the statements about Karina's interview true or false? (10 minutes)

- Read the statements together. Encourage initial predictions about whether they are true or false.

- Replay the interview for learners to check their ideas/work out whether the statements are true or false.

- Give class feedback on the answers. Ask learners to say and note down how they worked out whether each statement was true or false. For example, for statement 5, part of the statement is correct (astronauts do get taller in space) but the reason is wrong (their backbone stretches rather than their legs getting longer). Explain they will need this information for the next activity.

Answers

a	True	d	False
b	False	e	False
c	True		

Use of English – Reported speech
(5 minutes)

- Read the Use of English box about the difference between direct and reported speech. Explain that two common reporting verbs are *say* and *tell* and explain backshift (see Language background).

> **Workbook**
>
> Learners do Activities 1–3 on pages 72–73.

> **Digital Classroom:** Use the grammar presentation 'Reported speech' to revise reported speech. The i button will explain how to use the grammar presentation.

5 Check your answers to Activity 4. Correct the false sentences using reported speech. (10 minutes)

- Demonstrate the activity using the first false statement from Activity 4 and the prompts in the example (see answer for statement 2).

- Circulate and offer support while learners correct the other false sentences (statements 4 and 5) in pairs using reported speech.

Answers

Suggested answers:

b Karina didn't say that. She said that astronauts do experiments in space (using the weightless atmosphere).

d Karina didn't say that. She said that she loves doing spacewalks outside the space station.

e Karina didn't say that. She said that astronauts get taller in space because their backbones stretch/ get longer.

6 Personal qualities. Listen to the next part of the interview. Put the adjectives in the order that you hear. (5–10 minutes)

- First, look together at the adjectives. Check learners know the meaning and the correct pronunciation of each adjective, using a dictionary if necessary.

- To consolidate understanding, ask learners to tick three adjectives from the list that they feel describe their character.

- Before listening to the next part of the interview, tell learners to focus on putting the adjectives in order and not to worry about understanding every word.

- If helpful, replay the recording, pausing after each adjective.

> **Audioscript:** Track 44
>
> See Learner's Book page 99
>
> Interviewer: So what qualities and skills do you need to become an astronaut?
>
> Karina: You need to study hard at science and maths – but there are different types of science and maths, so find out what you find most exciting and focus on that. You need to be adventurous and enthusiastic about exploring and discovering new things. You need to be hardworking and work well in a team; it's very important that everyone works together to get the job done. Oh, and confident … there are risks in the job and you have to believe that you can do it. Oh yes, and you have to be very physically fit – the conditions in space are very hard on the body, especially when you come back down to Earth!

Answers

1 exciting, 2 adventurous, 3 enthusiastic, 4 hardworking, 5 confident, 6 fit

7 Match the adjectives in Activity 6 with their opposites. (5 minutes)

- Read through the adjectives together and practise their pronunciation.

- Allow learners time to do the activity in pairs, before giving class feedback on the answers.

Answers

a	boring – exciting
b	unfit – fit
c	unadventurous – adventurous
d	lazy – hardworking
e	shy – confident
f	unenthusiastic – enthusiastic

> **Digital Classroom:** Use the activity 'Personal qualities – opposites' to revise personal qualities vocabulary. The i button will explain how to use the activity.

8 How many of the opposite adjectives are made with a prefix? Play a game! (5–10 minutes)

- Check that learners understand what a *prefix* is (a group of letters added to the start of a word to make a new word). Identify which of the opposite adjectives are made with a prefix (see answers – *unfit, unadventurous, unenthusiastic*).

- Learners can play the game in teams or pairs. First, remind learners of other prefixes, e.g. *pro, pre, dis, im, ir*. Then give them one minute (or increase the time if appropriate) to write down as many adjectives as they can that are made with a prefix.

- Share answers as a class and congratulate the winning pair/team!

Answers
Opposite adjectives made with a prefix:
*un*adventurous, *un*enthusiastic, *un*fit.
Learner's own answers

9 What have you learned from the interview with Karina? (5 minutes)

- Circulate and offer support while learners tell their partner something they have learned from the interview.

- Have a quick class survey to share ideas.

Answers
Learner's own answers.

10 Write other questions you would like to ask an astronaut about their work. (15 minutes)

- First, brainstorm ideas for questions, for example the food astronauts eat, the clothes they wear, practicalities, everyday life in space, education and training to become an astronaut, general risks, etc.

- Before learners start the activity, remind them about question words like *How long … ?, Where …?, When …?*, etc.

- Circulate and offer support while learners work in pairs to write three questions and imagine the astronauts' answers.

> **Differentiation ideas:** Extend the activity for more confident learners by challenging them to write five questions and answers.

- Learners share their questions and answers with the class.

Answers
Learner's own answers.

11 Interview someone you know about their job. (15 minutes + 30 minutes at home + time for learners to report back to class in the next lesson)

- **Communication:** This is a good opportunity for learners to find out more about the job of someone they know. They need to take notes in order to report their findings to the class in the next lesson.

- Demonstrate the activity by getting learners to ask you the questions.

- Invite learners to ask the questions to a family member or friend. Tell them to make a note of the answers.

> **Differentiation ideas:** Extend the activity by inviting more confident learners to ask three additional questions.

- In the next lesson, learners report back to their class.

- To provide learners with the opportunity of practising written answers to interview questions, please see **Photocopiable 17**.

Answers
Learner's own answers.

12 Tell your class about your interview using reported speech. (15–20 minutes, additional time for larger groups)

- Ask learners for examples of their interviewees' answers and write them on the board in direct speech. Elicit how to transform these sentences into reported speech. For example: She said that …

- Circulate and offer support while learners transform the answers to the questions they asked into reported speech.

- Starting with more confident speakers, allow each learner time to report back to the class on their interviews.

- Give class feedback on common errors.

Answers
Learner's own answers.

Plenary ideas

Consolidation (5 minutes)

- Learners discuss what they enjoyed about the lesson.

- You could also use this time to talk through anything learners feel unsure about, such as the pronunciation of space vocabulary, prefixes or reported speech.

Homework ideas

Learners interview someone they know about their job (see Activity 11).

> **Workbook**
>
> Learners do Activities 1–3 on pages 72–73.

6.4 Write about it: Let's get a job!

LEARNING PLAN		
Learning objectives	**Learning intentions**	**Success criteria**
6Ro.01	• **Reading:** Recognise, with support, the opinions of the writer(s) in short and extended texts.	• Learners can understand the main points in some simple job advertisements.
6Wor.03, 6Wca.04	• **Writing:** Use appropriate layout for a limited range of written genres. Use grammatical structures correctly, allowing for occasional mistakes.	• Learners can write a job advert using the present continuous (for actions happening now), in appropriate layout and style.
6Ug.05	• **Use of English:** Use an increasing range of present continuous forms with present and future meaning.	
	• **Vocabulary:** *a zookeeper, an acrobat, an inventor, a gardener*	
21st-century skills		
Creative thinking: Imagine own professional future and explain reasons for choice.		

Materials: Learner's Book pages 100–101; Workbook pages 74–75; **Photocopiable 18**; internet access or information about sports person in magazines; Unit 6 sample answer

Starter ideas

Job interview feedback (10–15 minutes)

- Learners share their responses from the interviews they did for homework in the last lesson.

- Encourage learners to talk in sentences and to use vocabulary and grammar points from the unit. Write any new vocabulary and expressions on the board.

Main teaching ideas

1 How do people find jobs? (5 minutes)

- Allow learners a minute, in pairs, to think of three different ways someone could find a job.
- Circulate and offer support with new vocabulary.
- As a class, share ideas. Write suggestions on the board.

Answers
Learner's own answers. Suggested answers:
- job advertisements – on websites, through social media, newspapers (not so common nowadays), noticeboards in public places (shops, libraries etc.)
- through a recruitment agency (people who are paid to find jobs for other people)
- through word-of-mouth (when someone tells you in person that a job is available).

2 Match the job titles in the box to the adverts (10 minutes)

- Read the job titles together and elicit what they mean.
- Tell learners that they are going to read an advert for each of the three jobs. Make sure they understand that 'advert' is a more commonly used abbreviation for 'advertisement'.
- Encourage learners to make predictions about what they will read – ask them what skills/qualities are needed for each job.
- Circulate and offer support while learners read the adverts and then do the matching activity.
- Give class feedback on the correct answers.

Answers
1 an acrobat, 2 an inventor, 3 a zookeeper

3 Read the adverts again. (10 minutes)

> **Critical thinking opportunity:** Read statements 1–4 together. Then ask learners to read the adverts again and decide which of the candidates are suitable for the jobs in Activity 2 and which one isn't suitable for any jobs. Check learners know the meaning of *candidate* (someone who applies for a job), *biology* (study of living things) and *natural science* (study of nature). Also check learners know the meaning of *keen on* by asking if they think Priya likes design and technology.

- Ask learners to do the activity individually then check answers with a partner.
- Give class feedback on correct answers.

Answers
1 Inventor, 2 Acrobat, 3 Zookeeper, 4 No suitable jobs

Use of English – Present continuous review (5 minutes)

- Read the Use of English box together. Elicit the uses of the present continuous, including that it can be used for something that is temporary.
- Build up examples of positive and negative statements, as well as questions. Elicit that we use the auxiliary *be* and the present participle.

> **Workbook**
> Learners do Activities 3 and 4 on page 75.

> **Digital Classroom:** Use the activity 'Present continuous fun!' to reinforce the use of the present continuous form. The i button will explain how to use the activity.

4 Read the Use of English box. How would the sentences change with the pronouns *I* and *he/she*? (5 minutes)

- Write the sentences from the Use of English box on the board. Together, talk through how the form of the verb *to be* changes according to the pronoun. Then invite learners to suggest how the sentences change with the pronouns *I* and *he/she*.

Answers
I am looking for a friendly zookeeper …; He / She is looking for a …
I am recruiting genius-level inventors …; He / She is recruiting …

Writing tip – Use shortened sentences in adverts (5 minutes)

- You might want to use this as extension material as this is beyond the requirements of the Cambridge Primary English as a Second Language curriculum framework.

- You might want to use this as extension material as this is beyond the requirements of the Cambridge Primary English as a Second Language Framework.

- First, write some full versions of sentences from the adverts on the board, for example *You must be able to do experiments; You must be brave and comfortable with …*

- Ask learners if these sentences are the same as the ones in the adverts from Activity 2. If they don't notice, ask them to find the sentences in the adverts and tell you how they are different.

- Ask learners why they think shortened sentences are used in adverts. Explain that adverts need to communicate a lot of information in as few words as possible. Sometimes advertisers have to pay for every word they use, which means they have to miss out some words.

- Together, look for more examples in the adverts.

5 Look at the advert. Find and correct the mistakes. (10 minutes)

- Look at the advert together. Check learners know the meaning of *spade, talented* and *crazy about*.

- Ask learners to find and correct the mistakes and, where possible, shorten the sentences. They should correct the text on their own and then check with a partner.

- Give class feedback before moving on to the writing activity.

Answers
Are you good with a spade? We **are** looking for a talented gardener.
- ~~You~~ **M**ust be crazy about flowers and plants.
- ~~You~~ **M**ust be calm and not afraid of bugs and insects.
- Experience is needed.
- We are interview**ing** now. Call us on 6976 5454.

6 Write a job advert (30–40 minutes)

- Tell learners they are going to write their own job advert. Support them while they follow the instructions in the Learner's Book.

- As a class, brainstorm unusual jobs and what skills are needed for them. Write notes on the board.

- Make sure learners have chosen a job; ask them to write similar notes to help them plan their advert.

> **Assessment ideas:** Before learners start Step 2, show them the Unit 6 sample answer without the mark scheme comments. As a class, evaluate the sample answer's strengths and weaknesses, and also look at the checklist on page 101 of the Learner's Book, so that learners know what they are aiming to achieve in their job advert.

- Offer support while learners write their adverts, using the prompts in the Learner's Book. Also encourage learners to look back at the adverts in Activity 2 to help them.

> **Assessment ideas:** Once learners have finished their first draft, ask them to work through the checklist on **Photocopiable 18** to self-assess their work. When they have made any updates, invite them to swap their draft with a partner, who will proofread it. Encourage learners to give feedback sensitively and to include at least one compliment.

> **Differentiation ideas:** If more confident learners finish the job advert quickly, extend the activity by asking them to do mock interviews based on their advert. In pairs, they should take it in turns to be the interviewer and interviewee.

- Display the adverts on the wall for learners to walk round and read.

Answers
Learner's own answer.

Plenary ideas

Reflection (10 minutes)

Creative thinking: Invite learners to look at the adverts and imagine their own professional future. Which job(s) would they like to do? Ask learners to share which job they would like to do and why.

Homework ideas

Learners write a paragraph explaining which job they would like to do and why.

> **Workbook**
> Learners do Activities 1–5 on page 74–75.

6.5 Read and respond: *You can be anything*

Learning objectives	Learning intentions	Success criteria
6Rd.01, 6Rm.02, 6Rm.01, 6Ro.01	• **Reading:** Understand, with support, most specific information and detail in short and extended texts/Read independently a range of short, simple fiction and non-fiction texts with confidence and enjoyment/Recognise, with support, the opinions of the writer(s) in short and extended texts. • **Vocabulary:** *builder, dentist, plasterer, firefighter, florist, architect, doctor, hairdresser, scientist, police officer, singer, actor*	• Learners can read and enjoy a poem mentioning a variety of jobs and understand the writer's message.

21st-century skills

Emotional development: Examine ideas around being ambitious, aiming high and setting goals.

Materials: Learner's Book pages 102–105; Workbook pages 76–77

Starter ideas

Jobs (10 minutes)

- Write the jobs from the vocabulary list poem on the board.

- Before the lesson, make cards for learners to match. One card should have the name of each job and the other card a definition of what the job is.

- In pairs, learners match the cards and the definitions. This should help them make predictions about what they will read in the poem.

> **Differentiation ideas:** Encourage more confident learners to make (simple) sentences about each job as they do the matching activity, for example *A builder builds homes.*

Main teaching ideas

1 When you are older, what kind of job would you like to have? (10 minutes)

- Write prompts on the board, for example *I would/wouldn't like to be … because I'm (not) keen on …*

- Circulate and offer support as learners discuss, in pairs, what kind of jobs they would/wouldn't

like to have when they are older. Check they understand the difference between *creative* and *practical* by eliciting examples of both kinds of job.

- Share ideas as a class and write the different jobs on the board.

Answers
Learner's own answers.

2 Read and listen to the poem. Does the poem mention jobs that you talked about in Activity 1? (10 minutes)

- Tell learners they are going to read and listen to a poem about different jobs. Look at the glossary and pictures together then read the question in Activity 2. Tell the class to listen for answers to the question and not to worry about other words they don't understand.

- After reading/listening, go through the answers with the class and ask them to match the jobs in the poem to the pictures.

Audioscript: Track 45

See Learner's Book pages 102–103

Answers
Learner's own answers. Jobs represented in page images:
a doctor, **b** builder, **c** dentist, **d** plasterer, **e** scientist

 3 Read and listen to the poem again. Discuss these questions in groups. (10 minutes)

*   Before learners read and listen to the poem again, read the discussion questions together and check learners understand what is being asked.
*   Once learners have read and listened to the poem, circulate and offer support while they discuss the questions in groups of 3–4.

> **Differentiation ideas:** You could divide the questions up, giving some groups questions 1 and 2 and the others 3 and 4. Questions 1 and 2 are more straightforward, so you could divide the questions up according to learner's abilities and levels of language.

*   At the end of the discussion, learners share their ideas with the class. Give class feedback on the correct answers.

Answers
a   The poem mentions ten jobs: doctor, builder, dentist, singer, actor, hairdresser, plasterer, firefighter, police officer, scientist. It also describes a blacksmith's job (line 5: *Or look after horses, mending sore hooves*), but doesn't state the title. Total: 11 jobs. Learner's own answers.
b   The writer infers that potentially there are many different jobs open to us all and that the possibilities are endless.
c   The writer advises that your job should make you feel happy and if you feel happy in your work, you will always be successful; that you should make an effort and have ambitious goals.
d   Learner's own answers.

4 Find ten words for jobs in the poem and look at the suffix (the ending). (10 minutes)

*   Circulate and offer support while learners highlight the ten jobs in the poem.

*   Focus on the first job, *doctor*, and elicit that the suffix (the ending) is *-or*. Tell learners to write it in the *-or* oval in the Learner's Book, or in their notebook.
*   Explain that *-er*, *-or* and *-ist* endings are common in words that describe the person doing a job.
*   Offer support while learners divide the other words into groups according to their suffixes and add five more jobs from other lessons.

Answers

-er	*-or*	*-ist*
builder singer hairdresser plasterer firefighter police officer	doctor actor	dentist scientist

Learner's own answers. Suggested answers: teach*er*, computer programm*er*, engine*er*, design*er*, zookeep*er*, garden*er*; invent*or*; marine biolog*ist*, physiotherap*ist*.

> **Digital Classroom:** Use the activity 'Suffixes' to revise suffixes. The i button will explain how to use the activity.

5 Listen to the second verse of the poem again. (10 minutes)

*   Before listening, ask learners if they can think of any words that rhyme in the poem.
*   Play the second verse of the poem again. What rhyming sounds can learners hear at the end of each line?
*   Ask learners to write down the rhyming words in their notebooks.

Audioscript: Track 45
See Learner's Book pages 102–103

Answers
1   try / sky
2   day / may
3   hair / dare
4   walls / halls

6 Say these words and match them to the sounds in Activity 5. (5–10 minutes)

- First, ask learners to repeat the rhyming words and sounds from Activity 5.
- Learners then work in pairs to match the words and sounds to the words in the word box.

Answers
way (day / may); my (try / sky); falls (walls / halls); share (hair / dare)

Audioscript: Track 47
See Learner's Book page 104

Narrator: way
Speaker: day, may

Narrator: my
Speaker: try, sky

Narrator: falls
Speaker: walls, halls

Narrator: share
Speaker: hair, dare

❭ **Digital Classroom:** Use the activity 'Rhyming words' to reinforce the concept of rhyming words, focusing on words in the poem. The i button will explain how to use the activity.

Language focus – *could (+ be)*, and 7 Choose the correct definition of *could*. (5 minutes)

- Read the two lines from the poem in the Language focus box. Ask learners to find other lines with *could* in the poem and identify five or six examples. This will stress how frequently the structure appears (emphasising the theme of possibility).
- Focus learners on the three definitions of *could* in Activity 7. Ask learners which they think is the correct one. If learners find this difficult, remind them of the main point from Activity 3, question 2,

i.e. that there are many types of jobs and therefore many possibilities.

Workbook

Learners do Activities 4–5 on page 77.

Answers
c It is *possible* that you will be a doctor or dentist.

---

8 Use the pictures to make two more sentences using the structure in the poem. Make the sentences rhyme! (10 minutes)

- Elicit the names of the jobs in the picture (florist and architect).
- First, brainstorm words to describe what each person does (e.g. *sells flowers*, *designs things*) and write them on the board. Offer support while pairs of learners use the pictures and words to make two more sentences using the structure in the poem. Encourage them to think of words that rhyme.
- Give class feedback on the sentences before brainstorming other jobs that learners could write sentences about.
- Support learners while they make two more sentences with their own ideas. Allow non-rhyming sentences if you think this would be more manageable for them.

❭ **Differentiation ideas:** If learners need support with this task, you could mix up rhyming sentences on a mini-whiteboard or worksheet and ask learners to match the rhyming pairs.

- During class feedback, ask learners to read out their sentences.

Answers
Sample answers:
You could be a <u>florist</u> who <u>sells beautiful flowers</u> and <u>plants</u>.
You could be an <u>architect</u> who <u>designs buildings</u> and <u>towers</u>.
You could be an artist who paints and draws.
You could be a footballer who kicks and scores goals.
Plus learner's own answers.

9 Working hard and setting goals. (20–30 minutes)

- **Emotional development**: This activity gives learners a wonderful opportunity to examine ideas around being ambitious, aiming high and setting goals.

- Read through the first question and topics together. If possible, give learners an example of something you have worked hard to achieve and how you felt afterwards. Then put learners into pairs to discuss the questions, drawing on their personal experiences.

- Conduct a short feedback – ask learners to volunteer answers.

- Next, focus learners on Amir's notes in question 2 and ask the class what they think Amir wants to achieve. If learners are slow to respond, check they remember what *strikers* mean and that they understand *United* is a sports club.

- Move on to question 3 and identify the actions that Amir is going to take to achieve his goal. If helpful, ask learners prompt questions, such as *How often is Amir going to practise? When are the trials for the new school team?*

- Now ask learners to write down two goals that they want to achieve. If they are stuck for ideas, focus them on the topic areas in question 1.

- Circulate and offer support while learners tell a partner about their goals and help each other to complete a list of actions to achieve them (using Amir's notes as a model).

Plenary ideas

Consolidation and reflection (5–10 minutes)

Ask learners to share their goals and how they would like to achieve them. Give lots of positive feedback and encouragement.

Homework ideas

Learners choose one of the jobs from the poem and write about the qualities needed to do this job.

> **Workbook**
>
> Learners do Activities 1–6 on pages 76–77.

6.6 Project challenge

LEARNING PLAN		
Learning objectives	**Learning intentions**	**Success criteria**
6Wca.02, 6Wca.03, 6Wca.04	• **Writing:** Spell most familiar words accurately on a range of familiar topics when writing independently. Plan, write, edit and proofread short texts, with little or no support. Use grammatical structures correctly, allowing for occasional mistakes.	• Learners can write a quiz about jobs for classmates to complete, paying attention to spelling, grammar and vocabulary.
6Sc.06, 6Sc.02	• **Speaking:** Begin to produce and maintain stretches of language comprehensibly, allowing for hesitation and reformulation, especially in longer stretches of free production. Describe people, places and objects, and routine past and present actions and events.	• Learners can deliver a presentation about an inspiring job.
21st-century skills		
Collaboration: Take responsibility for own contributions in a group task.		

Materials: Learner's Book pages 106–107; Workbook page 78; access to the internet/library access or video clips of people talking about inspiring jobs; examples of other learner's work; large sheets of paper; pictures that learners can cut out and use; presentation software or poster card; Unit 6 project checklists; End of Unit 6 test; Progress test 2

Starter ideas

Raise interest in the projects (10–15 minutes)

- Tell learners they are either going to create a quiz about different jobs (Project A) or deliver a presentation about an inspiring job (Project B).

- If possible, raise interest in the projects by presenting examples of learner's work on similar topics from other classes or the internet.

- Revise new vocabulary from the unit, which learners may need for the challenges, in a fun way. For example, create a word search for learners to complete, or put anagrams of the new vocabulary on the board.

Main teaching ideas

Introduce and complete the projects (60 minutes)

Encourage learners to choose one of the projects and then follow the steps for their chosen project.

Project A: A quiz about different jobs

- Divide learners into pairs or small groups. Support them while they brainstorm information about jobs in the different categories.

- Circulate and support learners while they write the clues.

- **Collaboration:** Make sure all learners have the chance to contribute and have chosen 4–5 suitable jobs to write questions for. Encourage learners to work together on the clues, or ensure each group/pair divides the clue writing fairly.

> **Differentiation ideas:** As long as there is an overall total of 10 questions per pair/group, you could vary the number of questions learners write for the quiz according to ability, and also restrict themes (for example, media and information technology only). More confident learners could write two or three questions for each category; other learners could write one question for each category or five each for two categories.

- Circulate and support learners while they work together on their rough draft.

> **Assessment ideas:** Ask learners to proofread their work (if learners have written their own clues, they could swap with another group member), focusing on spelling, vocabulary and grammar, for example the present simple.

- Learners write the quiz in a presentable form and decorate it with pictures.

- Finally, they hand the quiz to another pair or group to complete.

> **Assessment ideas:** Learners use the Unit 6 project checklist to evaluate each other's quizzes.

Project B: A presentation about an inspiring job

- Depending on your class and the time available, learners could do this task individually or in pairs/groups. Although the presentation theme is personal to individual learners, they could still work together and choose a job that interests them both/all.

- As a class, read through the project instructions. Then brainstorm different jobs that are inspiring and write them on the board.

- Make sure each learner, pair or group has chosen a job to research.

- Circulate and offer support while learners make notes on the three topics.

- When learners are drafting their presentations (either using presentation software or poster card), circulate and make sure they are using sequencing phrases to guide the audience through the presentation.

> **Assessment ideas:** When learners have finished their first drafts, they could swap their part with another group member/partner and give tactful feedback on grammar, vocabulary and spelling errors.

- Learners draw or find pictures to go with their presentation.

- Give learners some time to practise their presentations before they deliver them to the class.

> **Assessment ideas:** Learners use the Unit 6 project checklist to evaluate each other's presentations.

Plenary ideas

Reflection (5–10 minutes)

> **Reflection:** As a class, learners discuss what they enjoyed about the projects and what they found most challenging. Did they enjoy working in pairs or small groups for these projects? Encourage learners to talk about what worked well and what the challenges were. Is there anything that they would do differently next time?

Homework ideas

Learners follow the instructions in the Learner's Book and complete the project they didn't do in class.

> **Workbook**
>
> Learners do Activities 1–2 on page 78.

6.7 What do you know now?

Why do people do the jobs they have?

- **Learning to learn:** Learners have the opportunity to reflect and evaluate their own learning success.

- Reintroduce the question from the start of the unit: *Why do people do the jobs they have?* Discuss learner's responses to the question now and compare with their comments at the beginning of the unit. How much has changed?

- Ask learners to work on the tasks in pairs.

- For questions 1, 2, 4, 5 and 6, encourage learners to look back through the unit if they can't remember. Offer support while learners answer the questions.

- When learners have finished, give class feedback on the answers.

Answers

1 (Compound nouns are underlined): a vet; a computer programmer; a physiotherapist; a science teacher; an engineer; a marine biologist.
2 The uniform in Lesson 2 is designed for a postman /woman.
   Learner's own answers. (Features described in Lesson 2: light; stripe; logo; zip; sleeve; zipped pocket; waterproof material; trainers; belt with pockets; alarm; inside pocket).
3 Learner's own answers.
4 An astronaut.
   Suggested personal qualities (four of): good at maths and science; adventurous; enthusiastic; hard-working; good team player; confident; physically fit. Plus learner's own suggestions.
5 Jobs advertised: acrobat, inventor, zookeeper. Learner's own answers. Example answers:
   Job 1: He/she is really good at gymnastics / flexible / strong / athletic.
   Job 2: He / she is really good at / fascinated by / interested in science / design technology.
   Job 3: He/she is really good at / fascinated by / interested in natural science; brave and confident with all kinds of animals.
6 You can be anything, but you must try, so never give up and reach for the sky.

Look what I can do

- There are five 'can do' statements. Learners read through the statements and tick the things they can do. Encourage them to reflect on how well they can do these things. Invite them to think of ways they can improve further, for example what strategies they can use or learn to use.

- If learners find it challenging to read the statements, look through the unit with them and help them to find the relevant information.

- Finally, ask learners to work through the questions on page 79 of the Workbook. Encourage them to talk about what they enjoyed and also about any further support they might need.

Check your progress 2

Learners answer the nine questions.

Answers

1   Across: 2. robot, 3. logo, 4. physiotherapist, 7. vet, 8. charity, 9. tablet, 11. brand
     Down: 1. satellite, 5. engineer, 6. save, 10. afford
     Unit 4 Inventions: robot, tablet, satellite
     Unit 5 Money: charity, brand, save, afford
     Unit 6 People and work: logo, physiotherapist, vet

2   Learner's own answers.

3   **a** I often buy things that I've saved for **myself**.
     b I am really keen **on** sport.
     c My friends say that I **am** good at drawing.
     d At the moment, my friend and I **are doing** this activity.
     e In ten years' time, I **will** probably learn to drive.
     f I spend money much **more** carefully if I save it myself.

4   Learner's own answers.

5   Past simple forms: win / *won*; have / *had*; buy / *bought*; save / *saved*; spend / *spent*;
     lose / *lost*; go / *went*; get / *got*; travel / *travelled*; visit / *visited*; try / *tried*; make / *made*;
     do / *did*; play / *played*.

6–9 Learner's own answers.

>7 Nature's power

Unit plan

Lesson	Approximate number of learning hours	Outline of learning content	Learning objectives	Resources
1 The power of volcanoes	2.0–2.5	Talk about what happens in an active volcano using past tenses.	6Ld.04 6Ug.06	Learner's Book Lesson 7.1 Workbook Lesson 7.1 ⬇ Photocopiable 19 **Digital Classroom:** video – Natural dangers; grammar presentation – Past continuous
2 Lightning strikes	1.0–1.5	Discover how lightning happens.	6Rd.01 1SIC.04 6Rd.02	Learner's Book Lesson 7.2 Workbook Lesson 7.2 **Digital Classroom:** activity – Lightning
3 Nature's forces	2.0–2.5	Give safety advice for natural dangers.	6Rd.01 6Ld.01 6Ld.03 6Sc.04 6Us.04 9ESp.01 6Wc.01	Learner's Book Lesson 7.3 Workbook Lesson 7.3 ⬇ Photocopiable 20 **Digital Classroom:** activity – What to do in a lightning storm
4 The effects of nature's power	1.5–2.0	Describe a special place using adjectives and prepositions.	6Wc.02 6Wc.03 6Uv.01	Learner's Book Lesson 7.4 Workbook Lesson 7.4 ⬇ Unit 7 sample answer ⬇ Photocopiable 21 ⬇ Differentiated worksheets 7A, B and C **Digital Classroom:** activity – Adjectives followed by prepositions
5 *Thank You Letter*	2.0–2.5	Read and enjoy a poem about the sun.	6Rm.01 6Rm.02 6Sc.05 6Wc.02	Learner's Book Lesson 7.5 Workbook Lesson 7.5 **Digital Classroom:** activity – Thank you letter

(continued)

| 6 Project challenge | 1.0–1.5 | Project A: An infographic text about a natural danger.

Project B: A presentation about a natural disaster. | 6Wor.03
6Wc.02
6Sc.06
6Sc.02 | Learner's Book Lesson 7.6
Workbook Lesson 7.6
[⤓] Unit 7 project checklists |

Cross-unit resources
[⤓] Unit 7 Audioscripts
[⤓] End of Unit 7 test
[⤓] Unit 7 Progress report
[⤓] Unit 7 Wordlist

BACKGROUND KNOWLEDGE

Unit 7 focuses on the power of nature. Learners talk about what happens in an active volcano, discover how lightning happens and give safety advice for natural dangers like earthquakes.

In Lesson 7.4, Hannah describes a visit to a special place to her – Pompeii. The ancient city of Pompeii in southern Italy was first discovered at the end of the 16th century. Mount Vesuvius is the huge volcano that erupted over Pompeii and other towns and settlements in CE 79, sending a poisonous ash cloud over the area. (CE stands for the common era. Common means that it is based on the most commonly used calendar, the Gregorian calendar. CE is also often referred to as AD.) In 24 hours, the poisonous ash covered the city, destroying buildings and killing thousands of people. The ash cloud encased people and objects, turning them to stone; this preserved whole bodies and the objects around them. Excavations have revealed valuable information about Roman life. Today, Pompeii is a UNESCO World Heritage Site and one of the most popular tourist attractions in Italy, with approximately 2.5 million visitors every year. Visitors can gain a dramatic insight into the tragedy of Pompeii and everyday Roman life.

In Lesson 7.5, learners read and listen to a thank you letter in the form of a poem, written by Eric Finney. Usually, children write thank you letters to friends or relatives to thank them for a gift they have received. Learners practise using descriptive language and alliteration to create a short poem about something meaningful to them.

TEACHING SKILLS FOCUS

Skills for life

Unit 6 introduced you to the *Cambridge Framework for Life Competencies*. Six of the key areas of competencies are covered in Unit 7:

- 7.1 Critical thinking: Make predictions about the actions of a volcano.
- 7.3 Communication: Give advice about responding to extreme weather or a natural danger.
- 7.4 Creative thinking: Describe a place that is special, giving reasons why.
- 7.5 Emotional development: Describe why something makes us feel happy.
- 7.6 Collaboration: Collaborate in a group task towards a shared outcome.

- 7.7. Learning to learn: Learners have the opportunity to reflect and evaluate their own learning success.

Remember, more information and a list of the *Can do* statements for each level are in the Cambridge Competency Booklets, which can be downloaded on the Cambridge University Press Language and Pedagogy Research for ELT website.

Your challenge

Look through Unit 7 and find opportunities to develop the *Social responsibilities* competency (or choose another skill that you think learners would benefit from practising).

7.1 Think about it: The power of volcanoes

LEARNING PLAN

Learning objectives	Learning intentions	Success criteria
6Ld.04 6Ug.06	• **Listening:** Understand, with support, most specific information and detail of short and extended talk. • **Use of English:** Use past continuous forms for background, parallel and interrupted past actions. • **Vocabulary:** *lava, explode, erupt, crack, ash, crater*	• Learners can understand specific information in an interview about documenting volcanoes. • Learners can use the past continuous to talk about events around volcanoes.
21st-century skills		
Critical thinking: Make predictions about the actions of a volcano.		

Materials: Learner's Book pages 111–113; Workbook pages 80–81; access to the internet or science books about volcanoes in learner's country (for Activity 9); Optional: matching cards for the Starter activity; **Photocopiable 19**

LANGUAGE BACKGROUND

Past continuous

The past continuous (also known as the past progressive) is used in several different ways:

- for interrupted past actions
- for parallel actions in the past
- for background actions.

For example, we use the past continuous to talk about an action taking place in the past that is interrupted by another action (which is seen as a background action): We **were making** a film <u>when the volcano suddenly exploded</u>.

We also use the past continuous to talk about two or more continuous (parallel) actions happening at the same time in the past – they provide a background to the story: We **were in** the area near the volcano while it <u>was erupting</u>.

Starter ideas

Matching cards (5–10 minutes)

- Explain to learners that in this unit they are going to look at the power of nature – including when volcanoes erupt and earthquakes happen.
- To prepare learners for the specialist vocabulary, pre-teach the following words:
  tsunami: a huge wave caused by an earthquake under the sea;

  risk: the possibility of something bad happening;
  erupt: when rocks and fire come out of a volcano;
  explode: when something breaks up into small pieces;
  active: might erupt at an time;
  dormant: not active now, but could be active later.

- Before the lesson, you could make cards for learners to match. One card should have the nature word and the other card a definition of what it means.
- In pairs, learners match the cards and the definitions.

Getting started (10 minutes)

- Together, look at the photos and ask learners to identify the natural events. Write new vocabulary on the board.

- Next, elicit ideas about the effects of the events.

- Circulate and offer support while learners ask and answer part c in pairs.

Answers
a   Main image: snow avalanche; smaller images (from left to right): volcano sending out an ash cloud; cracks in the earth from a drought or earthquake; an electric storm with lightning.
b   Learner's own answers.
c   Learner's own answers.

> **Digital Classroom:** Use the video 'Natural dangers' to introduce the topic of natural dangers and disasters. The i button will explain how to use the video.

Main teaching ideas

1   Look at the photos of volcanoes in action. Who do you think takes these pictures? (5 minutes)

- As a class, look at and talk about what is happening in the photos. Elicit the meaning of vocabulary like *lava, erupt(ion), explosion, close encounters* and *smoke* that learners will hear in the listening activity.

- In pairs, learners answer the questions.

- As a class, share feedback. Pre-teach the word *drones* and discuss how they can minimise the risks of taking these kinds of pictures.

Answers
Learner's own answers

2   Find images of these words in the photos. (5 minutes)

- Use this as an opportunity to pre-teach/check that learners understand the meaning of the words they will hear in the listening activity.

- Write the words on the board and invite learners to explain what they mean. As a class, find images of the words in the photos.

Answers
Photo a: lava / explode / erupt / crack / ash / crater (*explode*: when something breaks up into small pieces)
Photo b: ash / erupt / crack / crater (*erupt*: when rocks and fire come out of a volcano)
Photo c: lava

3   Read the sentences with your partner. Do you think they are true or false? (5–10 minutes)

- Read the sentences together and check learners remember the meaning of new words like *tsunami*.

- In pairs, learners discuss whether the sentences are true or false.

> **Critical thinking opportunity:** Learners consider the actions of a volcano and use these ideas to help predict what they will hear in the listening activity.

- Don't give the answers away yet, as learners will check their ideas in the next activity.

4   Listen to the photographer talking about his experiences filming volcanoes. (5–10 minutes)

- Tell learners they are going to listen to a photographer talking about his experiences filming volcanoes.

- Play the recording so learners can check their answers to Activity 3. Make it clear they should concentrate on listening specifically for this information without trying to understand every word they hear.

- After listening, give learners a few minutes to discuss their responses again in pairs before you share the answers.

Audioscript: Track 48

See Learner's Book page 113

| Presenter: | You risk your life to get so close to the volcano … what is the most dangerous experience you've had? |
| Photographer: | Oh, there's been a lot! We were making a film in Indonesia when the volcano suddenly exploded. We weren't expecting that because |

it had been quiet. The explosion was so huge that it blew the front of the volcano off. We were almost a kilometre away when the lava was rolling towards us. Molten lava can travel at a speed of 450 km an hour! There was water in front of it too, so there was the danger of a tsunami. Luckily the lava stopped and didn't reach us.

Presenter: What an experience! Any other close encounters?

Photographer: Yes! In Hawaii in 2018, we were in the area near the volcano while it was erupting. It was terrifying. Houses were disappearing as the earth opened up in huge cracks. We watched lava cover the places where the houses once were. Lava burns everything in its path. It moves very fast and it is extremely hot – about 2000 °C.

Presenter: … extremely hot! But you don't always know when a volcano is going to erupt, do you?

Photographer: No, that's right. And sometimes an active volcano is more dangerous when it is silent. That's when you know that pressure is building. Then it throws out huge clouds of smoke and ash – sometimes as high as 30 km into the air!

Answers
a True
b True
c False (2000 °C)
d False (30 km)

Use of English – Past continuous (10 minutes)

- Read the Use of English box together. Make sure learners remember how to form the past continuous and explain the different ways in which it can be used (see Language background).

- Learners could practise using the past continuous using **Photocopiable 19**.

Workbook
Learners do Activity 1 on page 82.

> **Digital Classroom:** Use the grammar presentation 'Past continuous' to revise using past continuous forms for background, parallel and interrupted past actions. The i button will explain how to use the grammar presentation.

5 Listen again and match the sentence halves. (5–10 minutes)

- Tell learners that this activity will help them practise using the past continuous to talk about an action taking place in the past that is interrupted by another action.

- Focus on the sentence halves and check learners understand their meaning.

- In pairs, learners match the sentence halves then listen to the recording again to check their answers.

Answers
1 c, 2 a, 3 b

6 What is it like to get so close to a volcano, do you think? (5–10 minutes)

- Circulate and offer support while learners discuss the questions in pairs.

- Encourage learners to use new vocabulary from the lesson and pre-teach/practise new words from Part 2 of the recording, such as *powerful, smell (strange), rotten, craters, soil* and *heat(ing)*.

> **Differentiation ideas:** Organise learners into pairs. Less confident speakers will benefit from language support and their partners will consolidate their understanding of the new vocabulary.

- Don't share feedback yet, as learners will check their ideas in the next activity.

Answers
Learner's own answers.

7 Listen to Part 2 and check your ideas in Activity 6. (5 minutes)

- Play Part 2 of the recording for learners to check their ideas from Activity 6.

- As a class, share feedback. Were learner's initial ideas similar to the recording?

Audioscript: Track 49

See Learner's Book page 113

Presenter:	So, with all the risks, why do you want to get so close to a volcano?
Photographer:	We want to show how beautiful and how powerful volcanoes are. They put on an amazing display – there are very beautiful colours and incredible sounds – like boiling water or fireworks! They smell strange too, because of all the gases that are coming out of the earth. And they can smell really bad too – like rotten eggs! That's the sulphur gas …
Presenter:	Ha ha! Yes, I have to say, I wouldn't want to go too near one!
Photographer:	And you're not alone! People are usually afraid of volcanoes. I often feel terrified when filming close to the craters, but for me, the volcanoes are really beautiful and fascinating too. And we must remember that they have done incredible things for the Earth. Billions of years ago, it was volcanoes that created most of the Earth's surface. Over time, they have produced very healthy soil, for plants and trees to grow and wildlife to live. They are very good for the ecosystems around us. And did you know that volcanoes can provide power for heating too?

Answers
See: *very beautiful colours.*
Hear: incredible sounds – like boiling water or fireworks.

Feel: terrified (when filming close to the craters) but finds volcanoes 'beautiful and fascinating too'.
Smell: really bad – like rotten (bad) eggs (the sulphur gas).

8 Listen again. What good things have volcanoes done for the Earth? (10 minutes)

- Ask the class if they can remember any good things volcanoes have done for the Earth, either from the recording or their own knowledge.

- Re-play the recording and check. Ask learners to focus specifically on this information.

Answers
Billions of years ago, volcanoes created most of the Earth's surface. They have produced very healthy soil (for plants, trees and wildlife). They are very good for the ecosystems around us. They can provide power for heating.

9 Are there any volcanoes in your country or region? Find out about the nearest volcano to you. (30–40 minutes)

- First, ask learners if they know about any volcanoes in their country or region. Write down key information on the board.

- Next, tell learners that they are going to choose a volcano and imagine they are film makers at the scene when it last erupted. They are going to write a description of what they saw and heard. Explain that in order to do this, they need information about the eruption and what happened.

- Allow pairs of learners time to research the information they need to write their descriptions.

- Circulate and offer support as they write notes and draft a description of the scene. Remind learners to use the past simple and past continuous to describe what happened. If helpful, you could also download the audioscripts of the recordings from the lessons for learners to refer to.

> **Differentiation ideas:** Provide less confident learners with some sentence starters. For example *'We were making a film in … when …', 'We were almost a kilometre away when …'.* Challenge more confident learners to use exciting adjectives.

> **Assessment ideas:** Before learners finalise their descriptions, ask them to swap their drafts with another pair, who will proofread for grammar, spelling and punctuation errors. Encourage learners to give feedback sensitively and include at least one compliment.

- Learners complete their drafts; you could display them in the classroom.

Answers
Learner's own answers.

Homework ideas

- If class time is short, learners could research and write about the volcano for homework.

> **Assessment ideas:** Write a short checklist as a class so that learners can self-assess their work before handing it in. For example: *Have I used new vocabulary from the lesson to describe the volcano? Have I used the past simple and continuous correctly? Have I used punctuation correctly? Have I checked my spelling?*

Workbook

Learners do Activities 1–6 on pages 80–81.

Plenary ideas

Consolidation (5–10 minutes)

Learners spend time reading their peers' volcano descriptions.

7.2 Physical science: Lightning strikes

LEARNING PLAN		
Learning objectives	**Learning intentions**	**Success criteria**
6Rd.01	• **Reading:** Understand, with support, most specific information and detail in short and extended texts. Read and follow instructions.	• Learners can understand, with support, specific information in a text about how lightning happens.
1SIC.04 6Rd.02	• **Science:** Talk about how science helps us understand our effect on the world around us.	• Learners can read and follow instructions.
	• **Vocabulary:** *bump into, storm, strikes, electricity, cloud, connect, positive, negative*	• Learners can talk about how science helps us understand our effect on the world around us.
21st-century skills		
Cross-curricular links: Physical science: Learners discover how lightning occurs during a storm.		

Materials: Learner's Book pages 114–115; Workbook pages 82–83; balloons and empty metal cans (Activity 6)

Starter ideas

Stormy weather (5–10 minutes)

- Explain that in this lesson you're going to find out how lightning happens.

- To prepare learners for the Hot Seat game (Activity 2), pre-teach *bump into, storm, strikes, electricity, cloud, connect*.

- Before the lesson, make cards for learners to match. One card should have the 'Hot Seat' word and the other card a definition of what it means.

- In pairs, learners match the cards and the definitions.

Main teaching ideas

1 How often do you see lightning in your country? (10 minutes)

- Ask learners how often they see lightning in their countries; discuss how they feel when they see it.

- Look at the picture and talk about how lightning can be dangerous. Elicit the expression *lightning strike* and discuss how lightning can strike trees, buildings and people. Support learners by giving them vocabulary such as *electric shock, falling buildings/trees, set fire to*, etc

Answers
Learner's own answers.
Dangers: Lightning can strike things on the ground, including trees, people and buildings. It can set things on fire and cause things to fall down.

2 Play the Hot Seat game! Act out the words for your team mates to guess. (10 minutes)

- Put learners into teams of four or five. Then demonstrate the game to the whole class.

- Choose one of the team to sit in the 'Hot Seat'.

- Ask the rest of their team to choose one of the words from the word box and act it out, using mimes, gestures, definitions or examples. They cannot say the word or use a translation.

- The learner in the Hot Seat guesses the word.

- Start by giving more confident learners the chance to volunteer to sit in the hot seat first.

Then give other learners the chance to have their turn. Circulate and offer support as learners play the game.

- Alternatively, you could play the game as a whole class, with one confident learner volunteering to sit in the 'Hot Seat' with their back to the board. You write one of the words on the board behind the student – then the rest of the class act out the word until the student in the 'Hot Seat' guesses it.

Answers
Learner's own answers.

3 Listen and read about lightning. Complete the text with the words from the box. (10 minutes)

- Offer support by writing useful vocabulary learners will hear and read about on the board, for example *electricity, electrical charge, warm air, rise, sink, drops, ice*, etc. Check learners know the meaning of these words/expressions and read the Key words: physical change box before they listen to the text.

- Play the audio and ask learners to listen and follow the text. They should focus particularly on listening out for the words from Activity 2.

- Learners work in pairs to read the text again and complete the gaps with words from the box.

- Play the recording again, so learners can check their answers.

> **CROSS-CURRICULAR LINKS**
>
> **Physical science:** Learners read the text to find out how lightning happens in a storm.

Audioscript: Track 50

See Learner's Book page 114

Answers
1 storm (Example), 2 electricity, 3 bump into, 4 cloud, 5 connect, 6 strikes

> **Digital Classroom:** Use the activity 'Lightning' to reinforce reading comprehension of the text from the Learner's Book. The i button will explain how to use the activity.

4 **Read paragraph 2 again. Use these words to complete the diagram. (10 minutes)**

- As a class, look at the words in the Key words box again and check learners understand their meaning.
- In pairs, learners reread paragraph 2 and use the words in the box to complete the diagram.
- Circulate and offer support as learners complete the activity.
- Give class feedback on the answers.

___

Answers
1 positive, 2 negative, 3 cold air, 4 hot air

___

5 **Read paragraph 3 again. Have you ever seen lightning strike the ground? Do the Lightning Quiz to find out how to stay safe. (10 minutes)**

- Tell learners they are going to do a fun quiz about how to stay safe from lightning.
- As a class, reread paragraph 3. Ask learners if they have ever seen lightning strike the ground and elicit ideas for staying safe.
- Check learners know the meaning of *shelter, avoid, landline, plugged in* and *charging* before they do the Lightning Quiz in pairs.
- Circulate and offer support with vocabulary.
- At the end of the activity, give the answers.

___

Answers
1 b, 2 a, 3 a, 4 a, 5 b, 6 a

___

6 **Try an experiment! You are going to produce static electricity. (10 minutes)**

- Write the expression *static electricity* on the board and elicit what it means.
- Tell learners they are going to do an experiment to produce static electricity. Look at the pictures and ask learners for ideas about what they might need to do.

- Divide learners into small groups and distribute a balloon and an empty metal can to each group.
- Read the instructions together and check learners understand *rub, blow up* and *move away.*
- Circulate and offer support while learners practise doing the experiment.
- Discuss the answers to questions b–d.
- Then ask learners to try the following variations. Or, if easier, demonstrate them to the class:
  - First, ask learners to 'charge' their balloons against different surfaces, for example a woollen jumper and a cotton t-shirt. Does it make a difference?
  - Next, ask learners to change the size of the balloon and then do steps b–d again. What changes do they notice?
  - Then see how much water learners can put in the can before the balloon can't move it.
  - They could also try other non-metal objects in place of the can (for example, paper, tissue, small plastic objects). What happens?
  - Finally, tell learners to have a can race with their friends! First, they should each line up several cans. Then ask them to charge a balloon and see which can reaches the edge of the surface first!

CROSS-CURRICULAR LINKS

Physical science: Learners do an experiment to produce static electricity.

___

Answers
b It creates static electricity.
c The can moves towards the balloon.
d The can follows the balloon.

___

Plenary ideas

Consolidation (10 minutes)

Learners report back to the class on what they learned and found out from the experiment using the past simple. For example: *We made our balloon smaller and …; We used tissue paper with the balloon and it … .*

Homework ideas

Under parental supervision, learners look for similar experiments on school/educational blogs in English.

Workbook

Learners do Activities 1–4 on pages 82–83.

7.3 Talk about it: Nature's forces

LEARNING PLAN

Learning objectives	Learning intentions	Success criteria
6Rd.01	• **Reading:** Understand, with support, most specific information and detail in short and extended texts.	• Learners can understand specific details in a short text about how earthquakes happen.
6Ld.01, 6Ld.03	• **Listening:** Understand a range of instructions	• Learners can understand earthquake safety instructions and deduce the meaning of key verbs from the context.
6Sc.04	• **Speaking:** Give a sequence of instructions.	
6Us.04	• **Use of English:** Use connectives (e.g. *while, until, as soon as*) in short texts.	• Learners can give a sequence of instructions using connectives.
9ESp.01	• **Science:** Explain the movement of tectonic plates in terms of convection currents.	• Learners can explain the movement of tectonic plates in terms of convection currents.
6Wc.01	• **Writing:** Write a sequence of instructions.	• Learners can write a sequence of instructions for a safety broadcast.
	• **Vocabulary:** *surface, fault line, tectonic plate, waves, shake, get down, cover, crawl, hold on*	

21st-century skills

Communication: Give advice about responding to extreme weather or a natural danger.

Cross-curricular link: Science: Learners explain the movement of tectonic plates in terms of convection currents.

Materials: Learner's Book pages 116–117; Workbook pages 84–85; access to the internet/library access or photocopied information about extreme weather or natural dangers that occur in your learner's country; recording equipment for podcast (Activity 7); **Photocopiable 20**

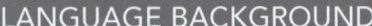

LANGUAGE BACKGROUND

Connectives

Connectives are words that are used to join other words and phrases. We use them constantly in written and spoken English.

In this lesson, they are referred to as *connecting words*. The main focus of the lesson is on three connectives:

- *until*: up to (a point in time)
- *as soon as*: immediately after
- *while*: at the same time as.

Common misconceptions

Misconception	How to identify	How to overcome
• Learners often use *while* instead of *when* to introduce a single action/ event. For example: ~~While~~ **When** *we meet, we go to the cinema.* • They also use *during* when *while* is correct. For example: ~~During~~ **While** *you're playing, maybe you can make some friends.* • In addition, learners use *after* when *until* is correct. For example: *I had an accident when I was riding my bicycle to school, so my bicycle was broken ~~until~~ **after** that.*	Write sentences with the connectives used correctly and identify the different implications in meaning: • *until, as soon as, while* (see Language background) • *after*: starting from a point in time • *when*: to say at what time single completed actions happened • *during*: from the beginning to the end.	Practise using: • Activities 1–5 on pages 84–85 of the Workbook • **Photocopiable 20.**

Starter ideas

Nature's forces matching activity (5 minutes)

- Tell learners that in this lesson they are going to give safety advice for if an earthquake happens.
- Ask them to think of other natural dangers, for example *storms, volcanoes, tornadoes, sandstorms and blizzards.*
- Before the lesson, make cards for learners to match. One card should have the natural danger and the other card a definition of what it means:
  Storm: bad weather – usually heavy rain, strong winds and often thunder and lightning;
  Volcano: a mountain with a hole in the top that lava flows out of;
  Tornado: a strong cone shaped wind that can destroy buildings;
  Sandstorm: a strong wind in the desert that carries sand with it;

Blizzard: a snow storm with a lot of wind;
Earthquake: a violent movement of the Earth's surface that can cause destruction.

- In pairs, learners match the cards and the definitions.

Main teaching ideas

1 What do you know about earthquakes? (10 minutes)

- Have a class discussion about what learners know about earthquakes. Learners talk about earthquakes they have seen on TV or in films.
- Learners may have had a frightening personal experience of an earthquake, so be sensitive and understanding during discussions.
- Use the photos to help learners describe what can happen during an earthquake.
- Build up useful vocabulary on the board.

Answers
Learner's own answers.

2 How do earthquakes happen? Read the text and label the diagrams with the words in bold. (10 minutes)

- Before reading the text, encourage learners to make predictions about how earthquakes happen, using their knowledge and the diagram.

- Elicit/pre-teach words learners will read in the text. For example, ask where earthquakes happen, to elicit *the Earth's surface* and *fault line*. Also, when discussing how earthquakes happen, elicit *moving plates* and *pressure builds up*.

- In pairs, learners read the text and label the diagrams with the words in bold.

> **Differentiation ideas:** If learners need support with this task, give them the four words with definitions to help them work out where each label goes.

- Give class feedback on the correct answers.

CROSS-CURRICULAR LINKS

Science: Learners explain the movement of tectonic plates in terms of convection currents.

Answers
1 (Earth's) surface, 2 tectonic plates, 3 waves, 4 fault line

3 What do you do if an earthquake happens? In pairs, write two instructions. Then listen to the public service broadcast and compare. (10 minutes)

- Before learners write instructions, have a general discussion about what to do if an earthquake happens. Learners in regions where earthquakes are common may feel more confident speaking about this.

- If learners aren't very responsive, ask questions to encourage them to think critically, or make a short quiz based on the announcement. For example: *If you are inside when an earthquake takes place, should you a) crawl under a strong table, b) stand near a wall or c) rush outside?*

- **Communication:** In pairs, learners write two instructions about what to do if an earthquake happens.

> **Differentiation ideas:** Challenge more confident writers to write three instructions.

- Play the public service broadcast and compare learner's ideas with the recording. Make sure learners understand what *the shaking* means.

- Give class feedback on the answers.

Audioscript: Track 51

See Learner's Book page 116

This is a public service broadcast! When an earthquake happens, the Earth starts to shake. You need to act quickly to protect yourself. As soon as the shaking starts, get down on your hands and knees. Cover your head with your arm. If you are inside, crawl under a strong table and hold on to the table legs until the shaking stops. Stay away from windows and outside doors and walls, where falling glass and bricks could hit you.

Stay inside until the shaking stops. Don't move from where you are while the earthquake is happening. This might sound surprising, but most people get injured when they try to move outside or to another part of the building.

If you are outside, stay where you are but move away from buildings, walls and other objects in the street.

Answers
Learner's own answers. Instructions from the broadcast:
- (As soon as the shaking starts), get down on your hands and knees.
- Cover your head with your arm.
- If you are inside, crawl under a strong table and hold on to the table legs until the shaking stops.
- Stay away from windows and outside doors and walls.
- Stay inside until the shaking stops. Don't move from where you are while the earthquake is happening.
- If you are outside, stay where you are but move away from buildings, walls and other objects in the street.

4   Listen to the first part again and act out the verbs of movement with a partner. Then act out the safety advice! (10 minutes)

- This activity should help learners understand the instructions by acting them out. If possible, complete the activity in the classroom.

- Listen to the first part of the public safety broadcast again. Ask learners to pay particular attention to the verbs of movement from the word box.

- Circulate and offer support as learners act out the verbs of movement with a partner.

- If learners haven't already written down the safety advice during the Activity 3 feedback, write the safety advice on the board: *Get down on your hands and knees; Cover your head with your arm; If you are inside, crawl under a strong table and hold on to the table legs until the shaking stops; Stay away from windows and outside doors and walls.*

- Circulate and offer support as learners practise acting out the safety advice with a partner.

Audioscript: Track 52

See Learner's Book page 117

This is a public service broadcast! When an earthquake happens, the Earth starts to shake. You need to act quickly to protect yourself. As soon as the shaking starts, get down on your hands and knees. Cover your head with your arm. If you are inside, crawl under a strong table and hold on to the table legs until the shaking stops. Stay away from windows and outside doors and walls, where falling glass and bricks could hit you.

Speaking tip – Giving important instructions, and 5 Complete these instructions from the broadcast, using verbs from Activity 4. (10 minutes)

- Before completing the instructions, read the Speaking tip and elicit more examples of positive/ negative imperative forms. Check learners know that the subject is not used in the imperative.

- Allow learners time to complete the sentences before giving class feedback on the answers.

Answers
1 Cover, 2 crawl, 3 Hold on

> **Digital Classroom:** Use the activity 'What to do in a lightning storm' to revise connecting words. The i button will explain how to use the activity.

Use of English – Connecting words (10 minutes)

- Elicit correct examples of connecting words and write example sentences on the board.

Workbook

Learners do Activities 1–4 on pages 84–85.

6   Listen again and complete the sentences with connecting words. (10 minutes)

- Listen to the public service broadcast again, asking learners to listen out for the connecting words.

- Read the sentences together and elicit suggestions about the missing connecting words.

- Learners copy and complete the sentences.

Audioscript: Track 53

See Learner's Book page 117

This is a public service broadcast! When an earthquake happens, the Earth starts to shake. You need to act quickly to protect yourself. As soon as the shaking starts, get down on your hands and knees. Cover your head with your arm. If you are inside, crawl under a strong table and hold on to the table legs until the shaking stops. Stay away from windows and outside doors and walls, where falling glass and bricks could hit you.

Stay inside until the shaking stops. Don't move from where you are while the earthquake is happening. This might sound surprising, but most people get injured when they try to move outside or to another part of the building.

If you are outside, stay where you are but move away from buildings, walls and other objects in the street.

Answers
a As soon as, **b** until, **c** while

7 Create a public service broadcast. Give safety instructions. (50 minutes)

- **Photocopiable 20** can be used before doing this activity to give learners ideas about what to write.
- First, check learners remember the meaning of *storms, volcanoes, tornado, sandstorms* and *blizzards* (from the Starter activity).
- Circulate and offer support while each group thinks of a type of extreme weather or natural danger that occurs in their country/region.
- Learners research why the natural danger/ extreme weather happens and write a short paragraph. If using the internet or library isn't practical, distribute photocopied information that learners can use.
- Offer support while learners create safety instructions to help people protect themselves when the event happens. Encourage them to use the public service broadcast as a model.

> **Assessment ideas:** When learners have finished their first draft, ask them to swap it with another group and check the work against the following list: *Have we used connecting words? Are the instructions short and simple? Have we used imperative verb forms? Have we used vocabulary from the lesson? Have we checked grammar, punctuation and spelling?*

- Once learners have completed their final drafts, ask them to divide up the instructions between them so that everyone has a turn to contribute to the podcast recording.
- **Communication:** Learners create a broadcast giving advice about what to do in extreme weather or if a natural danger occurs.

Answers
Learner's own answers.

Plenary ideas

Consolidation (20 minutes)

- Learners listen to their podcasts. Give them plenty of praise and positive feedback.

> **Assessment ideas:** As you listen to the podcasts, focus particularly on learner's pronunciation, use of instructions, connecting words and imperative verb forms. Make notes on areas where learners might need further support.

Homework ideas

Learners write a paragraph about what they have learned from another group's podcast.

Workbook

Learners do Activities 1–5 on pages 84–85.

7.4 Write about it: The effects of nature's power

LEARNING PLAN

Learning objectives	Learning intentions	Success criteria
6Wc.02, 6Wc.03 6Uv.01	• **Writing:** Write, with support, short texts which describe people, places and objects, and routine past and present actions and events. Express opinions and feelings. • **Use of English:** Use common dependent prepositions following adjectives. • **Vocabulary:** *fascinated by, interested in, amazed by, sad about*	• Learners can describe a special place using adjectives followed by prepositions to express feelings.
21st-century skills		
Creative thinking: Describe a place that is special, giving reasons why.		

Materials: Learner's Book pages 118–119; Workbook pages 86–87; pictures of places like Machu Picchu, the Taj Mahal, etc. (Starter activity); access to the internet and/or library, or to information about special places (Activity 7); Unit 7 sample answer; **Photocopiable 21**; **Differentiated worksheets 7A**, **B and C**

Starter ideas

Special places (10 minutes)

• Show pictures of special places like Machu Picchu, the Taj Mahal, the Temples of Angkor, the Alhambra, the AyaSofya, etc.

• Ask learners to share their experiences of visiting these places. Have a class vote for the place learners would most like to visit (again).

Main teaching ideas

1 Think of a special place that you've been to. (10 minutes)

• Ask learners to think of a special place they have visited, either in their own country or another country. Give them some guiding questions and prompts, for example *Who did you go with? What things did you do? How did you feel when you were there? What made it so interesting/beautiful?*

• Allow learners one minute to write as many adjectives as they can to describe the place.

• Build up a list of adjectives on the board that learners can use in Activity 7 when they write their description of a special place.

Answers

Learner's own answers.

2 Do you know anything about the city of Pompeii in Italy? (10 minutes)

• Help learners make predictions about what they will read in Hannah's description (Activity 3). Ask if they have heard of the city of Pompeii in Italy and if anyone knows what happened there.

• Look at the pictures and elicit ideas. Ask questions like: *What do you think happened to the people? What's that in the background? Is it a volcano? What about the buildings/pots – how old are they? Why have they been almost destroyed?* Elicit that Pompeii is a Roman city and that no one has lived there for thousands of years. If learners don't know the story, encourage them to speculate why/how it could have been destroyed. Write learner's ideas on the board.

• Revise *ash* and *erupted*, and elicit *poisonous*, which learners will encounter in the reading.

Answers
Learner's own answers. For information about Pompeii, see Background knowledge.

3 Read Hannah's description of her visit to Pompeii. (10 minutes)

- Tell learners they are going to read a description of the city by a teenager, Hannah, who visited Pompeii last summer.

- Allow a few minutes for learners to skim through Hannah's description so that they can check their predictions /find out what happened there.

- Tell learners not to worry about understanding every word, as they will read the description in more detail in Activity 4.

Answers
In CE 79 (nearly 2000 years ago), a huge volcano erupted in the south of Italy. The ash cloud from the volcano was over 20 kilometres high. It was a poisonous mixture of ash and gas, with a temperature of 300 °C. In 24 hours, it covered the city. It destroyed houses and killed thousands of people almost immediately. The ash covered people and objects and turned them to stone.

4 Read the description again and match each part with a heading. (10 minutes)

- Before learners reread the description, read through the headings together.

- In pairs, learners discuss which heading goes with each part.

- Give class feedback on the correct answers.

Answers
Part 1 – c, Part 2 – a, Part 3 – d, Part 4 – b

5 Find three interesting facts from the first part of Hannah's description. (10 minutes)

- Learners reread the first part of the description and find three interesting facts.

- In pairs, they share their ideas and talk about which fact surprised them the most.

- Have a class vote on the most surprising fact.

Answers
Interesting/surprising facts (three from):
- In CE 79, nearly 2000 years ago, a huge volcano erupted in the south of Italy.
- The ash cloud was over 20 kilometres high.
- It was a poisonous mixture of ash and gas.
- In 24 hours it covered the city of Pompeii.
- The temperature of the ash cloud was 300 °C.
- It destroyed houses and killed thousands of people almost immediately.
Learner's own answers.

Language focus – Adjectives + prepositions, and 6 Match the adjectives and prepositions, then find examples in Hannah's description. (10 minutes)

- Read the Language focus together. Make sure learners understand what prepositions are and what kind of words come before the prepositions (adjectives).

- To check learner's understanding, ask them to match the adjectives and prepositions in Activity 6.

- Then, in pairs, ask them to find and underline examples of the adjectives + prepositions in Hannah's description.

- Circulate and offer support while learners write one sentence of their own using each adjective + preposition from the word boxes.

> **Differentiation ideas:** Challenge more confident writers by asking them to write two sentences using each adjective + preposition from the word boxes.

- Use **Differentiated worksheets 7A, B and C** to practise prepositions after adjectives.

Answers
fascinated by, interested in, amazed by, sad about
Examples in sentences from text:
- But when we got there, I was really amazed by what I saw.
- I was really interested in the history and information about how the people lived so long ago. I was fascinated by the stone figures of the people, …
- … I felt very sad about them at the same time.
- I felt sad about normal people like you and me doing normal everyday things …

> **Digital Classroom:** Use the activity 'Adjectives followed by prepositions' to reinforce the use of adjectives followed by prepositions. The i button will explain how to use the activity.

7 Write a description of a special place. (30 minutes)

- **Creative thinking:** Learners write their own description of a place that is special to them and give reasons why it is special.

- Brainstorm places that learners could write about and make sure each learner has chosen somewhere that is special to them.

- Learners research interesting facts about their special place on the internet/in the library. Circulate and check that they have included adjectives, verbs and nouns to describe this place and how it makes them feel.

- Encourage learners to use the headings in Activity 4 to help plan their descriptions. Circulate and offer support as learners match their notes to the headings.

> **Assessment ideas:** Before learners start Step 3, show them the Unit 7 sample answer without the mark scheme comments. As a class, evaluate the sample answer's strengths and weaknesses. Also look at the list of steps on page 119 of the Learner's Book, so that learners know what they are aiming to achieve in their description.

- Before learners start writing, review the suggestion in the Writing tip. Circulate as learners write their drafts and make sure they include adjectives plus preposition phrases to describe their feelings.

> **Assessment ideas:** Once learners have finished their first draft, ask them to work through **Photocopiable 21** to self-assess their work. When they have made any updates, invite them to swap their draft with a partner, who will proofread it for grammar and spelling errors. Encourage learners to give feedback sensitively and to include at least one compliment.

Answers
Learner's own answers.

Plenary ideas

Reflection (10 minutes)

Learners read some of the other descriptions. Encourage them to ask each other questions about the special place using the vocabulary and grammar from the lesson, for example *Why were you amazed by … ?; I would love to go to …; Were you interested in …?*

Homework ideas

Using the information they have learned from their research and reading other learner's descriptions, learners make a quiz about special places; for example, *Which special place is in Italy? (Pompeii)*.

> **Workbook**
> Learners do Activities 1–6 on pages 86–87.

7.5 Read and respond: *Thank You Letter*

LEARNING PLAN

Learning objectives	Learning intentions	Success criteria
6Rm.01, 6Rm.02	• **Reading:** Understand, with support, most of the main points of short and extended texts. Read independently a range of short, simple fiction and non-fiction texts with confidence and enjoyment.	• Learners can read and enjoy a poem about the sun, understanding the main points.
6Sc.05	• **Speaking:** Pronounce familiar words and phrases clearly; begin to use intonation and place stress at word, phrase and sentence level appropriately.	• Learners can recognise matching sounds from the poem and use them in their own poem.
6Wc.02	• **Writing:** Write, with support, short texts which describe people, places and objects, and routine past and present actions and events. • **Vocabulary:** *blazing, dawn, glow, sunset, ripening*	• Learners can write a 'thank you' verse using the poem as a model.

21st-century skills

Emotional development: Describe why something makes us feel happy.

Materials: Learner's Book pages 120–123; Workbook pages 88–89

Starter ideas

Thank you letters (5 minutes)

- Tell learners that in this lesson they are going to read a thank you poem.

- Ask learners if thank you letters are used commonly in their culture and if they have ever written/received one. If so, ask what the letter said 'thank you' for.

- Learners look at other ways of saying thank you for something in Activity 10.

Main teaching ideas

1 Before you read the poem, make a list or mind map of words and phrases about the sun. (10 minutes)

- Tell learners that the thank you poem they are going to read is about the sun.

- Ask learners to work in pairs or small groups to make a list or mind map of words about the sun. Encourage them to use the pictures in the Learner's Book to generate ideas.

- Conduct class feedback, asking learners to share their words/phrases and to add to their lists/mind maps. At this stage, elicit/pre-teach words from the poem, such as *dawns, sunsets, blazing days on beaches, ripening apples, glow*, etc.

- Ask learners to look at their lists/mind maps and underline positive things that you might thank the sun for.

Answers
Learner's own answers.

2 Read and listen to the poem. (10 minutes)

- The aim of this activity is for learners to enjoy the poem and check whether their ideas from Activity 1 are mentioned.

- First, look at the words in the glossary (*dismal, slate* and *noble*) and check learners understand the meaning/know the correct pronunciation.

- Make it clear that at this stage it is not important to understand everything – learners just need to check their predictions.

- Learners read and listen to the poem. Spend a few minutes discussing which of their ideas from Activity 1 are mentioned in the poem.

Audioscript: Track 54
See Learner's Book pages 120–121

Answers
Learner's own answers.

3 Read and listen again. Discuss the questions. (10–15 minutes)

- Before learners read and listen to the poem again, look at the questions together and check that learners understand their meaning.

- Circulate and support learners while they work through the questions in pairs, for example by offering vocabulary support and encouraging them to use modals like *could* when speculating about where the author lives.

> **Differentiation ideas:** For question 1, challenge more confident readers to find five things that the writer thanks the sun for.

- Go through the answers as a class.

Answers
a Three from:
- every day that it shines (*Thanks for this / And every day*)
- dawns and sunsets that always arrive at the same time (*Your dawns and sunsets / Are just great – / Bang on time, / Never late. / For sunsets – the / Loveliest things I know*)
- brightening grey, cold days (*On dismal days, / As grey as slate, / Behind the cloud / You calmly wait, / Till out you sail …*)
- bright, hot days on beaches (*Blazing days on beaches*)
- ripening fruit and making it ready to eat (*For ripening apples, / Pears and peaches*)

- the beauty of sunlight (*For sharing out / Your noble glow*).

b How the sun looks: *Your noble glow / For sunsets – the / Loveliest things I know.*
What it does: *Your dawns and sunsets / Are just great – / Bang on time, / Never late. / To put a smile / On the whole world's face / Blazing days on beaches, / For ripening apples, / Pears and peaches; / For sharing out / Your noble glow.*
How it moves: *Till out you sail / With cheerful grace.*

c The poem indicates that the writer lives in a country with a temperate climate, which has cold, dull weather as well as hot (*On dismal days, / As grey as slate*). It is a country that grows apples, pears and peaches (*For ripening apples, / Pears and peaches*), so could be a European country.

d Learner's own answers.

4 Match a word in blue from the poem with a definition. (10 minutes)

- Read through the definitions together. Then focus on the first two blue words, *dawns* and *sunsets*. Elicit that they are both nouns.

- Look through the definitions and elicit which ones match the two words. If learners don't know, help them to eliminate the definitions that don't match.

- In pairs, learners match the other blue words with their definitions.

- Tell learners to add the words in blue to their lists/mind maps from Activity 1.

- Give class feedback on the correct answers.

Answers
a blazing
b dawn
c glow
d sunset
e ripening (verb – to ripen)

> **Digital Classroom:** Use the activity 'Thank you letter' to reinforce reading comprehension and vocabulary from the poem in the Learner's Book. The i button will explain how to use the activity.

5 Listen and repeat these lines from the poem. Which matching sounds do you hear? (5 minutes)

- Learners listen and repeat the lines from the poem, several times if necessary.

- Ask: *Which sounds are the same? Which sounds are similar?*

- Explain that learners will combine words and sounds in the following activities to create their own poems.

Audioscript: Track 55

See Learner's Book page 122

Answers
Same sounds: 'b', 'a' sounds.
Similar sounds: 'th' – soft (*thanks*) and hard 'th' sound (*those*).

6 Which other lines in the poem have matching sounds? (10 minutes)

- Read the poem and ask learners to call out *Stop!* when they hear a matching sound.

- You could re-play the audio (track 54) so that learners can appreciate the way the words sound and how this enhances the descriptive quality of the poem.

Answers
Thanks for **this**, On **d**ismal **d**ays, As grey as slate, For ripening **a**pples, **P**ears and **p**eaches, Your noble glow

7 Put the words with the same sound together. Listen and check. (5 minutes)

- In pairs, ask learners to look at the words and practise saying them.

- They then match the words that have the same sound.

- Play the recording so learners can listen and check, before giving class feedback.

Audioscript: Track 56

See Learner's Book page 122

Answers
warm / wonderful, magical / makes, bright / shining

8 Write a short verse about the sun in your notebook. Use the matching sounds from Activity 7. (5–10 minutes)

- First, focus learners on the picture and ask them what words come to mind, eliciting words from Activity 7 and other ones learners suggest.

- Now draw learner's attention to the verse and point out the gaps. Tell them they are going to complete the gaps with words from Activity 7. They need to choose words with the same matching sound to complete each line.

- Do the first one as an example, eliciting which word has the same sound as *bright* (*shining*). Then read the completed line together (*Your bright shining light*).

- Offer support while learners complete the other lines in the same way, working in pairs.

- During feedback, read out the completed verse, emphasising the matching sounds.

Answers
Suggested answer:
Thanks for
Your *bright, shining* light,
In the morning
Your warm, wonderful glow
In the evening
That makes colours magical.

9 Write a 'thank you' verse. (30 minutes)

- Tell learners they are going to write their own thank you verse.

- **Emotional development:** This is a good opportunity for learners to think about why something makes them feel happy.

- Give learners time to choose a topic; support them by eliciting and inputting ideas and suggestions for each one.

- When learners have thought of a topic, ask them to brainstorm nouns, adjectives and adverbs associated with it. They should record their ideas on a mind map. Circulate and offer support with vocabulary and by helping learners make connections between words with the same or similar sounds.

- Ask learners to put the words together to make descriptive phrases in a verse, using the same model and structure as the verse in Activity 8. Remind them how to start the verse and let them know that it doesn't need to rhyme.

> **Differentiation ideas:** If less confident writers need support with this task, provide sentence starters.

- When learners are happy with their first draft, ask them to write the verse on clean paper and decorate it with pictures, ready to make a display.

- Learners read other verses and write down two new and/or interesting words or phrases from each one.

Answers
Learner's own answers.

10 Saying thank you. What other ways can we say thank you for something? (10 minutes)

- Read through the questions together.

- Circulate and offer support while learners discuss, in pairs, the bullet-pointed list of ways to say thank you with reference to the questions.

Answers
Learner's own answers.
Depending on your culture and/or the conventions of the country you live in, ways to say thank you include: making a phone call; sending a thank you message via social media, text, email; sending a thank you card; buying someone flowers, giving chocolates, buying a small gift to show appreciation for something; doing something for someone in return; simply saying 'thank you' face-to-face.

Plenary ideas

Reflection (10 minutes)

As a class, discuss what learners enjoyed best about reading/writing the poems. Which reading strategies helped them the most? What did they find challenging about reading/writing the poems?

Homework ideas

Learners look for other interesting poems about the sun (or another star or a planet, or the wind or rain, etc.).

> **Workbook**
>
> Learners do Activities 1–5 on pages 88–89.

7.6 Project challenge

LEARNING PLAN

Learning objectives	Learning intentions	Success criteria
6Wor.03, 6Wc.02	• **Writing:** Use appropriate layout for a limited range of written genres. Write, with support, short texts that describe people, places and objects, and routine past and present actions and events.	• Learners can create an infographic text about a natural danger, using appropriate layout.
6Sc.06, 6Sc.02	• **Speaking:** Begin to produce and maintain stretches of language comprehensibly, allowing for hesitation and reformulation, especially in longer stretches of free production. Describe people, places and objects, and routine past and present actions and events.	• Learners can deliver a presentation about a natural disaster.

21st-century skills

Collaboration: Collaborate together in a group task towards a shared outcome.

Materials: Learner's Book pages 124–125; Workbook page 90; access to the internet and/or library, or information about natural dangers/news reports and photos of natural disasters; poster card; examples of other learner's work; Unit 7 project checklists; End of Unit 7 test

Starter ideas

Raise interest in the projects (10–15 minutes)

- Tell learners they are either going to create an infographic text about a natural danger (Project A) or deliver a presentation about a natural disaster (Project B).

- If possible, raise interest in the projects by presenting examples of learner's work on similar topics from other classes or the internet.

- Revise new vocabulary from the unit, which learners may need for the challenges, in a fun way. For example, create a crossword for learners to complete, or put anagrams of the new vocabulary on the board.

Main teaching ideas

Introduce and complete projects (60 minutes)

- Encourage learners to choose one of the projects and then follow the steps for their chosen project.

- **Collaboration:** Both of the projects in this unit require collaborating in pairs/small groups towards a shared outcome. Remind them about the importance of sharing the project tasks fairly and ensuring that all learners have the chance to have their say and contribute.

Project A: An infographic text about a natural danger

- Organise learners into pairs or small groups. Look at the natural dangers together and encourage each group to choose one to write about.

- Circulate and support learners while they research and make notes on their chosen natural danger, including looking for photo images and diagrams to accompany their text. Make sure each group member has their own question to research/make notes on. If using the internet or library is impractical, distribute photocopied information.

- Support learners while they select the most important information from their research, organise their notes into paragraphs and write short texts with headings. Remind learners that the texts only need to be short because the visuals will help demonstrate/explain their points.

⟩ **Assessment ideas:** Group members could check each other's texts for spelling, grammar and punctuation.

- Distribute poster card so learners can finalise their infographic texts.

⟩ **Assessment ideas:** Learners use the project checklist to evaluate another group or pair's infographic text, including two interesting facts they learned.

Project B: A presentation about a natural disaster

- Organise learners into small groups. Look at the pictures and ideas, and encourage each group to agree on a natural disaster for their presentation.

- Support learners while they brainstorm what they already know about the disaster. Elicit the kinds of questions they could ask as part of their research, for example *Where/When did it happen? How many people were involved? Were there any survivors?*

- Circulate and support learners while they research the natural disaster, including thinking about visuals that might work in their presentation. Make sure each group member has a question to research. If using the internet or library is impractical, distribute photocopied information.

- Continue to offer support while learners plan and write their presentations. Make sure learners know when to use the past simple and past continuous tenses in their writing.

- Allow time for learners to create visuals to go with their presentations. Encourage critical thinking about which visuals will engage/interest their audience.

⟩ **Assessment ideas:** Group members could check each other's presentation parts for spelling, grammar and punctuation, and give feedback on whether it is engaging for the audience in terms of visual interest/effects.

- Give learners time to practise their presentations, using the visuals. Make sure each group member has a part to present.

- Learners deliver their presentations as a group to the class, with each group member delivering a part.

⟩ **Assessment ideas:** Learners use the project checklist to evaluate another group's presentation, including noting down the name of the natural disaster.

Plenary ideas

Reflection (10 minutes)

⟩ **Reflection:** As a class, learners discuss what they enjoyed about the projects and what they found most challenging. What were the most interesting/shocking pieces of information from the texts in Project A? What helped to make the presentations engaging in Project B?

- Did learners enjoy working in pairs or small groups for these projects? Encourage them to talk about what worked well and what the challenges were. Is there anything that they would do differently next time?

Homework ideas

With adult supervision, learners watch (short) videos about a natural disaster or danger in English.

Workbook

Learners do Activity 1 on page 90.

7.7 What do you know now?

What are the effects of nature's power?

- **Learning to learn:** Learners have the opportunity to reflect and evaluate their own learning success.

- Reintroduce the question from the start of the unit: *What are the effects of nature's power?* Discuss learner's responses to the question now and compare with their comments at the beginning of the unit. How much has changed?

- Ask learners to work on the tasks in pairs.

- For questions 1–3, 5 and 6, encourage learners to look back through the unit if they can't remember. For question 4, learners could write about the place they wrote about in Lesson 7.4.

- When learners have finished the questions, give class feedback on the answers. Build up a sample answer for 1 and 2 and a list of suggestions for the other questions.

Answers

1 Learner's own answers.
Sample answer: When a volcano **erupts**, hot **lava** and **ash** come out of the **crater** and move down the volcano. The lava makes the earth **crack** because it is so hot. If the force is very strong, the lava and ash **explode** high into the air and there is a huge ash cloud.

2 Learner's own answers.
Sample answer: Lightning happens when warm air rises to the sky. In the sky, the tiny drops of water cool and form thunder clouds. At the top of the clouds, the water turns to small pieces of ice because the temperature is very cold. The ice pieces move around in the storm winds and bump into each other. This action makes an electric charge. The cloud fills up with electrical charges. The tiny ice crystals have a positive charge and rise to the top of the cloud; the bigger pieces of ice have a negative charge and sink to the bottom. When the positive and negative charges grow very big, a huge spark of lightning happens inside a cloud.

3 Three from:
- (As soon as the shaking starts), get down on your hands and knees.
- Cover your head with your arm.
- If you are inside, crawl under a strong table and hold on to the table legs until the shaking stops.
- Stay away from windows and outside doors and walls.
- Stay inside until the shaking stops. Don't move from where you are while the earthquake is happening.
- If you are outside, stay where you are but move away from buildings, walls and other objects in the street.

4 Learner's own answers.

5 Four from:
- dawns and sunsets
- the way the sun brightens grey, cold days
- the way it moves out from behind a cloud
- bright, hot days on beaches
- the way it ripens fruit and makes it ready to eat
- the beauty of sunlight.

Learner's own answers.

6 Five from: blazing, glow, sunset, dawn, ripening fruit, cheerful grace.

Look what I can do

- There are seven 'can do' statements. Learners read through the statements and tick the things they can do. Encourage them to reflect on how well they can do these things. Also invite them to think of ways they can improve further, for example what strategies they can use or learn to use.

- If learners find it challenging to read the statements, look through the unit with them and support them to find the relevant information.

- Finally, ask learners to work through the questions on page 91 of the Workbook. Encourage them to talk about what they enjoyed and also about any further support they might need.

>8 Entertainment

Unit plan

Lesson	Approximate number of learning hours	Outline of learning content	Learning objectives	Resources
1 Entertainment at home	2.0–2.5	Talk about on-screen entertainment.	6Lm.01 6Lo.01 6Ug.13	Learner's Book Lesson 8.1 Workbook Lesson 8.1 ⬇ Differentiated worksheets 8A, B and C **Digital Classroom:** video – On-screen entertainment; activity – Participle adjectives
2 The first films	1.5–2.0	Explore the history of films.	6Rm.01 6Rd.04 6Ug.03 6Ug.04	Learner's Book Lesson 8.2 Workbook Lesson 8.2 ⬇ Photocopiable 22 **Digital Classroom:** grammar presentation – Past simple passive; activity – Which year do you hear?
3 Too much tech?	1.5–2.0	Present a history timeline using the past simple passive. Discuss how to manage screen time.	6Ld.04 6Sor.01 6Sor.02 6Uv.04	Learner's Book Lesson 8.3 Workbook Lesson 8.3 ⬇ Photocopiable 23 **Digital Classroom:** activity – Adverbs of time and frequency
4 Creating film scenes	2.0–2.5	Create a storyboard to show scenes from a film.	6Rd.04 6Wor.01	Learner's Book Lesson 8.4 Workbook Lesson 8.4 ⬇ Unit 8 sample answer ⬇ Photocopiable 24 **Digital Classroom:** activity – Match the sound effects
5 *Jurassic Park*	1.5–2.0	Read and enjoy a film storyline.	6Rd.01 6Rm.02 6Rd.04 6Sc.05	Learner's Book Lesson 8.5 Workbook Lesson 8.5 **Digital Classroom:** activity – Lizards and dinosaurs!
6 Project challenge	1.0–1.5	Project A: A film or video game review presentation. Project B: Create a film poster and voiceover.	6Sc.06 6Sc.02 6So.01 6Wc.02	Learner's Book Lesson 8.6 Workbook Lesson 8.6 ⬇ Unit 8 project checklists

(continued)

Cross-unit resources

 Unit 8 Audioscripts
 End of Unit 8 test
Unit 8 Progress report
 Unit 8 Wordlist

BACKGROUND KNOWLEDGE

Unit 8 focuses on different kinds of on-screen entertainment. *Screen time* is used in the Learner's Book to describe how long we spend using our phones, TVs, tablets or computers.

In Lesson 8.2, *movie* and *movie theatre* are the US English equivalents to the British English *film* and *cinema*. Learners also look at a timeline for the history of films in this lesson, which involves the pronunciation of years. Usually we pronounce the first two digits of a year as a number followed by the second two digits as another number, e.g. 1895 is *eighteen ninety-five*. Twenty-first century dates usually follow this rule, although variations are not uncommon, e.g. 2020 – *two thousand and twenty*. In the first nine years in a century, e.g. 1907 – *nineteen oh seven*, the '0' is pronounced.

In Lesson 8.4, learners create their own storyboard. This is a method for planning films, or television shows, especially those which are animated. A storyboard also shows the artist's ideas. Walt

Disney first used storyboards; he drew up a series of numbered panels to explain the sequence for the film *Plane Crazy* (1928).

In Lesson 8.5, learners read an extract from the 1990 novel *Jurassic Park* by the American author Michael Crichton. The extract comes from an adaptation that is aimed at learners with Intermediate-level English. The film, which was based on the book, is considered to be a milestone in cinema history, as it made major advances in digital film-making, specifically the use of computer-generated imagery (CGI). In the film, a group of scientists visit an almost complete theme park, with (cloned) dinosaurs, on a fictional island near Costa Rica. A power failure causes the dinosaurs to run loose, endangering the people on the island, including the scientists. *Jurassic Park* has a PG/PG-13 guidance rating, so you may not want to show the whole film to your class.

TEACHING SKILLS FOCUS

Reading skills to help with language awareness

Lack of language proficiency can become a barrier to learning. It can affect understanding and communication, and mean that learners find reading and listening activities challenging. Learners start to feel demotivated and lose interest, which can significantly affect their progress.

Learners are often tempted to translate every word of a text into their own language as they read, thinking it is the only way to understand. However, focusing too much on new words and becoming distracted looking up words in a dictionary can make reading tedious. Learners will also struggle to develop valuable language skills, like inferring meaning from context.

To become competent readers, learners should try to treat a sentence as a whole, consisting of several elements. They should also realise that the meaning of each 'separate' word depends on the other words in the sentence.

Your challenge

Try to develop strategies to make reading the extract from Jurassic Park a more enjoyable experience for learners.

- If you have learned a new language, remember the challenges that you (or your peers) faced.
- Look at the extract from *Jurassic Park* from the perspective of someone with the same language, age and knowledge as your learners.

CONTINUED

- Try to predict the new words (and concepts) that will challenge your learners.
- Devise strategies to make the reading activity enjoyable. Ask yourself 'How can I support my learners?'

Before reading:

- Pre-teach the main key words (not all of them, though, as this activity could then become tedious).
- Create fun vocabulary activities, such as crosswords, matching card activities (for example, see Lesson 1, Activity 3).
- Encourage learners to make predictions from what they know about the novel/film and by looking at the illustrations.

- Look at the words in the glossary and invite learners to guess how they fit into the story.

While reading:

- Add two or three key words in a glossary.
- Mime some of Tina's actions (see Lesson 7.5).
- Give learners a limited time for reading to discourage them from trying to look up every word.

After reading:

Devise activities to encourage and support learners to infer meaning from context. For guidance on this, see the teacher's notes for Lesson 7.5, Activity 7, and the Reading tip 'Guess meaning from context' on page 139 of the Learner's Book.

8.1 Think about it: Entertainment at home

LEARNING PLAN

Learning objectives	Learning intentions	Success criteria
6Lm.01, 6Lo.01	• **Listening:** Understand, with support, most of the main points of short and extended talk. Recognise, with support, the opinions of the speaker(s) in short and extended talk.	• Learners can understand most of the main points, and recognise the opinions of the speaker, in a conversation about video games.
6Ug.13	• **Use of English:** Use an increasing range of participle adjectives and a range of adjectives in the correct order in front of nouns.	• Learners can use participle adjectives to talk about free time activities at home.
	• **Vocabulary:** *characters, actors, a plot, animation, sound effects, special effects, soundtrack, graphics, cast, costumes, setting, screen time*	

21st-century skills
Emotional development: Understand the effects of too much screen time and apply to own personal experience.

Materials: Learner's Book pages 127–129; Workbook pages 92–93; film trailers (for Starter activity); a dice for each group of four learners; **Differentiated worksheets 8A, B and C**

LANGUAGE BACKGROUND

Participle adjectives

Some participles, for example *interesting/interested*, can be used as adjectives.

We usually use the **past** participle (-ed) to say **how** a person **feels**.

We use the **present** particle (-ing) to talk about the situation/person/thing that **caused** the feeling.

These adjectives are used with the verb *be*.

*Susanna was **frightened** of the giant spider in the kitchen. (Susanna **felt** frightened.)*

*The giant spider in the kitchen was very **frightening**. (The spider **caused** the feeling.)*

Common misconceptions

Misconception	How to identify	How to overcome
Learners sometimes confuse the past participle with the present participle. For example: • *The giant spider in the kitchen was very ~~frightened~~ frightening.* • *Susanna was ~~frightening~~ frightened of the giant spider in the kitchen.*	Write two sentences on the board, like these, that demonstrate the difference between the past participle and the present participle, and elicit the different meanings.	Practise using: • Activities 5–6 on page 93 of the Workbook • **Differentiated worksheets 8A, B and C.**

Starter ideas

Favourite film trailers (10 minutes)

• Gain interest in the subject of films and using screens for entertainment. Show learners a few film trailers for films that are popular and suitable for this age group, using subtitles, if possible. Please note that *Jurassic Park* has a PG/ PG-13 rating, so you may not want to show the whole film to your class.

• Ask learners what they think of the films and elicit participle adjectives to describe the films, for example *exciting/boring/interesting/frightening*.

Getting started (10 minutes)

• Focus on the big question: *How do we use screens for entertainment?* Check learners know what *screens* and *screen time* mean and ask them to give examples of activities that people do using screens.

• Circulate and offer support while learners discuss the questions in pairs.

> **Differentiation ideas:** Write sentence starters on the mini-whiteboard or in a worksheet for less confident speakers to use, for example: *I think / don't think the family are watching; I like … + ing because …*

• At the end of the activity, share responses as a class.

Answers
Learner's own answers.

> **Digital Classroom:** Use the video 'On-screen entertainment' to introduce the subject of on-screen entertainment. The i button will explain how to use the video.

Main teaching ideas

1 What do you like watching or playing at home? Which activities do you spend the most time on? Why? (10 minutes)

• Look at the pictures together and elicit what is happening in each one. Use the -ing form, for example *watching video clips online, listening to music, playing board games*.

• Do a quick class survey. Learners answer the questions and say what they like watching or playing at home, which activities they spend the most time on and why.

> **Differentiation ideas:** Write example sentences on the board for less confident speakers to refer to, for example: *I like listening to music and watching TV; I spend most time watching films because they are exciting.*

Answers
Learner's own answers.

2 Play the Dice Game! (10 minutes)

- Distribute a dice to each group of 3–4 learners. Tell learners they are going to talk about one of the topics in groups.

> **Differentiation ideas:** Prepare a worksheet with sentence starters and prompts for less confident speakers, for example: 1 *The funniest clip I have seen was about …; It was funny because …; I saw … last week/yesterday.*

- Circulate and offer support while learners take turns to roll the dice and talk about the activity next to the number. Make sure each learner has at least one opportunity to roll the dice and start talking about an activity.

Answers
Learner's own answers.

3 Which activities in Activity 2 have these features? Which can you see in the photos? (10 minutes)

- First, check learners understand the meaning of the words.

- If you expect learners will find the vocabulary challenging, make cards for learners to match. One card should have the feature words and the other card a definition of what it means: *characters* – the people in the film; *actors* – the people who play the characters; *plot* – the film's story; *animation* – a way to make drawings look like they move; *sound effects* – noises to make a film seem real; *special effects* – images or sounds that represent something real or imaginary; *soundtrack* – the music/songs from a film; *graphics* – images and designs from books/films; *cast* – another name for the actors; *costumes* – the clothes the actors wear; *setting* – the place where the film is.

- Circulate and offer support while learners match the features to the activities from Activity 2 and the photos.

- Alternatively, rather than everyone looking at all six activities, you could give groups of learners one or two categories from Activity 2 and ask them to share feedback with the rest of the class.

- As a class, share possible answers.

Answers
Activity 2 (possible answers):
Online video clip: *animation / sound effects / special effects / soundtrack / graphics*
Board game: *characters / graphics*
Books: *characters / a plot / graphics / setting*
Video games: *characters / a plot / animation / sound effects / special effects / soundtrack / graphics / setting*
Film or TV programme: *characters /actors / a plot / animation / sound effects / special effects / soundtrack / graphics / cast / costumes / setting*
Music: *sound effects / soundtrack*
In photos: *characters / a plot / animation / graphics / setting / special effects / sound effects / costumes*

4 Which activity in Activity 2 is Rory talking about? (10–15 minutes)

- Tell learners they are going to listen to a boy, Rory, talking to his aunt about something he likes doing.

- Encourage ideas about things that 11-year-olds like doing on a screen and features of these activities.

- Play the audio. Tell learners to listen for the activity and the features. Then see if anyone guessed correctly.

Audioscript: Track 57

See Learner's Book page 128

Auntie Rosie: Hi Rory. Maybe you can help me? I'm looking for an idea for my nephew's birthday. I don't see him very often, so I don't really know what he likes. He's the same age as you. What kind of things do you like doing at home?

Rory:	Lots of things, but when I'm not playing outside, I'm really into gaming …
Auntie Rosie:	Ah, video games … there's an idea! What kind of games do you like?
Rory:	Well, my favourite at the moment is Mega Max Zero. It's awesome!
Auntie Rosie:	OK … What's it about? Is there any kind of plot or story to it?
Rory:	Yeah, there is kind of a plot to it. It's basically about a superhero – that's Zero – who fights with an army of robots against humans who want to destroy them.
Auntie Rosie:	That sounds frightening! Is it violent at all?
Rory:	Well, there's fighting in it, but players fight with robots, so it's not real. But my mum was a bit worried, so she watched it with me, and saw that the animation and graphics are like cartoons, so it doesn't look real. But she still doesn't let me play it all the time.
Auntie Rosie:	OK, that's interesting. I can see her point. But what things do you like about it?
Rory:	There's loads of action and the graphics are amazing! I also like it because it's quite difficult to play and that makes it more exciting. When you play it, you have to think hard about your moves. There's no time to get bored! But you have to know when to stop …

Answers
Rory is talking about video games.
Features: he mentions characters, a *plot*, *animation* and *graphics*.

5 Listen again. Name three good points that Rory says about his video game. (10 minutes)

- Elicit features that learners would consider 'good points' and ask if they remember whether Rory mentioned any of these.

- Learners listen to check their ideas and write down the three good points that Rory says about his video game.

- If necessary, re-play the audio and pause after each good point.

Answers
1 Loads of action, 2 Graphics are amazing,
3 Difficult to play and that makes it more exciting

6 Why was Rory's mum worried about the game? (10 minutes)

- Look at the photo and briefly discuss as a class why Rory's mum might feel worried about him playing the game.

- Read the three questions. For each one, build up suggestions from the class on the board. Do a quick class survey for the third question.

Answers
Learner's own answers.
Suggested answers: Video games can be addictive, so it isn't a good idea to play them all the time. She was also worried that it might be violent so wouldn't be suitable for a young person. Too much screen use can be bad for eyesight and general well being; it is better to occupy your free time with a variety of activities that include physical activity and being outside. Learner's own answers.

Language focus – Participle adjectives (5–10 minutes)

- Write the two sentences from the Language background on the board: *Susanna was frightened of the giant spider in the kitchen. The giant spider in the kitchen was very frightening.*

- Elicit the difference between *frightening* and *frightened*.

- Read the Language focus together and check.

- Identify and write more participle adjectives on the board, for example *worried about, interested in*.

- In pairs, learners ask and answer questions using the participle adjectives on the board, such as: *Are you frightened of spiders? Are you worried about the English test? Are you interested in gaming? Yes, I am. / No, I'm not.*

> **Digital Classroom:** Use the activity 'Participle adjectives' to revise participle adjectives. The i button will explain how to use the activity.

- For extra practice, learners can use **Differentiated worksheets 8A, B and C**.

7 Can you complete the sentences with the correct participle adjective? (5–10 minutes)

- Circulate and offer support while learners decide which participle adjective to use. Check they are applying the principle that the *-ing* form refers to the person/thing that *causes* the feeling and *-ed* refers to the person who *feels* the feeling.

- Play the recording so that learners can listen and check.

Answers

a	frightening	c	exciting
b	interesting	d	bored

Audioscript: Track 58

See Learner's Book page 129

Narrator:	1
Auntie Rosie:	That sounds frightening! Is it violent at all?
Narrator:	2
Auntie Rosie:	OK, that's interesting. I can see her point.
Narrator:	3
Rory:	… it's quite difficult to play and that makes it more exciting.
Narrator:	4
Rory:	There's no time to get bored!

8 What do you like doing at home? Answer the questions about you and compare with your partner! (10 minutes)

- Give learners a few minutes to consider their responses to the questions before they compare their answers with a partner.

Answers

Learner's own answers.

9 Work in a small group. Compare your experiences and ideas. (10–15 minutes)

- First, brainstorm and list activities using screens on the board.

- Before learners get into small groups, read the questions and check learners understand them. Then ask learners, in their groups, to answer the questions.

- Circulate and encourage learners to reason critically about whether the amount of time they spend in front of screens is 'a lot' and why they think this is.

- **Emotional development:** Use this as an opportunity for learners to consider how much time they spend on a screen each day, and alternative activities they could be doing.

- At the end of the activity, ask the groups to share their responses. As a class, try to agree on an 'acceptable time' learners should spend in front of screens each day. Also discuss the problems/disadvantages of spending too much time in front of screens.

- On the board, build up a list of activities you can do that are away from screens.

Answers

Learner's own answers.

Plenary ideas

Reflection (5–10 minutes)

- In groups, learners reflect on the lesson and whether it has changed their attitudes towards screen time.

- Encourage learners to commit to doing at least one of the activities away from a screen from Activity 9.

Homework ideas

- Learners write a paragraph (up to 100 words) about their favourite screen activity.

> **Assessment ideas:** Write a short checklist as a class so that learners can self-assess their work before handing it in. For example: *Have I included how often / when / where I do the activity? Have I said why I like doing it? Have I used vocabulary from the lesson? Have I used participle adjectives?*

> **Workbook**
> Learners do Activities 1–7 on pages 92–93.

8.2 History: The first films

LEARNING PLAN

Learning objectives	Learning intentions	Success criteria
6Rm.01, 6Rd.04	• **Reading:** Understand, with support, most of the main points of short and extended texts. Deduce meaning from context, with support, in short and extended texts.	• Learners can understand, with support, most of the main points in a text about the history of film, deducing key words on the topic from context.
6Ug.03	• **Use of English:** Use a range of present simple active forms and begin to use passive forms.	• Learners can use past simple passive forms to talk about events on a film history timeline.
6Ug.04	• **Use of English:** Use a range of past simple active forms for habits and states and begin to use passive forms. • **Vocabulary:** *film projector, audience, screens, pianist, make up, popcorn*	• Learners can use a range of past simple active forms for habits and states and begin to use passive forms.

21st-century skills

Cross-curricular links: History: Learners choose a form of entertainment and find out about its history.

Materials: Learner's Book pages 130–31; Workbook pages 94–95; **Photocopiable 22**; a brief clip from a silent movie (e.g. Charlie Chaplin) and/or black and white film for Starter activity; for Activity 6, access to the internet/library access or photocopies with key facts about the history of these forms of entertainment: television, computer or video games, music players, **Photocopiable 22**

LANGUAGE BACKGROUND

Past simple passive

The passive is formed by the verb *be* (and sometimes, in informal English, the verb *get*) + the past participle. This lesson focuses on the past simple passive: *The film **was made** in 2019.*

The active form of this sentence is: *They **made** the film in 2019.*

In this case, the main verb of the active sentence is in the simple past, so the auxiliary *be* is in the simple past.

The passive is common in English because we don't need to say who does the action. When using the active voice, we need to include the person who did the action.

The passive focuses on an action/event, not the person who did it.

To say who did the action, we can add *by*; for example *The film was made in 2019 **by** Neal Moritz*

Common misconceptions

Misconception	How to identify	How to overcome
Learners use the active form instead of the passive. For example: *She [**was**] allowed to have a party at home.* *He [**was**] born four days later than me.*	Write active and passive sentences on the board and ask concept check questions about them. For example: • *Su was allowed to have a party at home.* • *Her parents allowed her to have a party.* • *Who allowed Su to have a party?* Ask: Which sentence tells us this? Which sentence is active/passive?	Practise using: • Activities 1–3 on pages 94–95 of the Workbook • **Photocopiable 22**.

Starter ideas

Cinema history (10 minutes)

• Introduce the topic of cinema history by showing a clip from a black and white film, and a clip from a silent movie.

• Explain that *movie* in American English and *film* in British English both have the same meaning. Elicit reasons why a *film* would be called a *movie,* for example there was no talking, only movement.

Main teaching ideas

1 Talk. How often do you go to the cinema? How else can you watch films? (10 minutes)

• Circulate and offer support while learners answer the questions in pairs. Challenge them to name all the places in 30 seconds.

• At the end of the 30 seconds, learners report back to the class. Build up a list of frequency expressions on the board, for example *hardly ever, every now and then, once a week,* etc; and establish how and where else you can watch films.

Answers

Learner's own answers.

Places to watch films (other than at the cinema): on TV, tablets, laptops, phones.

---

2 What do you know about the history of films? (10–15 minutes)

• Before learners read and listen to the text, ask them if they know anything about the history of films. Read the key words together and pre-teach the words from the Vocabulary list.

• Play the audio and ask learners to read along.

• Then ask learners, in pairs, to match the words in bold to the pictures.

> **Differentiation ideas:** If learners need support with this task, give them simple definitions for the six blue words to help them match the words to the pictures.

- Help learners consolidate their understanding of the text through a fun true/false quiz. Here are a few example questions.
  The first film projector was invented in 1981. **False (1891).**
  An audience first paid to watch moving pictures in 1985. **False (1895).**
  It cost a dollar to watch the first films. **False (5 cents).**
  From 1907 to 1927, films were silent. **True.**
  Films with sound were called 'speakies'. **False ('talkies').**
  Films were only made in black and white until 1935. **True.**

Audioscript: Track 59

See Learner's Book page 130

Answers
a make-up, b popcorn, c audience, d screens, e pianist, f film projector

---

3 How many years are mentioned in the text? Why are they important in the history of film? (10 minutes)

- Focus on the first year that is mentioned (1891). Check learners know how to say it, i.e. eighteen ninety-one.

- Elicit why this year is mentioned (it is when the first film projector was invented).

- Allow time for learners to scan the text and underline the rest of the years, before they discuss with their partner why each year is important in the history of film.

Answers
Years are mentioned seven times in the text.
1891: the first film projector was invented (by the Edison company).
1895: an audience could watch moving pictures for the first time.
1907: people watched silent films in cinemas on big screens.

1912: audiences could buy popcorn to eat in cinemas for the first time.
1927: sound first appeared in films.
1928: Mickey Mouse made his first appearance in a film.
1935: the first movies appeared in colour.

Use of English – Past simple passive (10 minutes)

- Introduce the past simple passive by asking learners: *When was the first film projector invented?* Write the answer on the board: *The first film projector was invented in 1891.*

- Highlight *was invented* in a different colour, or circle the words.

- Repeat the process with another sentence, such as *When were the first moving pictures shown to an audience? The first moving pictures **were shown** in 1895.*

- Then ask learners some concept check questions to establish meaning and function. For example: *Are the sentences in the present or past tense? In the sentences, what is the action?* (invented, shown). *Do we know who did the action? Is it important?* (No)

- Talk about when and how we use the past simple passive (see Language background). Make sure learners notice that *was* can change to *were*.

Workbook

Learners do Activities 1–3 on pages 94–95.

> **Digital Classroom:** Use the grammar presentation 'Past simple passive' to revise the past simple passive. The i button will explain how to use the grammar presentation.

4 Read the Use of English box. How do we make a past simple passive sentence? (10 minutes)

- Focus learners on Activity 4 and ask them, in pairs, to complete the rule for forming a past simple passive sentence.

Answers
was or <u>were</u> + the <u>past</u> / ~~present~~ **form** of the verb

---

5 Create a timeline! (5–10 minutes)

- Demonstrate the activity by looking at the example together.

- Circulate and offer support while learners complete the sentences using the correct form of the verbs. Remind them that if the verb refers to a plural noun, they should use the plural of *be* (*were*).

- Allow time for learners to match the sentences to the years on the timeline. Encourage them to look back at the text on page 130 to help them.

- Give class feedback on the correct answers.

Answers
a where shown (Example), b was filmed, c was sold, d were made, e was played
1 1895 – a (Example), 2 1907 – e, 3 1912 – c, 4 1927 – d, 5 1935 – b

> **Digital Classroom:** Use the activity 'Which year do you hear?' to reinforce listening skills. The i button will explain how to use the activity.

6 Create your own timeline. (20–30 minutes)

- Explain to learners that they are going to create their own timeline, like the one they completed in Activity 5.

- Allow learners a few minutes to choose one of the forms of entertainment.

- Circulate and offer support while learners research its history. Remind them to focus on the key events.

> **Differentiation ideas:** Challenge more confident learners to choose six key events. Support less confident readers and writers by asking them to focus on four events.

- Circulate and offer support while learners make sentences, write the years and create a timeline.

> **Assessment ideas:** Provide written feedback on the timelines, focusing on the use of appropriate vocabulary and on how well learners have used past tenses, especially the past simple passive.

CROSS-CURRICULAR LINKS

History: Learners choose a form of entertainment and find out about its history (for example, television, video games).

Answers
Learner's own answers.

Plenary ideas

Share the timelines (10 minutes)

- Ask learners to share information about their timelines with the rest of the class, so that they can find out about the history of the forms of entertainment they didn't research.

- Encourage learners to use the past simple passive and to practise saying the different years. Give learners lots of praise for presenting their timelines to the rest of the class.

- Learners practise using the past simple passive to talk about films using **Photocopiable 22**.

Homework ideas

Using the past simple, learners write an entertainment quiz to help them remember what they have learned in the lesson; for example, *What first appeared in films in 1927? (Sound.)* Photocopy and distribute sentences that learners wrote about each form of entertainment so that questions on all the forms of entertainment can be included in the quizzes.

Workbook
Learners do Activities 1–3 on pages 94–95.

8.3 Talk about it: Too much tech?

LEARNING PLAN

Learning objectives	Learning intentions	Success criteria
6Ld.04	• **Listening:** Understand, with support, most specific information and detail of short and extended talk.	• Learners can understand specific points made in a discussion about scheduled screen time.
6Sor.01, 6Sor.02	• **Speaking:** Link sentences using an increasing range of connectives. Briefly summarise what others say, with support, in a range of exchanges in order to achieve a shared outcome.	• Learners can express opinions and reactions to the points made in the audio about scheduled screen time.
6Uv.04	• **Use of English:** Use a wide range of adverbs of definite and indefinite time.	• Learners can summarise points made from a group discussion and communicate them to another group.
	• **Vocabulary:** *schedule, screen time*	• Learners can use adverbs of definite and indefinite time to express their own screen habits.

21st-century skills

Social responsibility: Understand ways that you can look after your own wellbeing.

Collaboration: Collaborate with others in group tasks, to work towards a shared outcome.

Materials: Learner's Book pages 132–133; Workbook pages 96–97; **Photocopiable 23**

Common misconceptions

Misconception	How to identify	How to overcome
The position of time adverbs in a sentence is not usually flexible, which learners find challenging. For example: *He ~~makes always~~ makes jokes.* *That was the best day I ~~ever have~~ ever had.* *The house ~~still is~~ still there, but nobody lives in it.* *I ~~watch usually~~ watch documentary programmes.* *I enjoyed the ~~last night~~ concert last night.* *She asked me, 'Would you sing with me at the ~~tomorrow~~ concert tomorrow?'*	Compile a worksheet with common errors. Go through each one and talk through the correct order.	Practise using: • Activities 1–4 on pages 96–97 of the Workbook.

Starter ideas

Screen time (5 minutes)

- Explain to learners that this lesson is going to continue the theme of Lesson 8.1 and discuss how to manage time spent on screen-time activities.

- Pre-teach expressions that learners will hear and read in the listening activity and the advert, for example *addicted to screens, (un)sociable, distract(ed), bad-tempered*.

Main teaching ideas

1 In pairs, discuss the questions. (5–10 minutes)

- Briefly review learner's ideas about screen time from Lesson 8.1.

- Give learners a few minutes to discuss the questions with a partner.

- Conduct class feedback and list key ideas on the board, particularly learner's comments about the effects of too much screen time. Establish the average time the class spends using screens per week.

Answers
Learner's own answers.

2 Read the advertisement. What is it selling? (10 minutes)

- Before learners read the advertisement, read the questions.

- Tell learners not to worry if they don't understand every word – they should focus on finding out what the advert is selling and comparing their ideas from Activity 1 with the advert, particularly in the *Hard truths about screen time!* section.

- When learners have finished reading the advert, ask them to check their answers with a partner. They should tick the points from the advert that apply to them.

Answers
The advertisement is selling a mobile phone app that allows parents to limit internet access/screen time on their children's devices.
Learner's own answers.

Possible effects of too much screen time: make you tired; stop you being sociable; make you bad-tempered; distract you from school work; stop you sleeping properly; make you addicted to your device.

3 Listen to Mr Stern's class discussing screen-time schedules. (5–10 minutes)

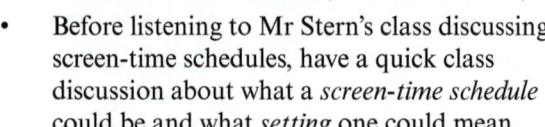

- Before listening to Mr Stern's class discussing screen-time schedules, have a quick class discussion about what a *screen-time schedule* could be and what *setting* one could mean.

- Ask learners to predict how long experts say children of their age should spend looking at screens.

- Play the audio and allow learners a minute to discuss the question with a partner.

- **Social responsibility:** Learners begin to understand ways that you can look after your own wellbeing by reducing screen time.

Audioscript: Track 60

See Learner's Book page 132

Mr Stern: OK everyone, we've talked today about what you do on your devices and how much time you spend looking at your screens. Now, according to the experts, children your age shouldn't have more than one or two hours of screen-time a day. Did you know that? Yes, a lot of us spend a lot longer than that – especially when we're not at school. So now we're going to talk about setting a screen-time schedule. This is a limit on the amount of time you spend on your devices, so you can have more time to do other things. We all know how hard it can be to leave our devices alone, and this isn't always very good for us. This time limit helps you balance it all out.

Girl: Do our parents set it?

Mr Stern: Yes, your parents or whoever looks after you at home. Yes, that's the idea …

Answers

A screen-time schedule is a limit on the amount of time children can spend on their devices. The schedule gives users an allocated amount of time to spend on devices.

4 Listen to the children discussing an example of a screen-time schedule. (10 minutes)

- Play the audio so learners can find out how many hours of screen time the children are allowed in one week.

- Tell learners not to worry about understanding every word, as they will have the chance to listen for more details later.

- Learners discuss their answer in pairs.

- As a class, share feedback.

Audioscript: Track 61

See Learner's Book page 132

Mr Stern: So let's imagine that you have a limit of one hour of screen time daily on schooldays, and two hours a day on weekends, or when you're not at school. But you get to decide how you are going to organise that time. Should it be equal time every day? Or more screen-time at weekends and less during the week? Now discuss in your groups, then summarise your points to share with the class at the end. Off you go …

Boy 1: OK, one hour a day and two hours at the weekend – that's nine hours total. So, what you do think? Equal time every day?

Girl 1: No, I think it's better to have more screen time at the weekend and less on a school day. Then you can watch and play more things at the weekend. What does everyone else think?

Boy 1: I think that's a good idea.

Boy 2: Me too. But what if you have a friend over on a school night and you want to play on the X-box? Then you need more time on a weekday.

Girl 1: Then you could have more time on that day and less time the next day. I think that's how it works.

Boy 1: Yes, that sounds right. But what about when you use your tablet or the internet for homework? Mr Stern … Does it count if you need to use the internet for homework? I often use my tablet for homework.

Mr Stern: No, that wouldn't count towards the weekly allowance – as long as you were just using your device for homework! The screen-time schedule is just for free time activities.

Boy 1: OK, that's good. OK, are we ready to do a summary of our points?

Answers

Nine hours of screen-time are allowed in a week.

5 Listen again. What have the children decided for their schedule? (10 minutes)

- Before learners listen to the audio again, check they understand the meaning of *allowance*.

- Circulate and offer support as learners work in pairs to correct the errors in the summary. Make sure they have a copy of the corrected summary in their notebooks, as they will need this for Activity 8.

> **Differentiation ideas:** Organise learners into pairs. Less confident listeners and writers will benefit from language support and their partners will consolidate their understanding of the listening text.

- Give class feedback at the end of the activity.

Answers

1 Hours of screen time per **week** = 9 hours (not 'weekend').
2 There is **more** screen time scheduled **at weekends**.
3 If you have more screen time on one day, **you have less time the next day.**
4 Screen time needed for homework is **not** included in the weekly allowance.

6 Listen. What two points do the children add to their summary? (10 minutes)

- Before listening, tell learners to imagine they are the children who are discussing the schedule summary and that they want to add two ideas to it. Elicit suggestions from learners about things they could add, like how they could 'earn' more screen time, when they should/shouldn't use screens, and if their parents should limit their screen time too.

- Play the audio to see if the children had the same ideas. Ask learners to discuss the question in pairs. Then share feedback as a class.

- Ask learners to add the two points to the summary they have written in their notebooks.

Audioscript: Track 62

See Learner's Book page 133

Boy 2:	Wait, one more thing … maybe we could earn extra hours for doing jobs around the house or getting good grades?
Girl 1:	Yes, great idea! So, we can earn more screen time for doing jobs or getting good grades – add that to our list.
Boy 1:	And I've got one more point to make. How about having no-tech zones in the house? So that means places or times when no technology is allowed. For example, when everyone is eating together. And everyone has to stick to the rules, not just us. And that includes parents! Parents must put their devices down too!

Boy 2 and

Girl 1:   Yes, agreed!

Answers

1. They can earn extra hours for doing jobs around the house or getting good grades at school.
2. Introduce no-tech zones in the house: places or times when no technology is allowed (for example, at mealtimes).

Use of English – Adverbs of time and frequency (5 minutes)

- Read the Use of English box together.

- Elicit other examples of adverbs of time and frequency (for example, *yesterday, tomorrow, weekly, yearly, often, sometimes, rarely, regularly*). Build up a list on the board under two headings – *Definite time* and *Indefinite time*.

- Learners can practise using adverbs of time and frequency using **Photocopiable 23**.

> **Workbook**
>
> Learners do Activities 1–4 on pages 96–97.

> **Digital Classroom:** Use the activity 'Adverbs of time and frequency' to revise adverbs of time and frequency. The i button will explain how to use the activity.

7 How do you and your family use your screen time? (5 minutes)

- Circulate and offer support while learners ask and answer the questions with a partner and circle the adverbs.

- Share feedback as a class. Ask learners whether each adverb describes a *definite time* or an *indefinite time*.

Answers
Adverbs:
a weekly, **b** normally, **c** usually, **d** sometimes, **e** tonight
Learner's own answers.

Speaking tip – Giving opinions and responding (5 minutes)

- Explain to learners that they are going to present their own ideas for managing screen time.

- Read the phrases and questions to give learners prompts and suggestions for giving opinions and responding to their group.

Answers
Learner's own answers.

8 Present it! Managing our screen time. (25 minutes)

- Before learners start their discussions, refer them to the summary in their notebooks from the listening activities.

- Circulate and offer support while learners discuss the children's ideas, saying if there is anything they would change. Encourage learners to use the phrases in the Speaking tip and time adverbs.

- Try to ensure that all group members contribute to making the summary.

- **Collaboration:** Learners work together to present a summary of their ideas on managing screen time.

- Learners compare their ideas with another group.

> **Assessment ideas:** Create a short checklist for learners to use before comparing their ideas with another group. They can also use the checklist to give feedback on the other group's summary. For example: *We have summarised whether the ideas would work for us; We have said what we would change; We have used the suggestions from the Speaking tip; We have used adverbs of time.*

- Over the next week, learners keep a diary and record how much time they spend on-screen each day.

- As a class, discuss activities that learners like doing at home away from screens. Refer back to discussions in Lesson 8.1 – have learners tried any of the activities mentioned there?

Answers
Learner's own answers.

Plenary ideas

Consolidation (15 minutes)
Learners use their summaries to make a poster about how to reduce screen time.

Homework ideas

Over the next week, learners record how much time they spend on-screen a day. They will compare with their classmates in the next lesson.

Workbook
Learners do Activities 1–4 on pages 96–97.

8.4 Write about it: Creating film scenes

LEARNING PLAN

Learning objectives	Learning intentions	Success criteria
6Rd.04 6Wor.01	• **Reading:** Deduce meaning from context, with support, in short and extended texts. • **Writing:** Punctuate short texts with some accuracy when writing independently. • **Vocabulary:** *science-fiction, comedy, horror, adventure, drama, action, historical, laughed, sniggered, insisted, sighed, whispered*	• Learners can match sentences and dialogue to storyboard pictures, using the pictures to help with comprehension. • Learners can continue the story on the storyboard, creating sentences and dialogue with the correct punctuation.

21st-century skills

Critical thinking opportunity: Identify a suitable title for a film.

Creative thinking: Create a storyboard and dialogue for a film idea (continuing on from a model storyboard).

Materials: Learner's Book pages 134–35; Workbook pages 98–99; poster card for the storyboards (1 sheet for each group of 3–4 learners); Unit 8 sample answer; **Photocopiable 24**

Starter ideas

Lesson 3 feedback and Film plot (10 minutes)

- First, share feedback about how long learners spend on-screen. When they started recording their screen time in a diary, were they surprised at how long they spent on-screen a day? How does screen time compare between learners?

- Then introduce the topic for this lesson: creating scenes for a film. Describe a film plot that is suitable for children of this age. If you aren't familiar with any, try looking for a review in English online. Don't say the name of the film but do say where (you think) the writer(s) got their ideas from. For example: *It's about a very fast, small blue animal from another planet. At the start, the animal escapes to Earth because someone wants to steal his superpowers … I think the writers got their ideas from a video game.* (Answer: Sonic the Hedgehog)

Main teaching ideas

1 What are your favourite film plots? (10 minutes)

- Circulate and offer support, including giving key vocabulary, while learners work in pairs and tell their partners about their favourite film plots. Encourage speculation about how film makers get their ideas.

> **Differentiation ideas:** If learners need support with this task, give them a worksheet with some sentence starters and useful vocabulary.

- At the end of the activity, invite learners to share their favourite film plots. Use this as an opportunity to give learners ideas and write useful vocabulary on the board, as they will be writing their own storyboard later.

Answers
Learner's own answers.

2 Listen to the film trailer and look at the storyboard. What kind of film is it? (10 minutes)

- Before listening to the audio, read the names of the types of films. Check learners understand them by eliciting names of films for each one.

- Look at the pictures. Explain that this is a *storyboard*; its purpose is to show the main scenes in a film. Point out that the pictures in this storyboard are not in the order of the story; learners will match them later.

- Elicit ideas about what kind of film it could be. Play the film trailer and check.

- If learners usually associate *scream* with *being frightened* and therefore *horror* films, explain that this is an expression for when something is extremely funny.

Audioscript: Track 63

See Learner's Book page 134

Get ready to fall down laughing! Terrible twins, Horis and Boris are back and they're crazier than ever! Dad thinks that a fun-filled weekend in the great outdoors will encourage the brothers to 'bond'. How wrong can he be?!

Answers
A comedy film.

3 Choose the best title or write your own. (5 minutes)

- Read the titles together. Check learners know the meaning of *revenge*. In pairs, give learners time to discuss which title they prefer and why, and/or to write an alternative title.

> **Critical thinking opportunity:** Rather than indicating that any one answer is *correct*, encourage learners to reason critically and give reasons to support/justify their opinions.

- Invite learners to share their opinions and titles with the class. Have a class vote for the 'best' title.

Answers
Learner's own answers (if choosing their own title) or any answer a–c. (Note: while c is the only title that picks up on the trick Boris plays on his brother, this will not be clear to learners at this stage of the lesson.)

4 Match the sentences to a picture or thought bubble on the storyboard. (10 minutes)

- Read the sentences together. Check learners understand the meaning of *putting up the tent, trouble in mind, cheerful, promise, nicest spot* and *spotted the ants' nest*.

- Match the first sentence to picture 1. Then ask learners to match the remaining sentences in pairs.

- Give class feedback on the correct answers.

Answers
Picture 1 – a, Picture 2 – c, Picture 3 – d, Picture 4 – b, Picture 5 – f, Picture 6 – e

> **Digital Classroom:** Use the activity 'Match the sound effects' to explore using sound effects in film. The i button will explain how to use the activity.

5 What sound effects and special effects could you add to these scenes? Make the sounds! (10 minutes)

- Look at Scene 1 together. Encourage learners to think of sounds and effects that would bring the scene to life, like noises for fighting, such as *thumping* sounds.

- Try to make this activity as light-hearted as possible. Rather than insisting on learners using words for sounds and effects, get them to actually make the sounds.

- Circulate and offer support while learners discuss, in pairs, what sound effects and special effects they could add to the other scenes. Encourage them to use phrases such as *Why don't we add …?* and *Let's put a … in.*

Answers

Learner's own answers. Ideas for sound/special effects:

Scene 1   brothers fighting: cartoon sound effects for fighting – punches, claps and thuds.

Scene 2   Dad's idea: a light bulb appears above his head with a pinging sound.

Scene 3   car journey: sound of car driving along with menacing music, signalling trouble ahead.

Scene 4   at the campsite: countryside sounds – birds singing, bees buzzing, crickets chirping (but with faint menacing music playing faintly in background).

Scene 5   the ants' nest: menacing music gets louder. Rustling and squeaking sounds for the ants.

Scene 6   Boris indicating spot for Horis's sleeping bag: menacing music gets louder.

Writing tip – Use direct speech and reporting verbs (5–10 minutes)

- Ask learners to close their books. Write the example sentences from the Writing tip on the board without punctuation.
- Read the lines to learners, emphasising *sniggered* and *sighed*.
- Invite learners to come to the board and add each item of punctuation to the sentences, i.e. speech marks, commas and then the exclamation mark.
- Read the Writing tip together, which explains the basic rules for using direct speech and reporting verbs. Also elicit that exclamation marks show emotions and feelings, especially when someone is shocked, surprised or upset, if they speak loudly or shout, or say something funny.

6   Read the Writing tip box and add punctuation to the next four scenes. Change said to a different verb from the box. (10–15 minutes)

- As a class, look at the reporting verbs in the box and elicit their precise meaning. Mime the verbs to help learners understand the meaning.
- Write the first sentence on the board. Elicit where the speech marks and exclamation mark should go.
- Discuss which reporting verb from the box could go here. (Elicit that what he is saying is a secret.)

- Circulate and offer support while learners punctuate the remaining sentences.
- Give class feedback – show the correct punctuation on the board.

Answers

Scene 7   'So that's why he wants me to sleep there … Well, I've got other ideas!' **whispered** Horis.

Scene 8   'No, Boris, I insist! I can't possibly take that place. You must sleep there!' **insisted** Horis. 'No Horis, really, I couldn't … YOU must sleep there!' **insisted** Boris.

Scene 9   'Tell you what, boys … I'll take that place,' **sighed** Dad.

Scene 10   'Hee hee … serves Boris right!' **sniggered** Horis.

7   Create a storyboard to continue the story. (30–45 minutes)

- **Creative thinking:** Learners follow the instructions to continue a storyboard and dialogue for a film idea.
- Offer support while each group brainstorms ideas for their scenes and write notes.

> **Assessment ideas:** Before learners start Step 2, show them the Unit 8 sample answer without the mark scheme comments. As a class, evaluate the sample answer's weaknesses and strengths. Also look at the checklist on page 135 of the Learner's Book, so that learners know what they are aiming to achieve with their storyboard.

- Circulate and offer support while learners create each scene, including dialogue and ideas for music and special effects. Try to ensure that each group member has a chance to contribute.

> **Differentiation ideas:** Extend the activity by asking more confident groups to create four scenes with three sentences each. Less confident groups could focus on creating three scenes with two sentences each.

- Remind learners to create a simple drawing for each scene.

> **Assessment ideas:** Once learners have finished their first draft, ask them to work through the checklist in **Photocopiable 24** again to self-assess their work.

- Learners create their final storyboard, transforming it into a poster.

Plenary ideas

Reflection (5–10 minutes)

*   Learners look at other groups' storyboards. Praise each group for the work they have completed.
*   As a class, discuss which ideas learners like best.

Homework ideas

Learners write about 100 words about how they created their film scenes using the past simple tense,

> **Workbook**
>
> Learners do Activities 1–6 on pages 98–99.

8.5 Read and respond: *Jurassic Park*

LEARNING PLAN

Learning objectives	Learning intentions	Success criteria
6Rd.01, 6Rm.02, 6Rd.04	• **Reading:** Understand, with support, most specific information and detail in short and extended texts. Read independently a range of short, simple fiction and non-fiction texts with confidence and enjoyment. Deduce meaning from context, with support, in short and extended texts.	• Learners can read and enjoy an extract from *Jurassic Park*, understanding specific details in the story and deducing unknown vocabulary from context.
6Sc.05	• **Speaking:** Pronounce familiar words and phrases clearly; begin to use intonation and place stress at word, phrase and sentence level appropriately. • **Vocabulary:** *shade, emerged, hind, palm, weight, scrambled*	• Learners can recognise and practise pronouncing hard and soft 'th' sounds in common words.

21st-century skills

Critical thinking opportunity: Identify characters, setting, plots and themes in fictional storylines for films and video games.

Materials: Learner's Book pages 136–139; Workbook pages 100–101; for the Starter: a suitable video clip for this age from *Jurassic Park*, with interesting special effects

Starter ideas

Special effects clip (10 minutes)

*   Explain to learners that in this lesson they are going to read a storyline of a film with special effects.
*   Interest learners in the topic by showing a video clip of a film with interesting special effects. Afterwards, briefly discuss the effects – what do learners think of them?

Main teaching ideas

1   What are the best special effects you've seen in films? (10 minutes)

*   On the board, build up the names of popular films (suitable for this age group) that contain special effects.
*   Vote for the film with the best special effects that learners have seen.
*   Encourage ideas about how learners think special effects are created in films. Teach key words such as *computer-generated, mechanical, photographic, pyrotechnics*.

Answers

Learner's own answers. Suggested answers:
How special effects are created in films:
traditionally (in films with no CGI), special
effects can be *photographic*, using techniques with
cameras to produce special visual effects; they can
be *mechanical*, using props, scenery, models and
special machines that produce weather extremes
or *pyrotechnics* (effects with fire). Special effects
can also be produced using make-up (to change
an actor's physical appearance) and set design (for
example, using special effects to build constructions
that will easily collapse). However, since the early
1990s, Computer Generated Imagery (CGI) has
played a major part in creating special effects; many
of the effects previously produced photographically
or mechanically are now produced with CGI,
resulting in cheaper and safer ways to create special
effects in film.

2 Have you ever seen the *Jurassic Park* films? (5 minutes)

- Ask learners if they have seen any of the films
  and/or know what they are about. Look at
  the pictures in the Learner's Book and ask
  questions to elicit information about the film.
  For example: *Who/What is in the first film?*
  (Dinosaurs, scientists) *What is Jurassic Park?*
  (An amusement/theme park with dinosaurs)
  How do the dinosaurs escape? (Someone breaks
  the code.) Write ideas on the board but don't
  say at this point if they are correct or not, as
  learners will check in the next activity.

- Elicit suggestions about why the first *Jurassic
  Park* film was important in cinema history. Ask
  *How did they create the dinosaurs? Was this a new
  or old method?* Again, write ideas on the board
  but don't say at this point if they are correct.

Answers

Learner's own answers. Suggested answer:
The *Jurassic Park* films are about a group of
scientists who visit an amusement park, which
is inhabited by cloned dinosaurs. The dinosaurs
are supposed to be confined in a controlled
environment, but sabotage sets them free, putting
the scientists and other people on the island in great
danger. They attempt to escape the island.

3 Read the introduction to find out. Were your predictions correct? (10 minutes)

- Play the recording. Learners read and listen
  to the introduction, then discuss the question
  with a partner.

- As a class, share feedback.

Audioscript: Track 64

See Learner's Book page 136

Answers

Learner's own answers. Suggested answers:
Why the first *Jurassic Park* film was important
in cinema history: it is generally regarded as the
first film to make major advances on digital film
making, in the use of CGI. Afterwards, many other
films followed its lead in creating special effects
primarily using CGI.

4 Read and listen to an extract from the novel, *Jurassic Park*. (10 minutes)

- Tell learners that they are now going to listen
  to and read part of the novel, *Jurassic Park*.

- Read the rubric. Make it clear that learners
  do not have to understand everything. They
  just need to identify the strange meeting Tina
  has near the beach. They will have the chance
  to read and listen to the extract again, and to
  answer the questions later.

- Play the recording so learners can listen
  and read.

- Learners answer the question in pairs.

- Share feedback as a class.

Audioscript: Track 65

See Learner's Book pages 137–138

Answers

Tina meets a strange lizard that she thinks is cute.

5 Read and listen again. Answer the questions after each section. (15 minutes)

- Read the questions together and check learners understand *notice*. Look at the glossary terms together. Then learners listen to and read the extract again.

- Circulate and offer support while learners answer the questions in pairs.

> **Differentiation ideas:** Organise learners into pairs. Less confident readers and listeners will benefit from language support and their partners will consolidate their understanding of the extract.

- At the end of the activity, give class feedback on the answers.

Answers
a   Tina and her parents were at the beach.
b   No, Tina was near the sea.
c   Bird tracks.
d   A lizard came out of the jungle.
e   It stood on two legs.
f   No, she thought it was cute.
g   No, it came towards her (without fear).
h   The lizard was about the same size as a chicken.
i   It jumped on Tina's hand and then moved quickly up her arm towards her face.

6 Discuss the questions below in groups. (10–15 minutes)

> **Critical thinking opportunity:** Read questions 1–3 together; then ask learners to work in small groups to discuss them. They should be prepared to give feedback to the class afterwards.

- After feedback, focus learners on questions 4–6 and follow the same procedure.

Answers
a–c Learner's own answers.
Suggested answers:
d   It has lots of exciting action scenes; the plot is original and contains a lot of drama, action and suspense (Will people on the island manage to escape the dinosaurs?); it is very exciting to look at (e.g. beautiful, dramatic, tropical landscapes; huge, fierce dinosaurs).
e   For example: *The Harry Potter books; Life of Pi; The Lion, the Witch and the Wardrobe; Diary of a Wimpy Kid; Disney classics –*

Adventures of Pinocchio, Bambi, Into the Woods, Snow White and the Seven Dwarves, etc. There are many other examples.
f   Stories with a simple plot structure (i.e. not too many twists and turns); a varied dramatic element, i.e. lots of 'highs' and 'lows'; a 'problem' and a quest for a solution; a variety of sympathetic characters and villains; interesting and varied settings; stories containing a moral element or 'life lesson'.

Reading tip – Guess meaning from context (5 minutes)

- Ask learners to name strategies they use when reading a text that contains lots of difficult words.

- Elicit that the most helpful strategy is to read the whole sentence to get an idea of the word's meaning and then guess the word. The words and phrases around the unfamiliar word usually give you clues. Tell learners it is also helpful to look at pictures around the text, the theme of the paragraph and at any headings or titles.

7 Look at the words in blue in the text. Guess their meaning by looking at the other words around them. (10 minutes)

- Focus learners on the words in blue in the story. Tell them to read the sentence before and after each word and look for clues in the meanings of other words. They should then choose the correct definition for each word.

- As a class, look at the first blue word, *shade*. Read the sentence before and after *shade*. Ask learners which words/phrases help them understand the meaning (e.g. *move out of the sun, palm trees*).

- Encourage learners to find the correct definition, i.e. a place with no sunlight.

- Circulate and offer support while learners complete questions 2–6 in pairs. If learners ask for help, point to the words/phrases around the word in question to help them see that the clues are in the text.

- Give class feedback on the correct answers.

Answers
1 a, 2 a, 3 b, 4 a, 5 b, 6 a

> **Digital Classroom:** Use the activity 'Lizards and dinosaurs!' to reinforce reading comprehension and vocabulary from the *Jurassic Park* extract in the Learner's Book. The i button will explain how to use the activity.

8 Listen and repeat these *th* words from the story. (10 minutes)

- Demonstrate a hard *th* sound ('th' in 'the') and soft *th* sound ('th' in 'thick'). Repeat until learners can hear the difference.

- Play the audio and ask learners to listen and repeat the words. Establish which have a hard and soft *th* sound.

- Put learners in small groups. Ask them to come up with as many other words as they can with words containing *th*. Give a short time limit. Then ask learners to read the words in their groups and establish whether the *th* is hard or soft.

Audioscript: Track 66

See Learner's Book page 139

Answers
Hard sound: **c** the, **f** then
Soft sound: **a** threw, **b** breath, **d** thick, **e** thought

9 Values. Looking after yourself. (15 minutes)

- Remind learners that in the extract, Tina is on holiday with her parents in Costa Rica. She wanders off from her parents and meets a lizard.

- As a class, read the first two questions. Check learners understand *wise* and *prevented*.

- Circulate and offer support while learners discuss the questions with a partner.

- Conduct class feedback. Then focus learners on question 3 and ask them to think of at least three points for each example. Encourage learners to use the sentence starters in the Learner's Book.

> **Differentiation ideas:** Challenge more confident pairs to think of five points. Less confident pairs should focus on thinking of two points.

Answers
General suggestions:
- Always let an adult you trust know where you are, where you are going and who you are with.
- Don't talk to people you don't know.
- Remember your home phone number.
- Know what number to call if there is an emergency.

Plenary ideas

Consolidation (10 minutes)

Ask learners to discuss what they would have done in Tina's situation.

Homework ideas

With parental supervision, invite learners to watch (short) video clips from the film *Jurassic Park*.

Workbook

Learners do Activities 1–6 on pages 100–101.

8.6 Project challenge

LEARNING PLAN

Learning objectives	Learning intentions	Success criteria
6Sc.06, 6Sc.02, 6So.01	• **Speaking:** Begin to produce and maintain stretches of language comprehensibly, allowing for hesitation and reformulation, especially in longer stretches of free production. Describe people, places and objects, and routine past and present actions and events. Express opinions, feelings and reactions.	• Learners can deliver a presentation reviewing a film or video game, expressing a personal recommendation or reaction.
6Wc.02	• **Writing:** Write, with support, short texts which describe people, places and objects, and routine past and present actions and events.	• Learners can create a dramatic voiceover and poster for a film idea.

21st-century skills

Collaboration: Collaborate with others in group tasks, to work towards a shared outcome.

Materials: Learner's Book pages 140–141; Workbook page 102; Optional: 1 dice per pair/group of learners (for Starter activity); poster card/presentation software; recording equipment; examples of other learner's work; Unit 8 project checklists; End of Unit 8 test

Starter ideas

Raise interest in the projects (10–15 minutes)

- Tell learners they are either going to make a film or video game review presentation (Project A) or create a film poster and voiceover (Project B).

- If possible, raise interest in the projects by presenting examples of learner's work on similar topics from other classes or the internet.

- Revise new vocabulary from the unit, which learners may need for the challenges. For instance, play the dice game from Lesson 8.1. This time, the numbers on the dice represent 'Talk for 30 seconds about …': *1 My favourite types of film; 2 Cinema history; 3 What I know about Jurassic Park; 4 The plot of my favourite film; 5 Screen time; 6 Where I watch films.*

Main teaching ideas

Introduce and complete projects (60 minutes)

Encourage learners to choose one of the projects and then follow the steps for their chosen project.

Project A: A film or video game review presentation

- Organise learners into small groups. Make sure each group chooses a film or video game to review – one they know enough about to write a presentation. Make suggestions to guide them if they can't decide.

- When learners are drafting their presentation, make sure they follow the headings in Step 2 to help them structure it; encourage them to use sequencing phrases and descriptive words. Circulate and help learners to summarise the plot so that this part of the presentation isn't too long. For example: It's a story … about a boy called … who …. One day he … but ….

- Give learners time to practise their presentations in their groups. Make sure each learner has a different section to talk about. Remind learners to start by giving the purpose of the presentation, for example: *Today we are going to talk about …*

- If adding slides with pictures or a short video clip isn't possible, learners can draw pictures.

- **Collaboration:** Learners collaborate to complete the presentation as a group; each group member has their own role in the project to work towards a shared outcome.

- Learners present their film or video game review to the class.

> **Assessment ideas:** Learners use the project checklist to evaluate the reviews, including the adjectives used to describe each film or game.

Project B: Create a film poster and voiceover

- Organise learners into small groups. Play the audio for the film trailers, so learners can match them to a film type and say what other kinds of films they know.

- Support learners while they choose a type of film to work on.

- Circulate and support learners as they discuss their ideas for a film storyline and write notes. Remind them that they only need a basic story idea.

- Encourage learners to use sentences and/or dialogue to make their voiceovers exciting and memorable. If helpful, play the audio from Step 1 again to give them ideas.

- Give learners time to practise reading their voiceover aloud – make sure each group member has a different part to say. Remind learners not to say the film title.

- Encourage learners to have fun creating the title and visuals for their film poster. Ask them to think about what makes them take notice of a film/video game advert/poster.

- **Collaboration:** Learners collaborate to complete the poster and voiceover as a group; each group member has their own role to work towards a shared outcome.

> **Assessment ideas:** Learners use the project checklist to evaluate the posters and voiceovers, including whether the link between the voiceover and the film poster is clear.

Audioscript: Track 67

See Learner's Book page 141

Narrator:	1
Man:	An adventure too big for one land …
Boy:	Torah – don't leave us …
Torah:	But I have to … I am defender of the Secret Scroll … I must do all I can to save it …
Man:	She knew what she had to do to protect the secret of her land … but would she survive the journey into the unknown …?
Narrator:	2
Mum:	Don't be sad … Suzi was an old cat and she had a good life … and besides, the ones we love never really leave us …
Little boy:	I sure hope she doesn't leave me …
Man:	Be careful what you wish for, little boy! Suzi is back and she has some unfinished business … not everyone was sweet to Suzi during her long life … now it's payback time!
Narrator:	3
Man:	Lost in an unknown galaxy, three billion light years from home …
Zigon:	The mutant force is upon us, Captain … we must release the ultra rays …
Captain:	Not yet, Zigon! If we release the ultra rays, we risk destroying ourselves as well as the mutant force …
Zigon:	But Captain, there is nothing else …
Captain:	Never say never, Zigon! I have a plan …
Narrator:	4
Man:	In a world with no rules, where no one is safe and nothing is certain, a mysterious visitor has arrived. But he is not alone …

Plenary ideas

Reflection (10 minutes)

> **Reflection:** Did learners enjoy working in small groups for these projects? Encourage them to talk about what worked well and what the challenges were. What could they do differently next time?

Homework ideas

With adult supervision, learners read an age-appropriate film review online in English.

> **Workbook**
>
> Learners do Activities 1–4 on page 102.

8.7 What do you know now?

How do we use screens for entertainment?

- **Learning to learn:** Learners have the opportunity to reflect and evaluate their own learning success.

- Reintroduce the question from the start of the unit: *How do we use screens for entertainment*? Discuss learner's responses to the question now and compare with their comments at the beginning of the unit. How much has changed?

- Ask learners to work on the tasks in pairs.

- For questions 1–6, encourage learners to look back through the unit if they can't remember. Circulate and offer support while learners answer the questions.

- When learners have finished the questions, give class feedback on the answers. Build up a list of suggested answers on the board.

Answers
1 Learner's own answers.
2 In 1895, the first moving pictures were shown to an audience. In 1927, the first film with sound was released.
3 Learner's own answers.
4 Dad takes the twins on a camping trip. They have been fighting a lot and he thinks the trip will help them be friends and work together. Boris sees an ants' nest in the camping field. He suggests Horis sets up his tent there. Horis doesn't know that the ants' nest is there.
5 The story is set on an island (Costa Rica), at the beach.
6 The strange lizard jumps onto Tina's hand and moves up her arm towards her face.

Look what I can do!

- There are six 'can do' statements. Learners read through the statements and tick the things they can do. Encourage them to reflect on how well they can do these things. Also invite them to think of ways they can improve further, for example what strategies they can use or learn to use.

- If learners find it challenging to read the statements, look through the unit with them and support them to find the relevant information.

- Finally, ask learners to work through the questions on page 103 of the Workbook. Encourage them to talk about what they enjoyed and also about any further support they might need.

9 Amazing arts

Unit plan

Lesson	Approximate number of learning hours	Outline of learning content	Learning objectives	Resources
1 Amazing art around us	2.0–2.5	Talk about amazing art in public places.	6Lm.01 6Us.02	Learner's Book Lesson 9.1 Workbook Lesson 9.1 **Digital Classroom:** video – Amazing arts; activity – Indefinite pronouns
2 The Recycled Orchestra	1.0–1.5	Discover how music is made from recycled rubbish.	6Rd.01 6Uv.07 6Ug.07	Learner's Book Lesson 9.2 Workbook Lesson 9.2 ⬇ Differentiated worksheets 9A, B and C **Digital Classroom:** activity – Musical instruments; activity – Concrete and abstract nouns; activity – Recycled art
3 Art attack!	2.0–2.5	Plan a day out to discover the arts, using future tenses.	6Lm.01 6Sc.06 6Ug.08	Learner's Book Lesson 9.3 Workbook Lesson 9.3 ⬇ Photocopiable 25 **Digital Classroom:** grammar presentation – Present forms with future meanings
4 Amazing architecture	1.5–2.0	Create a poem about amazing architecture.	6Rd.01 6Wc.02 6Wor.03 6Uv.03	Learner's Book Lesson 9.4 Workbook Lesson 9.4 ⬇ Unit 9 sample answer ⬇ Photocopiable 26 **Digital Classroom:** activity – I like it!
5 Willow	2.0–2.5	Read and enjoy a story about creative thinking.	6Rd.01 6Rm.02 6Rd.04 6Ug.13 6Sc.05	Learner's Book Lesson 9.5 Workbook Lesson 9.5 ⬇ Photocopiable 27 **Digital Classroom:** activity – Willow
6 Project challenge	1.0–1.5	Project A: Artwork for a public space. Project B: Create colour compositions about the senses.	6Sc.06 6Sc.02 6Wc.02 6Wc.03	Learner's Book Lesson 9.6 Workbook Lesson 9.6 ⬇ Unit 9 project checklists

(continued)

Cross-unit resources

⬇ Unit 9 Audioscripts
⬇ End of Unit 9 test
⬇ Progress test 3
⬇ Unit 9 Progress report
⬇ Unit 9 Wordlist

BACKGROUND KNOWLEDGE

Unit 9 focuses on the arts and their importance in our lives. On the unit opener page, the image of the mosaic bench is in *Park Güell,* a large public park with buildings of architectural interest, in Barcelona, Spain. The mural is in the Lodhi Colony, New Delhi. The Lodhi colony is India's first open-air art district.

In Lesson 9.2, learners discover how music can be made from recycled rubbish. At the end of the lesson, they make *maracas,* also known as *maraca, a (Rumba) shaker, chac-chac* or *rattle.* It is a percussion instrument, which is held in the hand by a long handle and shaken. The sound made by the maracas is a feature of several types of Latin music.

In Lesson 9.3, learners listen to Dom's plans for a day out during half-term. *Half-term* is a week-long school holiday taken by learners in the UK three times a year, in the middle of each of the three school terms.

In Lesson 9.4, learners read about amazing buildings. *Sydney Opera House* is the iconic building in Sydney harbour that was designed by Jørn Utzon in the 1950s and finally completed in 1973. The *Casa Battló* in Barcelona is famous for its renovation by the architect Antoni Gaudí. Among its features are the façade decorated in a mosaic technique that uses broken tiles; and the roof, which is shaped like a colourful dragon.

In Lesson 9.5, learners read an extract from the children's book *Willow* by Denise Brennan-Nelson and her sister, Rosemarie Brennan. They were brought up in Michigan, USA, with five sisters and a brother. Denise Brennan-Nelson has written several other children's books and works with schools to foster a love of literacy. Rosemarie Brennan is a writing teacher and an author.

In Lesson 9.6, Project B involves *collage.* This is a picture in which various materials or objects, for example, paper, cloth or photographs, are stuck onto paper or another surface.

TEACHING SKILLS FOCUS

Differentiation: Reading activities

Differentiation is the process of making an activity less, or more, challenging for the different skills of your learners. This can help maximise the potential of all your learners.

Reading activities can be challenging for some learners. If a reading activity is demanding, there is the danger of less confident readers becoming de-motivated. More confident readers can become bored if you spend a lot of time teaching vocabulary to less confident readers.

Your challenge

- Look at the *Reading* learning objectives from Lesson 5 of this unit:
  Understand, with support, most specific information and detail in short and extended texts.
  Read independently a range of short, simple fiction and non-fiction texts with confidence and enjoyment.
  Deduce meaning from context, with support, in short and extended texts.
- Next, look at the success criteria for these learning objectives:
  Learners can read and enjoy a story with a message about creative thinking, understanding

---

CONTINUED

specific details and deducing the meaning of key words from context.
See how the activities in the Learner's Book have been planned to take learners through these processes step by step.

- Think about your learner's strengths and weaknesses. Can you think of any other differentiation ideas for the reading activities in Unit 9, particularly in Lesson 9.5? For example, you could:

  - adapt the content, for example shorten it for less confident readers

- adapt the learning process, for example give learners a summary of the story before reading

- adapt expectations of what learners will be able to achieve, for example how much specific information they are expected to find

- put learners with different abilities into pairs or groups and ask them to discuss their answers before class feedback

- add extra tasks to challenge more confident speakers, or give less confident speakers fewer tasks or more time.

9.1 Think about it: Amazing art around us

LEARNING PLAN

Learning objectives	Learning intentions	Success criteria
6Lm.01 6Us.02	- **Listening:** Understand, with support, most of the main point of short and extended talk. - **Use of English:** Use reciprocal pronouns (each other, one another) and a range of indefinite pronouns. - **Vocabulary:** *a sculpture, a 3D artwork, metal, textiles, a mural, pattern, doorway, textiles, 3D, steel, spray paint, mosaic, paper, metal, concrete, lace.*	- Learners can understand the main points in a series of descriptions of artworks in public places. - Learners can understand how indefinite pronouns are used in sentences about art in public places.

21st-century skills

Critical thinking: Recognise and evaluate the purpose and message in public space artworks.

Materials: Learner's Book pages 143–145; Workbook pages 104–105; pictures of different art forms, including things not traditionally thought of as art – for example, enter these terms into a search engine: *graffiti, spray paint murals, street art, poster art, sticker art, chalk art, yarn bombing, recycled sculptures*

Starter ideas

Amazing art! (5–10 minutes)

- Show learners pictures of different forms of art. Include traditional art from different regions, including Aboriginal art, as well as more modern/ creative techniques (see Materials).

- On the board, write the names of the types of art and the materials that can be used to create them. Try to elicit/pre-teach some new words for the lesson, for example *a sculpture, a 3D artwork, a mural, textiles, pattern, mosaic, steel, spray paint, paper, metal, concrete*.

- Have a quick class survey to see which forms of art learners consider to be the most amazing.

Main teaching ideas

Getting started (10 minutes)

- Look together at the Big Question: *What is the effect of art on us?* Elicit suggestions.

- Look at the photos and answer questions a–c together. For a, ask learners why people might think of them as art, as they're not traditional in style. If helpful, ask some questions for c. For example: *How does art make you feel? Can you imagine your town without the art you described in b?*

- Support learners by writing useful vocabulary on the board.

***

Answers
a   1 Main image: painted wall mural (New Delhi, India). 2 Statue/sculpture of a robot. 3 Decorative mosaic bench, (Park Güell, Barcelona, Spain).
b   Learner's own answers.
c   Learner's own answers.

***

> **Digital Classroom:** Use the video 'Amazing arts' to introduce the subject of the arts. The i button will explain how to use the video.

1   Talk to your partner. Look at the artworks in the photos. (5 minutes)

- If you haven't done the Starter activity, write the words in bold on the board and talk through their meaning with learners.

- Circulate and offer support while learners look for the words in bold in the photos.

- Give class feedback.

***

Answers
a A mural on a wall. b A 3D artwork with metal and textiles. c A sculpture. d Paper flags with a lace pattern. e A decorative doorway.

***

2   Each artwork has a purpose or a message. What do you think it is? (5–10 minutes)

- Read the activity rubric. Check learners understand the meaning of 'purpose'.

> **Critical thinking opportunity:** In pairs, learners ask and answer *Wh*-questions about the artworks in the photos to help them think about their purpose or message. For example: *What does the artwork show? Who do you think the artwork was for? Is the artwork colourful? Why? What do the colours represent? Where is the artwork? How was the artwork made?* Make it clear that learners don't need to know the definitive answer for each artwork; the emphasis is on coming up with ideas.

> **Differentiation ideas:** Write sentence starters and conjunctions on a worksheet or mini-whiteboard for less confident speakers to refer to in their answers. For example: *The purpose could be … because …; I think the message could be … because … .*

- Circulate and offer support and encouragement. Guide learners to think about the function of each piece. For instance, is the aim of the doorway artwork to show the way into the building, or is it more to do with how the decoration makes you feel? Ask: *Is there a direct message in any of the artworks* (for example the LOVE sculpture)?

- Invite learners to share their ideas; encourage them to support their ideas with reasons.

***

Answers
Learner's own answers

***

3   Listen and match the descriptions to the artworks. Which of your ideas are mentioned? (10 minutes)

- Before playing the audio, encourage learners to make predictions about the words that will be used to describe the artworks. Write suggestions on the board, for example *rubbish, collected, sculpture,* etc.

- Tell learners not to worry about understanding every word; they should focus on matching each description to one of the artworks and seeing if any of their ideas from Activity 2 are mentioned. They will have the chance to listen to the recording again in the next activity.

- Play the audio. As a class, share the answers.

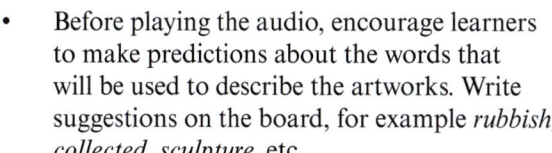

Audioscript: Track 68

See Learner's Book page 144

1   Look carefully at this 3D artwork of a fish. What is it made of? Look and you will see shells, but also rubbish collected on the beach. This interesting sculpture shows us that, sometimes, we can make something beautiful out of someone else's rubbish!

2   This beautiful doorway is decorated with blue tiles arranged in a mosaic pattern. The big bold doorway attracts the attention of people walking past and lets them know that this is the entrance to an important building. What kind of building could it be?

3   Look at the strong steel letters in the famous red sculpture. The letters in the red sculpture remind people to be kind to each other. What do the letters spell? If you can work it out, then you will get the message of this sculpture, loud and clear. And that was the intention of the artist. What is the message?

4   Anyone who visits festivals in Mexico will often see lines of colourful paper flags fluttering in the sunshine. These special flags, with their distinctive cut-out patterns, tell everyone that it is a special day and a celebration is taking place – it could be a wedding, a national holiday or a special festival party.

5   This bright colourful mural is on the walls of the World Trade Center in New York, USA. The metal walls were hard and grey to look at, so local artists were asked to paint bold colourful murals to make them look bright and beautiful for people walking by the site. The murals send positive messages to everybody who visits this famous landmark.

Answers
Description 1 – Image b; Description 2 – Image e; Description 3 – Image c; Description 4 – Image d; Description 5 – Image a

4   Listen again to find out the purpose or message of each artwork. Are the statements true or false? (10–15 minutes)

*   Read the statements together. Check learners understand the vocabulary, including *decorative*, *doorway*, *remind* and *care for each other*.

*   Replay the audio so learners can decide whether the statements are true or false and correct the false statements.

*   If helpful, replay the audio, pausing after each description.

*   Learners work in pairs to correct the false statements.

> Differentiation ideas: If learners need support with this task, ask them to focus just on identifying whether the statements are true or false.

*   Give class feedback on the correct answers.

Answers
1   False. The fish sculpture is made of shells and rubbish collected on the beach (showing us that something beautiful can be made out of someone else's rubbish).
2   True.
3   True.
4   False. People decorate the streets with coloured flags on special days when celebrations are taking place (for example festivals, weddings, national holidays).
5   False. Before the mural, the metal walls were hard and grey.

5   Types of art and materials (5 minutes)

*   Read the words in the word box and ask learners to repeat them. Check learners understand what the words mean.

*   Circulate and offer support while learners, in their pairs, find examples of the words in the photos.

> Assessment ideas: As learners do the activity, circulate and check they are using the correct pronunciation.

*   Use the photos to give class feedback. If helpful, practise the pronunciation of the words again.

Answers
Image a (WTC mural): spray paint, concrete (plus metal walls).
Image b (fish): textiles, 3D, metal.
Image c (LOVE sculpture): 3D, steel, metal.
Image d (flags): paper.
Image e (doorway): mosaic.

6 Look at the photos. Which works of art do you like best? (5 minutes)

- As a class, discuss which artworks learners like best, which they don't like and why.

- Build up suggestions on the board, for example: *I like the doorway best because it's colourful/ interesting. I don't like the flags because …*

Answers
Learner's own answers.

Language focus – Indefinite pronouns (10 minutes)

- Before looking at the Language focus box, elicit what learners know about indefinite pronouns.

- Read the Language focus box, then explain that pronouns ending in -*body* or -*one* are used for people; pronouns ending in -*thing* are used for objects.

- Build up a list of the other indefinite pronouns on the board: *anybody, nobody, somebody, everyone, no one, someone, anything, everything, nothing, everywhere, anywhere.*

> **Digital Classroom:** Use the activity 'Indefinite pronouns' to revise indefinite pronouns. The i button will explain how to use the activity.

7 Read the Language focus and choose the correct pronoun. (10 minutes)

- Invite learners to read the sentences, choose the correct pronouns and tick the sentences that are true for them. Circulate and offer support.

- Learners should then compare their answers with a partner.

- As a class, share feedback.

Answers
1   'I think art in public spaces is a good idea because **everyone** can enjoy it.'
2   'There are art displays **everywhere** in my school.'
3   '**Nobody** in my family likes art.'
4   'There isn't **anywhere** in my town or city where you can see street art.'
5   'There is **someone** in my family who is good at drawing and painting.'
Plus learner's own answers.

8 Work in small groups. Choose two of the questions to discuss. (15 minutes)

- Organise learners into small groups.

- Read the questions as a class and check learners understand the meaning of new words.

- Make sure each group has chosen two of the questions to discuss. Alternatively, allocate two questions to each group.

- Circulate and offer support with vocabulary and pronunciation as learners discuss the questions.

- Learners compare their answers with other groups who have discussed the same questions. Offer support during this process – try to ensure that each learner has the opportunity to speak.

- As a class, share ideas for each question. Did the groups broadly agree? Write some key points for each question on the board.

Answers
Suggested answer to point 2: Artists usually want to display their work in public places so that a lot of people will see it. Art in public spaces is more accessible to everyone regardless of age, background, education, etc. (in comparison to galleries and museums).

Plenary ideas

Reflection (5–10 minutes)

In groups, learners reflect on the lesson. Has it inspired them to try and see a particular artwork? Or create an artwork of their own?

Homework ideas

Learners write a paragraph (up to 100 words) about an artwork in their town, or an artwork that they would like to see.

Workbook

Learners do Activities 1–6 on pages 104–105.

> **Assessment ideas:** Write a short checklist as a class so that learners can self-assess their work before handing it in. For example: *Have I used the new art vocabulary from the lesson? Have I used indefinite pronouns? Have I checked my grammar and punctuation?*

9.2 Music: The Recycled Orchestra

LEARNING PLAN

Learning objectives	Learning intentions	Success criteria
6Rd.01 6Uv.07, 6Ug.07	• **Reading:** Understand, with support, most specific information and detail in short and extended texts. • **Use of English:** Use a limited range of abstract nouns and compound nouns. Use present perfect forms to express recent, indefinite and unfinished past. • **Vocabulary:** *cans, spoons, forks, rubbish, (musical) instruments, education, creativity, concentration, teamwork, imagination, pride*	• Learners can understand, with support, specific information in a text about the Recycled Orchestra. • Learners can recognise and use concrete and abstract nouns in the text. • Learners can recognise and understand the use of the present perfect simple (for unfinished past) in the text.

21st-century skills

Cross-curricular: Music education. Learners make a simple musical instrument from recycled materials.

Materials: Learner's Book pages 146–47; Workbook pages 106–107; **Differentiated worksheets 9A, B and C**

LANGUAGE BACKGROUND

Present perfect for unfinished past

As stated in Unit 1, the present perfect tense describes events when the time of the event is not important, or to show a connection between the present and the past.

We can also use the present perfect to talk about things that started in the past and continue in the present time. For example: *I have played the guitar in a band for many years. The instruments have given the children the chance to enjoy different kinds of music.*

Common misconceptions

Misconception	How to identify	How to overcome
Learners use the past simple to refer to things that started in the past and continue in the present time, or the present perfect to refer to finished time periods. For example: Now I ~~started~~ **have started** to study full time. I ~~have made~~ good friends there.	Write two sentences – one for each form. Ask concept check questions to elicit the difference in meaning. For example: A I **made** good friends there. B I**'ve made** good friends this year. Ask: *Which sentence refers to a finished time?* (A) *Which refers to a time that is not finished?* (B) *Which is past simple?* (A) *Which is present perfect?* (B)	Practise using: • Activities 1–3 on pages 106–107 of the Workbook • **Differentiated worksheets 9A, B and C.**

Starter ideas

Musical instruments (10 minutes)

- Explain that in this lesson, learners are going to find out how music can be made from items that people throw away.

- Revise/pre-teach vocabulary for musical instruments (and people who play them), for example *cello (cellist), saxophone (saxophone player), guitar (guitarist), trumpet (trumpeter/trumpet player)* and *drums (drummer)*.

- Briefly discuss whether learners play a musical instrument and if they like listening to particular music. Invite learners to ask and answer questions about the instruments, for example *Can you play the …? How long have you played?*

Main teaching ideas

1 Look at the musical instruments in the photos. (5–10 minutes)

- As a class, look at the photos on page 146 of the Learner's Book and identify what the instruments are made of. Build up a list of materials on the board.

- Ask learners to look at their lists from Activity 1 and compare them to the list on the board.

Answers

Some examples: old metal tins (for violins, cellos, guitars and drums); old pipes, keys, bottle tops and coins (saxophones and trumpets).
Learner's own answers.

2 Read and listen to the article about the Recycled Orchestra. Which instruments do they play? What is special about them? (5–10 minutes)

- Before reading and listening, tell learners they are going to find out about the Recycled Orchestra from Paraguay, South America. Check learners know where Paraguay is on a world map and elicit predictions about what kind of instruments learners expect to find in the orchestra.

- Play the audio and tell learners to read along. Make it clear that they are just listening out for the types of instruments and what is special about them. They will look at the article in more detail later in the lesson.

- Learners discuss their answers in pairs.

- Give class feedback.

> **Audioscript: Track 69**
>
> See Learner's Book page 147

Answers

String, wind and percussion instruments.
The orchestra is special because they play with instruments made entirely from recycled rubbish.

3 Read the article again and answer the questions. (10 minutes)

- Read through the questions as a class and ask learners if they have any initial ideas about the answers.

- Circulate and offer support while learners are looking for the answers in pairs.

> **Differentiation ideas:** Organise learners into pairs. Less confident readers and listeners will benefit from language support and their partners will consolidate their understanding about the article.

- Go through the answers as a class and invite learners to share their responses.

Answers

a When the music school started, there weren't enough instruments for all the children to play, so a local carpenter started making instruments out of recycled rubbish (materials that were free and easily available). The children and teenagers in the orchestra couldn't afford standard instruments. The rubbish came from a nearby landfill site.

b Violins, cellos, guitars (string); drums (percussion); saxophones, trumpets (wind). Learner's own answers.

c The orchestra plays famous pieces of classical and rock music. Learner's own answers.

d Learner's own answers. Suggested answer:
People are proud of the orchestra because their
hard work, dedication and talent have produced
something beautiful, literally out of rubbish.
The orchestra shows that something special can
be achieved in adverse situations. The orchestra
has brought positive attention and respect
to the town from the rest of the country and
internationally.

> **Digital Classroom:** Use the activity 'Musical
instruments' to revise musical instruments vocabulary.
The i button will explain how to use the activity.

4 **Language focus – Concrete and abstract
nouns, and 5 Read the Language focus
box. Then look at the nouns in green
and blue in the article. (5–10 minutes)**

- Discuss what learners already know about
concrete and abstract nouns, and elicit
examples.

- Read the Language focus box and check.

- Look together at the nouns in green and
blue in the article and elicit which nouns are
abstract and which ones are concrete.

Answers
Concrete nouns are green. Abstract nouns are blue.

> **Digital Classroom:** Use the activity 'Concrete
and abstract nouns' to revise concrete and abstract
nouns. The i button will explain how to use
the activity.

5 **Discuss the questions in a small group.
(5–10 minutes)**

- Read the questions as a class and check
learners understand the meaning.

- Circulate and offer support with vocabulary
and pronunciation while learners discuss the
questions in small groups. Try to ensure that
all learners have the chance to contribute.

- At the end of the discussion, invite learners to
share their ideas with the class. Note down key
words and vocabulary on the board and ask
learners to write them in their notebooks.

Answers
a Learner's own answers
b Learner's own answers.
c Learner's own answers.
Suggested answer for c: Concentration is needed to
practise the instrument, read the music and coordinate
with the rest of the orchestra. Teamwork is needed
to coordinate with each other and keep up the same
level of practice. Other skills: appreciation of music;
understanding of how to communicate with music;
stamina to play for long periods; willingness to work
hard at practising (dedication).

**Use of English – Present perfect for
unfinished past, and 6 How many examples
of the present perfect can you find in the
text? (10 minutes)**

- Review the use of the present perfect simple
from Unit 1, including the form (see Language
background).

- Together, look at the Use of English box to see
another way the present perfect is used.

- Check understanding by giving learners a few
minutes to look at the text and find and underline as
many examples of the present perfect as they can.

- For extra practice, learners can use **Differentiated
worksheets 9A, B and C**.

┌───┐
│ **Workbook**   │
│   │
│ Learners do Activities 1–3 on pages 106–107. │
└───┘

Answers
*This **has transformed** their lives …*
*Ada Rios **has played** in the Orchestra for many years.*
*Since then, Cola **has used** old metal tins to make …*
*The instruments … **have given** hundreds of children
the gift of music.*
*Since it started, the Recycled Orchestra **has gone**
from strength to strength.*
*… it **has performed** many concerts all over South
America …*
*Something very beautiful **has come** out of the
rubbish …*

> **Digital Classroom:** Use the activity 'Recycled art' to revise the present perfect. The i button will explain how to use the activity.

7   Make a musical instrument out of recycled materials. (10–15 minutes)

- First, look at the photos as a class and elicit the names of the waste materials.

- Learners discuss in groups of 3 or 4 what instruments can be made from them.

- Circulate and offer support while learners brainstorm ideas about how to make the instrument and how to change the sound it makes. If helpful, encourage them to draw simple diagrams to help explain their thoughts.

- As a class, share feedback.

CROSS-CURRICULAR LINK

Music education: Learners explore how to make a simple musical instrument from recycled materials.

Answers

Maracas can be made from these waste materials. For further details, type *maracas from waste materials* into a search engine. You can change the sound it makes by filling the bottle with different-sized materials, different amounts of materials, and varying the weight and texture of the materials.

Plenary ideas

Reflection (5 minutes)

As a class, discuss other instruments that learners could make from waste materials.

Homework ideas

Under adult supervision, learners look online and follow instructions to make maracas or another instrument from waste materials.

> **Workbook**
>
> Learners do Activities 1–3 on pages 106–107.

9.3 Talk about it: Art attack!

LEARNING PLAN

Learning objectives	Learning intentions	Success criteria
6Lm.01 **6Sc.06, 6Ug.08**	• **Speaking:** Understand, with support, most of the main points of short and extended talk. • **Use of English:** Begin to produce and maintain stretches of language comprehensibly, allowing for hesitation and reformulation, especially in longer stretches of free production. Use a range of future forms, including present continuous and present simple with future meaning. • **Vocabulary:** *architecture, theatre, performance art, statue, street art, painting, a treasure hunt, a quiz, a workshop*	• Learners can understand the main points in a conversation about plans for a day out. • Learners can understand and use the present simple and present continuous in the context of future plans and scheduled events, when explaining plans for a day out.

21st-century skills
Communication: Use appropriate language to describe plans for a day out with a cultural theme.

Materials: Learner's Book pages 148–49; Workbook pages 108–109; **Photocopiable 25**; leaflets; access to the internet (for Activity 10)

Common misconceptions

Misconception	How to identify	How to overcome
Learners use the present simple for arrangements instead of the present continuous, for example: *What ~~do you bring~~ **are you bringing** to the party?*	Write sentences on the board and elicit the difference in meaning, for example: *Does the train leave at 6.30?* (an event that is fixed on a timetable) *Are you leaving at 6.30 tomorrow?* (a future arrangement)	Practise using: • Activities 1–3 on pages 108–109 of the Workbook • **Photocopiable 25**.

Starter ideas

Days out (10 minutes)

• Explain to learners that in this lesson they are going to listen to a conversation about plans for a day out.

• Discuss the kinds of days out learners go on in their countries, connected with the arts or creative activities.

Main teaching ideas

1 **Have you ever seen any of these artworks? Talk with a partner. (5–10 minutes)**

• Briefly review different types of artwork from Lesson 1.

• Look at the artwork names together and check learners understand what they are. The idea of this activity is to encourage learners to notice how much art is around them – in their town/city/school, etc. Before learners talk in pairs, have a general discussion, pinpointing examples of artwork in their own environment. For example: *What statue can you see in the town square? What photos are there in the school hall? What mural did Class 4 paint last year?* If there is a city in your country with a lot of cultural icons, draw this into the discussion. *Has anyone ever been to …? What famous building can you see there?* If possible, provide visuals of artworks in learner's environment or country that they will recognise.

- Circulate and offer support while learners talk about the artworks with a partner.

> **Differentiation ideas:** Write prompts/example sentences on a worksheet or mini-whiteboard for less confident speakers to use. For example: *Have you ever seen …; Yes, last week/last year, I saw …; No, never …; Why was it interesting?; It was interesting because …*

- Invite learners to summarise their discussions with the class.

Answers
Learner's own answers.

2 Now play a game with your classmates. Describe an example of art but don't say what it is. (15–20 minutes)

- Tell learners that each member of the class should think of an example of art, without saying what it is. Look at the example in the Learner's Book together.

- Circulate and support learners while they make notes about their chosen work of art. If they find it hard to think of one, offer suggestions.

> **Differentiation ideas:** Challenge more confident learners to choose two examples of art to describe.

- Demonstrate the activity. Describe a work of art yourself, or ask a confident speaker who has chosen two examples to describe one of them and get the class to guess what it is.

- Offer support while learners take it in turns to describe/guess the example(s) of art to a partner/group of 3 or 4.

Answers
Learner's own answers.

3 Read the adverts for cultural events and match to a type of art. (10 minutes)

- Before you read each advert as a class, look at the photos and encourage predictions about what learners will read.

- After you have read each advert, give learners a couple of minutes, in pairs, to match each event to a type / types of art from Activity 1 and decide whether the event is inside or outside.

- Share feedback as a class.

Answers
1   Art Safari: paintings, sculptures, murals.
2   Star Circus: theatre or performance art
3   Sculpture Park: sculptures
Event 2 takes place inside; Events 1 and 3 take place outside.

4 Read the adverts again. Answer the questions about the activities in blue. (10 minutes)

- First, read the questions together.

- Allow learners time to answer the questions in pairs.

- Give class feedback on the answers.

Answers
a   A *workshop*, which teaches you how to create a sculpture out of natural materials.
b   An *art treasure hunt*, with clues to find animal-themed artworks by local artists.
c   A *quiz* about the Star Circus.

5 Talk with your partner. Which event would you like to take part in? Why? (10 minutes)

- Circulate and support learners as they answer the questions with a partner.

> **Differentiation ideas:** Write sentence starters and vocabulary on a worksheet or mini-whiteboard for less confident speakers to refer to when answering the questions. For example: *I would like to take part in the … because it looks more exciting/relaxing/creative. The other events don't look as exciting/relaxing/creative. I think the events include activities because …*

Answers

Learner's own answers. Suggested answers:
- The events include activities to attract attention and encourage more people to take part.
- The Art Safari treasure hunt guides people to the artworks and makes sure they see all of them.
- The Star Circus quiz offers the opportunity to win two free tickets to the circus (and also gets people to look at the website).
- The Sculpture Park workshop gives people the experience of creating a sculpture and something to take home with them from the Park.

 6 Listen to Dom's plans for a day out. Which art event is he going to? (10–15 minutes)

- Before listening, tell learners that Dom is planning a day out during half-term. Explain that half-term is a week's holiday from school in the UK, usually each October, February and May.

- Tell learners that Dom is going to one of the three days out from the reading activity. Make predictions about the words he could use connected with each event.

- Play the audio so learners can hear which art event he is going to do.

- Learners compare their ideas with a partner before you share ideas as a class.

Audioscript: Track 70

See Learner's Book page 149

Friend: So when are your friends coming to stay?

Dom: Next week, in the half-term holiday. They're arriving on Sunday and staying until Wednesday. Their train leaves early on Wednesday morning, so we only have two full days together.

Friend: What are you going to do with them?

Dom: Well, we're planning to do this Art Safari treasure hunt in the city centre on Monday. They've never been to our city before and this looks like fun.

Friend: So what do you do on this Art Safari treasure hunt thing?

Dom: Well, there are these animal artworks hidden in places around the city centre. They're made by artists that live in the city – my mum's friend has done one. You get a map and a bunch of clues – that's the treasure hunt – and you work out where the artworks are from the clues …

Friend: OK … sounds different …

Dom: It'll be cool! One of my friends is really into art, so she'll love this. It's a good way for our friends to see places in our city – better than just walking around and they hate shopping. We'll hunt around for these paintings and sculptures and things and they'll get to see other cool places in the city at the same time.

Answers

The Art Safari treasure hunt.

Use of English – Present tenses with future meaning, and 7 Look at sentences 1 and 2 and complete the explanation with present simple or present continuous. (10 minutes)

- Check what learners already know about present tenses with future meaning. Then look at the example sentences in the Use of English box. Explain that the present simple is used for events in the future that are scheduled (sentence 1). The present continuous is used for plans and arrangements (sentence 2). Check understanding by asking learners to think of other example sentences using the present simple and present continuous in this way (for instance, *The holidays **start** next week*; *They **are coming** to see us on Tuesday*).

- Read the explanation sentences in Activity 7. Check learners know what *a fixed schedule* is. Give learners a couple of minutes to complete the explanation.

- Give class feedback on the correct answers.

Workbook

Learners do Activities 1–3 on pages 108–109.

Answers

a   Present simple

b   Present continuous

> **Digital Classroom:** Use the grammar presentation 'Present forms with future meanings' to revise present forms with future meanings. The i button will explain how to use the activity.

 8   Listen and complete the sentences from the next part of the conversation. (10 minutes)

- Before listening, read the sentences together. Encourage learner's predictions about what the speakers will say.

- Play the audio and ask learners to note down the answers.

- Learners check their answers with a partner before you share feedback as a class.

- If helpful, replay the audio so that learners can listen to the answers again.

Audioscript: Track 71

See Learner's Book page 149

Friend:	How long's the Art Safari? Is it all day?
Dom:	No, we're just doing it in the morning. Then we're meeting my mum's friend – the artist one – for something to eat at the Nova Café. After that, we're going to the Film and Photography Museum. It has virtual reality film sets! The Virtual Experience starts at 4pm.
Friend:	Sounds awesome.
Dom:	Do you want to come?
Friend:	Yes, please. My cousin is visiting next week – can he come too?

Answers

a are meeting, **b** are going, **c** starts, **d** is visiting

---

9   Present it! Plan a cultural tour or event in your town or city. (20–30 minutes)

- As a class, brainstorm the kinds of activities learners could include in their cultural tour or event. Encourage learners to think about a range of 'art' that might be available to see in their town or city, for example interesting buildings, galleries, museums, statues and monuments. Also consider theatre and performance events. If possible, bring in some leaflets or have a look online at performances coming to local theatres or other venues. Learners could also focus on a concert, play or art exhibition at school.

- Circulate and offer support while learners plan their itineraries in small groups. Make sure that all learners have the chance to contribute ideas.

- **Communication:** Before learners share their ideas with the class, give them time to make notes about the event and decide what each group member is going to talk about. Check they feel confident about using present tenses with future meaning to describe their plans for a cultural tour or event.

> **Assessment ideas:** As you listen to the presentations, focus on learner's pronunciation, use of new vocabulary and how they are using present tenses with future meaning. Make notes on areas where learners might need further support.

- Have a class vote on the most interesting day out.

Answers

Learner's own answers.

Plenary ideas

Consolidation (15 minutes)

Learners make a poster to advertise their day out. Encourage them to use the vocabulary from the lesson.

Homework ideas

Learners write around 100 words about a trip that one of the other groups planned.

Workbook

Learners do Activities 1–3 on pages 108–109.

9.4 Write about it: Amazing architecture

LEARNING PLAN

Learning objectives	Learning intentions	Success criteria
6Rd.01	• **Reading:** Understand, with support, most specific information and detail in short and extended texts.	• Learners can understand specific information in short poems about famous buildings.
6Wc.02, 6Wor.03	• **Writing:** Write, with support, short texts which describe people, places and objects, and routine past and present actions and events. Use appropriate layout for a limited range of genres.	• Learners can write a short poem about a famous building following a writing and layout framework.
6Uv.03	• **Use of English:** Use prepositions (for example *as, like*) to indicate manner.	• Learners can understand the use of 'like' as a preposition, in the context of the poems.
	• **Vocabulary:** *sapphire, shimmering, gleaming, illuminated, curved*	

21st-century skills

Creative thinking: Create a simple poem about an interesting building using creative imagery.

Materials: Learner's Book pages 150–51; Workbook pages 110–111; Optional: interesting buildings for learners to write their poem about (Activity 6); Unit 9 sample answer; **Photocopiable 26**

Common misconceptions

Misconception	How to elicit	How to overcome
Learners confuse prepositions, for instance *as/like*. For example: She's **as like** my older sister. My friends are interested in kung fu **as like** you.	Write two sentences on the board. Ask concept check questions to elicit the difference between *as* and *like*. For example: **As** your teacher, I think you should study more. (= I am your teacher) **Like** your mother, I think you should study more. (= I am not your mother, but I agree with her)	Learners practise by writing about six sentences about themselves – three with 'like' as a preposition and three using 'as'.

Starter ideas

Amazing buildings in my country (10 minutes)

- Explain to learners that they are going to read poems about amazing buildings in this lesson, and then create a poem of their own.

- Have a brief discussion about famous buildings that learners know in their country. What makes them amazing?

Main teaching ideas

1 Look at the famous buildings from around the world. (10 minutes)

- Look at the famous buildings in the photos – ask learners to name them.

- Then, as a class, look at the shapes and colours in each building and build up a list of vocabulary on the board.

- Elicit the meaning of *It reminds me of* … by looking at the example in the Learner's Book.

- In pairs, invite learners to say what the buildings remind them of. Encourage them to be creative with their ideas.

- Come back together as a class and share feedback.

Answers
Learner's own answers.

2 Read the poems. Can you match each one to a photo? (10 minutes)

- Tell learners they are going to read poems about two of the buildings from Activity 1. Encourage predictions about the kinds of words each poem might include.

- Explain that learners don't need to understand every word – they should just focus on matching each poem to a photo.

- Learners read the poems and match each one to a photo.

- Go through the answers as a class – encourage learners to give reasons for their answers.

Answers
Poem 1: Photo b – Sydney Opera House.
Poem 2: Photo d – Casa Batlló.

3 Read the poems again and answer the questions. (10 minutes)

- Before rereading the poems, read the questions and check that learners understand what they are asking.

- In pairs, learners answer the questions.

> **Differentiation ideas:** Organise learners into pairs. Less confident readers will benefit from language support and their partners will consolidate their understanding about the poems.

- As a class, go through the answers.

Answers
a   1 Sydney Opera House – 'the sails on a huge white ship'. 2 Casa Batlló – 'a magic house in a story book'.
b   1 white, concrete, glass. 2 mosaic, sapphire (blue) glass.
c   The use of 'I' gives the buildings a character or personality.

4 Now close your eyes! How many images can you remember from each poem? (5 minutes)

- Creative imagery is beyond the requirements of the Cambridge Primary English as a Second Language curriculum framework so you might want to use this activity as extension material.

- Ask learners to sit quietly and close their eyes for a few moments. What images can they remember from each poem?

- Learners share their ideas with a partner. Which images were the strongest? How did their ideas compare?

Answers
Learner's own answers.

5 Can you match the descriptive adjectives in blue with a description? (5–10 minutes)

- Circulate and offer support as learners work in pairs to match the descriptive adjectives in blue with a description.

- If learners find this task challenging, encourage them to look at the words in their context, for example *illuminated at night*. If necessary, eliminate the wrong answers to help learners further.

Answers
a sapphire, b shimmering, c gleaming, d illuminated,
e curved

Language focus – Uses of *like* (5 minutes)

- Look at the Language focus box together.

- Check understanding by asking learners to provide more examples of *like* used as a verb and preposition.

- Also check learners know the difference between *like* and *as* for talking about similarities (see Common misconceptions).

> **Digital Classroom:** Use the activity 'I like it!' to revise the different uses of *like*. The i button will explain how to use the activity.

Writing tip – Plan your work (5 minutes)

- Explain to learners that they are now going to create their own poem about an amazing building.

- Look at the Writing tip together. Encourage learners to take some time to think about and plan their poems before they start writing, for instance by making a list of useful adjectives, key points that they want to include, etc.

- Also invite learners to use dictionaries as they research ideas for the poem, in order to explore the use of different words.

6 Write a poem about an amazing building. (25–30 minutes)

- Brainstorm interesting buildings that learners could write their poem about, including ones they mentioned in the Starter activity. Alternatively, you could supply images of alternative buildings from the ones in the lesson for learners to choose from.

- Make sure each learner has chosen a building to write about. Then ask everyone to be quiet for a few moments. Learners close their eyes and think about how their building would describe itself.

- Ask learners to spend a few minutes noting down some descriptive words/ideas that make them think of the building. Ideally, they should look for words that rhyme or start with the same letter, for example *gleaming glass*. Encourage more confident writers to look at

the poems in Activity 2 for alliteration, for example <u>sh</u>immering o<u>c</u>ean, and try to replicate this in their own poems.

- Next, learners write notes that answer the four questions in Step 2. The writing frame is just a guide; learners can express themselves in different ways and add extra lines if they want to. However, the line with the use of 'like' as a preposition should stay the same.

> **Differentiation ideas:** Ask more confident writers to create a poem with 8–10 lines.

> **Assessment ideas:** Before learners start Step 3, show them the Unit 9 sample answer without the mark scheme comments. As a class, evaluate the sample answer's strengths and weaknesses. Also look at the checklist on **Photocopiable 27**, so that learners know what they are aiming to achieve in their poem.

- **Creative thinking:** Learners use their notes to write a simple poem about an interesting building using creative imagery and descriptive words. They shouldn't include the name of the building on the poem, as learners will try to guess this in the Plenary.

> **Assessment ideas:** Once learners have finished their first draft, ask them to work through the checklist on **Photocopiable 26** again to self-assess their work.

- Learners update their drafts and finalise their poems.

Answers
Learner's own answers.

Plenary ideas

Consolidation (10 minutes)

Make a display of the poems. Learners read each other's poems. Can they match them to a building?

Homework ideas

Learners write a poem about another famous building, or look for interesting poems about famous buildings to share with the class.

Workbook

Learners do Activities 1–7 on pages 110–111.

9.5 Read and respond: *Willow*

LEARNING PLAN

Learning objectives	Learning intentions	Success criteria
6Rd.01, 6Rm.02, 6Rd.04	• **Reading:** Understand, with support, most specific information and detail in short and extended texts. Read independently a range of short, simple fiction and non-fiction texts with confidence and enjoyment. Deduce meaning from context, with support, in short and extended texts.	• Learners can read and enjoy a story with a message about creative thinking, understanding specific details and deducing the meaning of key words from context.
6Ug.13	• **Use of English:** Use an increasing range of participle adjectives and a range of adjectives in the correct order in front of nouns.	• Learners can understand and use adjectives in the correct order in front of nouns when writing short descriptive phrases.
6Sc.05	• **Speaking:** Pronounce familiar words and phrases clearly; begin to use intonation and place stress at word, phrase and sentence level appropriately. • **Vocabulary:** *giggled, a scowl, shivered, glared, a frown*	• Learners can recognise and practise different pronunciation of the vowel 'i' with words from the story.

21st-century skills

Emotional development: Understand the value of creative thinking.

Materials: Learner's Book pages 152–55; Workbook pages 112–113; **Photocopiable 27**

Starter ideas

Art introduction (5 minutes)

- Tell learners that in this lesson they are going to read a story about a girl called Willow and her art class.
- Ask learners if they enjoy doing artistic activities at school/home. What do they like/not like about them? Encourage them to use art vocabulary from the story, for example *crayon, paper, paint brushes, paint*.

Main teaching ideas

1 Do you have an art room at school? What's it like? (5 minutes)

- Ask learners if they have an art room at school. Discuss what it's like and what activities they do there.

- If learners don't have an art room, ask them to describe how they would like it to look/be like.

Answers
Learner's own answers.

2 Read and listen to the story about Willow's art class. (10–15 minutes)

- There are a number of new and challenging words in the text. First, read the glossary words together. However, make it clear that learners are not expected to understand everything when they first read and hear the story. They should focus on answering the two questions in the activity, i.e. what Willow's art teacher, Miss Hawthorn, is like, and why she gets annoyed with Willow.

- Before you play the audio, look at the pictures and encourage predictions about what Miss Hawthorn and her art class might be like.

- After learners have read/listened to the story, circulate and offer support while learners discuss the answers in pairs.

- Share feedback as a class. If learners find it hard to answer the questions, ask prompting questions such as: *Is Miss Hawthorn strict or warm? Does she encourage creativity?*

Answers

Miss Hawthorn is strict and cold. She doesn't encourage her students to be creative in her art class. She gets annoyed with Willow because Willow doesn't paint her pictures according to Miss Willow's examples. She always does something different.

Audioscript: Track 72

See Learner's Book pages 152–153

---

3 Read again and answer the questions in pairs. (10 minutes)

- Read each question together. Check learners understand words like *behaviour* and ask them for ideas using the pictures to help them predict the answers. Learners may be able to answer some of the questions already, but don't worry if they can't, as it was not the focus of the previous activity.

- Give learners time to read the text and answer the questions in pairs.

> **Differentiation ideas:** You could divide the questions up so that pairs focus on answering two or three questions.

- Share feedback on the questions with the class.

Answers

a The students sit in strict orderly rows. They don't talk or move much. Their paintings are copies of Miss Hawthorn's examples and no one tries anything different.

b Willow doesn't follow Miss Hawthorn's examples. She paints in her own imaginative style. She doesn't sit still – she likes to move in her seat and look out of the window.

c She owns an art book with paintings by famous artists – her 'well-loved art book'.

d Miss Hawthorn doesn't like Willow. She tells her off for moving in her seat and makes negative comments about her paintings.

e She gives Miss Hawthorn her well-loved art book.

f Learner's own answers. At the end of the story, having spent time with Willow's art book, Miss Hawthorn gathers paints, brushes, pencils and a sketch pad and starts to 'doodle'. It is the first time she has ever drawn anything in a relaxed informal style. (The inference is that Willow's art book has opened her eyes to a more creative way of expressing herself through drawing.)

Reading tip – Repetition, and 4 Read the Reading tip box. (10 minutes)

- First, check learners know the meaning of *repetition.* Then look at the Reading tip together. Invite learners to find the repeated example sentences in the story. Ask: *What do the repeated sentences tell us about Willow's character?*

> **Differentiation ideas:** Put less confident learners in pairs and ask them to find one example of repetition, rather than looking for multiple examples.

Answers

The repeated sentences tell us that Willow thinks, behaves and paints differently, and more creatively, to the other students.

---

5 Words that show emotions and feelings. (10 minutes)

- The objective of this activity is to practise deducing the meaning of key words from context.

- First, read the definitions together and check learners understand their meaning.

- Then look at the words in blue in the story. Encourage learners to look at other words around the verbs to help them guess the meaning.

- Match the first word, *glared*, to a definition (d) together.

- Offer support while learners work in pairs to match the rest of the blue words to a definition.

Answers

a giggled, b scowl, c shivered, d glared, e a frown

6 Find other words and phrases to describe Willow and Miss Hawthorn's characters. (10 minutes)

- In pairs, learners scan the story to look for and underline words to describe Willow's and Miss Hawthorn's characters.

- Before giving class feedback, learners use the words they underline as the basis to discuss whether Miss Hawthorn's attitude changes Willow's character.

› **Differentiation ideas:** Learners could just focus on finding words and phrases to describe Willow and Miss Hawthorn's characters.

Answers
Willow: 'Rosy-cheeked Willow'; 'her most magical smile', 'skipped off'
Miss Hawthorn: 'Miss Hawthorn's icy blue eyes'; 'Miss Hawthorn's moods were as dark as her clothing'; '"Horrid little girl," she muttered'; 'long bony finger'.
Despite Miss Hawthorn's negative attitude towards Willow, her character doesn't change throughout the extract: she continues to be bright and happy. At the end she generously gifts Miss Hawthorn her much-loved art book.

› **Digital Classroom:** Use the activity 'Willow' to reinforce reading comprehension of the text *Willow* from the Learner's Book. The i button will explain how to use the activity.

7 What do you think of the story? What message do you think there is in the story? (5–10 minutes)

- Circulate and offer support with vocabulary and pronunciation while learners discuss, in small groups, what they think of the story and what message there is in the story.

Answers
Learner's own answers. There is a strong message of support for the processes of creative thinking in the story, and to carry on being creative, even if someone puts you down.

8 Pronunciation: 'i' sounds. (5 minutes)

- Write *smile* and *pink* on the board. Elicit the different pronunciation of the 'i' sounds (/ai/ and /I/).

- Tell learners they are going to listen to more words from the story and say how the 'i' is pronounced in each word.

- Play the recording. Encourage learners to listen and repeat the words. If helpful, play the recording a few times.

- Learners write the words in the correct column.

Audioscript: Track 73
See Learner's Book pages 154

Answers
/ai/ silent, icy, smile
/I/ still, twisted, pink, stinks, giggled, skipped, gift

Use of English – Adjective order (5 minutes)

- Before looking at the Use of English box, remind learners that they can use more than one adjective before a noun. Ask them why they might want to do this (to add more detail).

- Write the adjectives *broken* and *single* and the noun *crayon* on the board (from the story). Elicit the correct word order.

- Read the Use of English box and the table in Activity 9 to see the correct adjective order.

Workbook
Learners do Activity 3 on page 113.

9 Read the story again. Can you find three more examples of adjective + adjective + noun? (10 minutes)

- Ask learners to reread the story and look for three more examples of adjective + adjective + noun.

- Learners copy the table in their notebooks and write the adjectives and nouns in the correct columns in the table.

- Learners practise the order of adjectives in a fun way using **Photocopiable 27**.

Answers

Number / quantity	Opinion	Size	Physical quality (e.g. texture, taste)	Colour	Material	Noun
single			broken			crayon
			icy	blue		eyes
			straight	brown		trunks
			rounded	green		tops
		long	bony			finger
			soft		furry	kitten
	beautiful			red		sunset
			sweet	golden		fruit
		huge	crashing			waterfall
	horrid	little				girl

10 Look at Gabi's list of things she likes painting. Which phrases have adjectives in the wrong order? (5 minutes)

- Look at the example. Elicit that *soft* is a physical quality and *furry* describes a material, so this order is correct.

- Circulate and offer support while learners check/correct the other phrases.

- Once learners have looked at each phrase, they should write it in the correct columns in the table.

Answers
A soft furry kitten ✓
A red, beautiful sunset ✗ *A beautiful, red sunset*
Sweet golden fruit ✓
A crashing huge waterfall ✗ *A huge crashing waterfall*

11 Play the crazy captions game! (5 minutes)

- Use this game to revise adjectives and nouns from topics in other units.

- As a class, brainstorm adjectives from each category in the table and nouns on any topic from Stage 6. Write them on the board for learners to refer to.

- Look at the examples of crazy captions in the Learner's Book. Tell learners they are going to make as many similar examples as they can in one minute. Remind learners that the adjective order must be correct.

- In pairs, learners make as many crazy captions as they can.

- Each pair reads their favourite crazy caption to the class.

- Build up a list on the board and have a class vote to decide the craziest caption.

Answers
Learner's own answers.

12 Values. Thinking in a creative way. How can we build creative thinking skills? (10–15 minutes)

- Put learners into groups. Tell them that by answering the questions, they will be helping to build their creative thinking skills.

- **Emotional development:** This activity is a engaging way for learners to understand the value of creative thinking and find out how to further improve their creative thinking skills.

- If class time is short, each group could concentrate on one question. Learners could then compare their answers as a class and complete the rest of the questions for homework.

Answers
Learner's own answers

13 Why do you think creative thinking is so important? (10 minutes)

- Invite learners to share their ideas and thoughts on why creative thinking is so important.

- If learners find it challenging to answer the question, ask them to think back to the story and to Activity 12.

Answers

Learner's own answers.

Suggested answer: When we think creatively, we learn to look at things from a fresh new perspective and this can help us improve what is already there. It is the key to progression, innovation and developing and improving our skills.

Plenary ideas

Reflection (5 minutes)

Ask learners to reflect on the story. What did they like about it? What parts did they find challenging?

Homework ideas

See suggestion in Activity 12.

Workbook

Learners do Activities 1–5 on pages 112–113.

9.6 Project challenge

LEARNING PLAN

Learning objectives	Learning intentions	Success criteria
6Sc.06, 6Sc.02	• **Speaking:** Begin to produce and maintain stretches of language comprehensibly, allowing for hesitation and reformulation, especially in longer stretches of free production. Describe people, places and objects, and routine past and present actions and events.	• Learners can create a design for an artwork for a public place and deliver a presentation.
6Wc.02, 6Wc.03	• **Writing:** Write, with support, short texts which describe people, places and objects, and routine past and present actions and events. Express opinions and feelings.	• Learners can write and display a short composition about images associated with a specific colour.

21st-century skills
Collaboration: Participate actively with other students in shared creative projects.

Materials: Learner's Book pages 156–157; Workbook page 114; examples of other learner's work; internet access; library books; old magazines; poster card; scissors; glue; Unit 9 project checklists; End of Unit 9 Test; Progress test 3

Starter ideas

Raise interest in the projects (10–15 minutes)

- Tell learners they are either going to create artwork for a public space (Project A) or create colour compositions about the senses (Project B).

- If possible, raise interest in the projects by presenting examples of learner's work on similar topics from other classes or the internet.

- Revise new vocabulary from the unit, which learners may need for the challenges, in a fun way. For example, create a crossword or wordsearch.

Main teaching ideas

Introduce and complete projects (60 minutes)

Encourage learners to choose one of the projects and then follow the steps for their chosen project.

Project A: Artwork for a public space

- Organise learners into groups of three or four and tell them about the context of the project (see Step 1).

- First, make sure all groups have chosen a disused or neglected space in their town. Circulate and support learners while they brainstorm what might make people want to use it again and what kinds of artwork could improve the space.

- Next, learners gather ideas for their artwork. If using the internet is not practical, learners could get ideas from old magazines or library books.

- Learners discuss the kind of message they want their artwork to communicate.

- **Collaboration:** Make sure each learner is participating actively in the project. Encourage learners to manage and share the tasks and decide as a team whether they want to make rough sketches or create a collage.

- Continue to support learners while they discuss ideas about the kind of artwork they want to create and the materials to use.

- Distribute poster card to each group. Learners work together in their groups and create their poster image.

- Before learners present their artwork to other groups, circulate and support them while they decide who is going to discuss the different aspects of the artwork, i.e. the type of artwork it is, the materials in the artwork, the message behind the artwork, and the name of the public space they want to improve with their artwork.

> **Assessment ideas:** Learners use the Unit 9 project checklist to evaluate another group's artwork idea.

- Give lots of praise to all group members for their presentations. When all the groups have presented their designs, vote for the winner of the competition.

Project B: Create colour compositions about the senses

- Organise learners into pairs. Ask them to choose two colours and look through magazines to find interesting images of the colours – see the Learner's Book for examples.

- Check learners understand what 'collage' means (see Background knowledge). Distribute scissors, poster card and glue for learners to create their collages.

- Circulate and support learners while they make mind maps of all the things they associate with the colours.

- Elicit what we mean by the five senses: what we see, hear, feel, taste and smell.

- **Collaboration:** Circulate and support learners as they categorise the ideas from their mind maps into sense groups, then decide which images they like best and which feel the strongest. Encourage them to share ideas with their partner. Tell them that they will use these ideas to write their compositions.

- Learners use the writing frame to create a composition for each colour. Reassure learners that the writing frame is there as a guide – they can use a different structure or add extra lines to their compositions. Look at the example writing frame from the Learner's Book together; remind students to use the different word types in each line.

> **Assessment ideas:** Before learners finalise their compositions, ask them to swap them with another pair, who will check that the compositions are easy to read, describe images for each colour linked to the senses, and use interesting ideas and descriptive words.

- Learners finalise their compositions on a poster.

- Display them in the classroom.

> **Assessment ideas:** Learners use the Unit 9 project checklist to evaluate the compositions, including making a note of what they think is the most interesting image.

Plenary ideas

Consolidation (10–15 minutes)

> **Reflection:** As a class, learners discuss which piece of work from their projects they like the best. Encourage them to explain why.

Homework ideas

Learners follow the instructions in the Learner's Book to complete the project they didn't do in class.

Workbook

Learners do Activities 1–2 on pages 114.

9.7 What do you know now?

What is the effect of art on us?

- **Learning to learn:** Learners have the opportunity to reflect and evaluate their own learning success. Reintroduce the question from the start of the unit: *What is the effect of art on us?* Discuss learner's responses to the question now and compare with their comments at the beginning of the unit. How much has changed?

- Ask learners to work on the tasks in pairs.

- For questions 1, 2, 5 and 6, encourage learners to look back through the unit if they can't remember. Encourage learners to use the sentence starters to help them answer questions 3 and 4. Circulate and offer support while learners answer the questions.

- Give class feedback on the answers.

Answers
1 Artworks / materials: (two from) sculpture (metal, steel) 3D artwork (textiles, metal); wall

mural (spray paint, concrete); festival flags (paper); decorative doorway (mosaic).

2   String (play by plucking or moving a bow across strings); percussion (play by beating); wind (play by blowing).

3   Learner's own answers.

4   Learner's own answers.

5   Willow gets a lot of her painting ideas from her much-loved art book. In the art class, she drew 1) a pink (flamingo) tree; 2) a tree with blue apples.

6   (Two from): *single broken crayon* (the art supplies or equipment); *icy blue eyes* (Miss Hawthorn); *straight brown trunks* (the trees in the students' paintings); *rounded green tops* (the trees in the students' paintings); *horrid little girl* (Miss Hawthorn's description of Willow); *long bony finger* (Miss Hawthorn)

Look what I can do!

•   There are six 'can do' statements. Learners read through the statements and tick the things they can do. Encourage them to reflect on how well they can do these things. Also invite them to think of ways they can improve further, for example what strategies they can use or learn to use.

•   If learners find it challenging to read the statements, look through the unit with them and support them to find the relevant information.

•   Finally, ask learners to work through the questions on page 115 of the Workbook. Encourage them to talk about what they enjoyed and also about any further support they might need.

Check your progress 3

Learners answer the eight questions.

Answers

1

Nature	Entertainment	Art and design
tornado	soundtrack	mural
lava	cast	mosaic
clouds	sound effects	creativity
crater	audience	textiles

2   **a** crater, **b** audience, **c** mural, **d** cast, **e** soundtrack, **f** lava

3   Learner's own answers. Sample answers:
    Tornado – a strong, dangerous wind that can destroy buildings.
    Clouds – You can see these in the sky – they are grey or white.
    Sound effects – sounds in a film that make it sound more real.
    Mosaic – a pattern made by putting together small pieces of glass, stone or tile.
    Creativity – the ability to produce new or unusual ideas.
    Textiles – something that is made of fabric or cloth.

4   Learner's own answers.

5   **a** was going, **b** amazing, **c** Everybody, **d** played, **e** am meeting, **f** beautiful old, **g** interested in, **h** was done

6   Learner's own answers.

7   **a–f** Learner's own answers.

8   Learner's own answers.

Index of photocopiables

The following photocopiables can be downloaded from Cambridge GO.

Unit 1

1   Map reading sentence halves
2   Have you ever ...?
3   Checklist for a description of a first-time experience

Unit 2

4   First conditional dominoes
5   Play a board game
6   Checklist for a biography about a sports person

Unit 3

7   Revision crossword: Food chains
8   Checklist for an infographic about an animal
9   Information exchange about baleen whales

Unit 4

10 Did you ...?
11 Who said we won't!?
12 Checklist for a persuasive essay about an invention

Unit 5

13 Are you a big spender?
14 Checklist for an opinion essay
15 How independent are you?

Unit 6

16 Snakes and ladders
17 Create a space expedition
18 Checklist for a job advert

Unit 7

19 What were they doing?
20 Connective dominoes
21 Checklist for a description of a special place

Unit 8

22 A film quiz
23 Snap!
24 Checklist for creating a storyboard

Unit 9

25 What's in your diary?
26 Checklist for creating a poem
27 Adjective order fun

Differentiated worksheets 1A, B and C: Verb patterns

Aim: To practise verb patterns.

Differentiated worksheet A is the least challenging worksheet, with the most support. This is recommended for the least confident learners.

Differentiated worksheet C is the most challenging worksheet, with the least support. This is recommended for the most confident learners.

Differentiated worksheet B is between Worksheets A and C.

Procedure:

- Learners can complete this worksheet at the end of Lesson 1.4.
- Each worksheet is designed to be self-explanatory.

Answers

Worksheet A

A 1 sent me (Example), 2 I told her, 3 gave, 4 to go, 5 to write, 6 us to buy

B 1 invited me to his party (Example), 2 taught my sister and I to swim, 3 asked Raj to give me a pencil, 4 wanted us to go to the concert, 5 friend sent me a postcard from her holiday

C Learner's own answers

Worksheet B

A 1 sent me (Example), 2 told her, 3 gave, 4 to go, 5 to write, 6 us to buy

B 1 invited me to his party (Example), 2 taught my sister and I to swim, 3 asked Raj to give me a pencil, 4 wanted us to go to the concert, 5 friend sent me a postcard from her holiday

C Learner's own answers

Worksheet C

A 1 sent me (Example), 2 told her, 3 gave, 4 to go, 5 to write, 6 us to buy

B 1 Seamus invited me to his party. (Example) 2 My dad taught my sister and I to swim. 3 I asked Raj to give me a pencil. 4 They wanted us to go to the concert. 5 My friend sent me a postcard from her holiday.

C Learner's own answers

Name _____ Date _____

Worksheet 1A: Verb patterns

verb + direct object + indirect object	He **gave** me a funny smile.
verb + direct object + infinitive (with *to*)	My friend **asked** me to go with him.

A **Choose the correct word or words.**

1   He **sent me** / **me sent** some information about the school trip.

2   I **told her** / I **her told** a secret about Carrie.

3   She **gave** / **to give** him an ice cream.

4   My friend asked me **to go** / **go** on the rollercoster.

5   Our teacher told us **writing** / **to write** the answers in our books.

6   She sent **to buy us** / **us to buy** a cake from the shop.

B **Reorder the words to make sentences.**

1   me / invited / his / to / party / Seamus

   Seamus invited me to his party. _____

2   to / My dad / swim / my sister and I / taught

   My dad _____

3   pencil / Raj / to / I / asked / me / give / a

   I _____

4   to / wanted / us / go / the concert / to / They

   They _____

5   a postcard / me / sent / friend / from her holiday / My

   My _____

C **Complete the sentences with your own ideas.**

1   My dad taught me to _____.

2   I gave my friend a _____ for her birthday.

3   _____ (friend's name) invited me _____.

4   My teacher asked me _____.

Name _____ Date _____

Worksheet 1B: Verb patterns

| verb + direct object + indirect object | He **gave** me a funny smile. |
| verb + direct object + infinitive (with to) | My friend **asked** me to go with him. |

A **Look at the underlined mistakes. Write the correct sentences.**

1 He <u>me sent</u> some information about the school trip. _____*sent me*_____

2 I <u>her told</u> a secret about Carrie. _____

3 She <u>to give</u> him an ice cream. _____

4 My friend asked me <u>go</u> on the rollercoster. _____

5 Our teacher told us <u>writing</u> the answers in our books. _____

6 She sent <u>to buy us</u> a cake from the shop. _____

B **Reorder the words to make sentences.**

1 me / invited / his / to / party / Seamus

   Seamus <u>*invited me to his party.*</u>_____

2 to / My dad / swim / my sister and I / taught

   My dad _____

3 pencil / Raj / to / I / asked / me / give / a

   I _____

4 to / wanted / us / go / the concert / to / They

   They _____

5 a postcard / me / sent / friend / from her holiday / My

   My _____

C **Complete the sentences with your own ideas.**

1 My dad taught me to _____.

2 I gave my friend a _____ for her birthday.

3 _____ (friend's name) invited me _____.

4 My teacher asked me _____.

Name _____ Date _____

Worksheet 1C: Verb patterns

| verb + direct object + indirect object | He **gave** me a funny smile. |
| verb + direct object + infinitive (with *to*) | My friend **asked** me to go with him. |

A **Find and underline the mistakes. Write the correct sentences.**

1 He <u>me sent</u> some information about the school trip. _____*sent me*_____

2 I her told a secret about Carrie. _____

3 She to give him an ice cream. _____

4 My friend asked me go on the rollercoster. _____

5 Our teacher told us writing the answers in our books. _____

6 She sent to buy us a cake from the shop. _____

B **Reorder the words to make sentences.**

1 Seamus / invite / me / his party

   Seamus invited me to his party. _____

2 My dad / teach / my sister and I / swim

   _____

3 I ask Raj / give / me / a pencil

   _____

4 they / want / us / go / the concert

   _____

5 my friend / send / me / a postcard / from holiday

   _____

C **Complete the sentences with your own ideas.**

1 My dad taught me to _____.

2 I gave my friend a _____ for her birthday.

3 _____ (friend's name) invited me _____.

4 My teacher asked me _____.

Photocopiable 1: *Map reading sentence halves*

Aim: Learners revise the content of Lesson 1.2, including the use of prepositions to show the connection between nouns by matching sentence halves.

Preparation time: 10 minutes

Language focus: Prepositions before nouns

Vocabulary: Map reading vocabulary from Lesson 1.2

Materials: One set of *Map reading sentence halves* per pair of learners

Optional: A large-scale version of a world map showing longitude and latitude lines, for learners to interact with in the extension activity

Procedure:

- Distribute one set of the sentence halves to each pair of learners. Tell them they are going to create full sentences by putting two sentence halves together.

- Learners mix up the sentence halves and spread them face up on the table. Pick up random sentences and elicit whether they go together until you find a suitable pair.

- Tell learners to work together and match the two halves of the sentences.

- Circulate and give support about which combinations are acceptable.

- **Extension:** (Optional) Using a large-scale world map, learners practise pinpointing the location of places, using words from Photocopiable 1, e.g. *longitude/latitude/minutes, seconds, from the North/South Pole.*

Photocopiable 1: *Map reading sentence halves*

We use **longitude** and **latitude** to pinpoint the exact location of places **on** …	… our planet.
We map the Earth's surface **with** …	… lines called *latitude* and *longitude*.
Lines of **latitude** circle the Earth **from** …	… east to west.
The lines of **latitude** are parallel **to** …	… the equator.
The **lines** are about 111 km apart …	… **from** each other.
The distance between the lines is measured in **degrees**, from 0–90 degrees **to** …	… the north, south, east and west.
Lines of **longitude** run **from** …	… the **North Pole** to the **South Pole**.
The lines of **longitude** divide the Earth's surface **into** …	… **vertical** sections.
The **vertical** sections are like pieces **of** …	… an orange.
When a location is **between** the lines, we divide the **degrees** into …	… **minutes** and **seconds**, so the exact location can be found.

Photocopiable 2: *Have you ever ...?*

> **Aim:** Learners practise asking and answering questions about experiences using the present perfect and past simple.
>
> **Preparation time:** 10 minutes
>
> **Language focus:** Present perfect and questions and short answers; past simple *wh*-questions and answers
>
> **Vocabulary:** Various experiences, including those from Lesson 1.4
>
> **Materials:** One set of conversation cards per pair of learners

Procedure:

- Tell learners they are going to ask and answer questions with a partner about things they have done.

- Distribute one set of cards to each pair of learners.

- Demonstrate the activity. Tell learners to look for Card 1 and focus on the question on the left (1a). Explain that we are asking about the experience in general and elicit a present perfect question and short answer, for example:

  Have you ever been on a rollercoaster?   *Yes, I have. / No, I haven't. / No, never.*

- Focus on the questions on the right (1b). Explain that these questions refer to the specific experience in the previous question. Elicit past simple questions and answers, for example:

  Where did you go on the rollercoaster?   *(I went on the rollercoaster) in ....*

  (Note: In the case of a negative answer to the 'Have you ever' question, learners do NOT need to ask the questions on the right.)

- Practise with more examples until you are satisfied learners have understood the task.

- Circulate and offer support while learners ask and answer the questions on the other cards in pairs.

Photocopiable 2: *Have you ever …?*

Conversation cards:

- *Have you ever …? (Present perfect simple)*

- *When / Where / Who did you …? (Past simple)*

1a go /a rollercoaster	**1b** Where? Who? … like it?	**2a** ride / horse	**2b** Where? When?
3a feel / excited	**3b** What / about? When? Why?	**4a** feel / scared	**4b** Why? When?
5a see the sea	**5b** Where? When? … like it?	**6a** cook dinner	**6b** When? Who? What?
7a be / proud of yourself	**7b** What? Why?	**8a** perform on stage	**8b** When? Where?
9a play / a school team?	**9b** Which? Who … with?	**10a** go to a concert	**10b** Where? When?

Name _____ Date _____

Photocopiable 3: Checklist for a description of a first-time experience

Checklist	Have I included it?	Example(s)
Use your answers to the questions to organise your description.		
Use different verb tenses.		
Use powerful adjectives and nouns to describe your feelings.		

Name _____ Date _____

End of Unit 1 test

Vocabulary 1

Circle the correct words.

Example:

0   There's lots of (excitement) / *excited* about the new computer game – everyone wants to play it!

_____

1   He was *pride / proud* of himself when he got to the top of the mountain.   [1]

2   Learning to play a new song on the piano gives me lots of *satisfied / satisfaction*.   [1]

3   I think my aunt is a very *bravery / brave* person.   [1]

4   That film was *amazement / amazing*! I'm glad we watched it!   [1]

5   That's a *beauty / beautiful* painting! Do you know the name of the artist?   [1]

Vocabulary 2

Complete the adjectives. There is one space for each letter in the word.
Some letters are already there.

Example:

0   I feel e _x_ _c_ _i_ _t_ _e_ _d_ when I go to the cinema.

---

6   I feel i __ __ __ __ __ s __ __ __ when I look at websites about animals.   [1]

7   I feel s __ __ __ __ __ when I see a snake.   [1]

8   I feel a __ __ __ __ when I read about pollution.   [1]

9   I feel n __ __ __ __ __ __ when I jump off a rock into the sea.   [1]

10 I feel h __ __ __ __ when I see my friends.   [1]

Grammar 1

Complete the sentences with the words in the box.

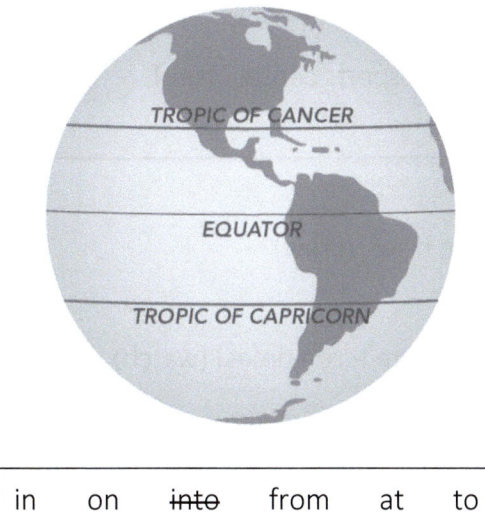

| in | on | ~~into~~ | from | at | to |

Example:

0   Let's divide the map ___*into*___ sections.

___

11 Let's look at some places _____ our planet.   [1]

12 Imagine that the North Pole is _____ one end of our planet.   [1]

13 The Equator is _____ the middle.   [1]

14 Imagine travelling _____ east to west.   [1]

15 How many degrees is Mumbai _____ the south of Kolkata?   [1]

Grammar 2

Complete the sentences with the present perfect form of the verbs in brackets.

Example:

0 ___Have___ you ___seen___ the new sports centre? (see)

_____

16 We _____ some trees. (draw) [1]

17 Laura _____ that film three times! (watch) [1]

18 _____ you _____ this song? (hear) [1]

19 I _____ that game before. (not play) [1]

20 _____ your brother _____ his homework? (finish) [1]

Name _____   Date _____

Progress test 1

Vocabulary 1

Read the descriptions and complete the words.
There is one space for each letter in the word. The first letter is already there.

Example:

0   This verb means 'think that someone is awesome'.

a _d m i r e_

---

1   This makes blood go round your body.

h __ __ __ __   [1]

2   This verb means to go up and down, like a ball.

b __ __ __ __ __   [1]

3   This part of your body is between your waist and your leg.

h __ __   [1]

4   This person stops the ball going into the goal, for example in football.

goal k __ __ __ __ __   [1]

5   This part of your body is between your arm and your neck.

s __ __ __ __ __ __   [1]

Vocabulary 2

Read the sentences and circle the correct word for each space.

Example:

0   Lamon's a fast runner so he's good at _____.

   A   chess   B   (athletics)   C   swimming

---

6   George felt very _____ when he finished his homework.

   A   satisfying   B   satisfaction   C   satisfied   [1]

7   Antarctica is a _____.

   A   country   B   continent   C   province   [1]

8   Lucy plays football really well – she has a lot of natural _____.

   A   talent   B   amazement   C   campaign   [1]

9   The South _____ is in Antarctica.

   A   Pole   B   Degree   C   Equator   [1]

10 I hope I _____ this game!

   A   ban   B   harm   C   win   [1]

Grammar 1

Complete the sentences with the correct form of the verb in brackets.

Example:

0 ___Do___ you ___know___ my friend Jonas? He's very funny. (know)

---

11 Where _____ you _____? (live) [1]

12 I _____ my homework – I'm going to do the last two exercises
tomorrow afternoon. (not finish) [1]

13 _____ your brother _____ swimming?
He can come to the pool with us. (like) [1]

14 If I sleep for eight hours tonight, I _____ better tomorrow
morning. (feel) [1]

15 _____ you ever _____ a dolphin? (see) [1]

Grammar 2

Complete the emails with **one** word in each space.

From: Alex

To: Chris

Chris,

It's great you can come _____with_____ me and my family to the beach tomorrow. You don't

need (16) _____ bring any food because my parents will have plenty for all of us.

There will be lots of sandwiches and some salad and fruit. My parents prefer food

(17) _____ is healthy, but they'll bring some chocolate for us to eat after

swimming!

See you soon,

Alex

From: Chris

To: Alex

Hi Alex,

Thanks! (18) _____ it's windy tomorrow, we can fly my kite together

at the beach. Would you like me to bring it? I made it myself and I'm really proud

(19) _____ it! Also, (20) _____ time should I come to your

house in the morning?

Let me know,

Chris

[Total: 5 marks]

Reading 1

Read the text and the sentences. Are the sentences true or false?

Circle A, B or C.

If there isn't enough information to answer 'True' (A) or 'False' (B), choose 'Doesn't say' (C).

First riding lessons

Rania and Meg are best friends. They love sport, and because Meg has to use a wheelchair, they're always looking for new ideas for sports activities that they can both do. When Meg's mother found a place where the girls could learn to ride horses, they were very excited.

When the girls went to the riding school for their first lesson, the horses looked enormous, so they were both a bit scared. They soon felt better when they met their teacher, Karen, who was really friendly and gave them some carrots for the horses. Karen told the girls to hold their hands flat, with their fingers together, and it was amazing because the horses took the carrots from their hands so carefully. 'I don't feel terrified now!' Meg laughed.

Karen gave them hats and boots to wear during the lesson, and then she helped the girls to get onto the horses and sit comfortably. Meg's horse was called Star, and Rania's was called Juno. Because this was their first lesson, Karen was in front of them on foot the whole time and they didn't go very fast. After they got off the horses, Karen showed the girls how to feed them. Both the girls thought it was a great experience, and now they go riding together every week.

Example:

0   Horse riding was the first sport that Rania could do with Meg.

   A   True   B   False   C   (Doesn't say)

---

21   When they arrived at the riding school, the girls felt quite nervous.

   A   True   B   False   C   Doesn't say   [1]

22   The girls liked their teacher, Karen.

   A   True   B   False   C   Doesn't say   [1]

23   Carrots were the horses' favourite food.

   A   True   B   False   C   Doesn't say   [1]

24   The girls had to buy special hats for their riding lesson.

   A   True   B   False   C   Doesn't say   [1]

25   Karen was on a horse while she was teaching the girls.

   A   True   B   False   C   Doesn't say   [1]

Reading 2

Look at the text in each question.
What does it say?

Circle the correct letter A, B or C.

Example:

0   Why is Imane texting?

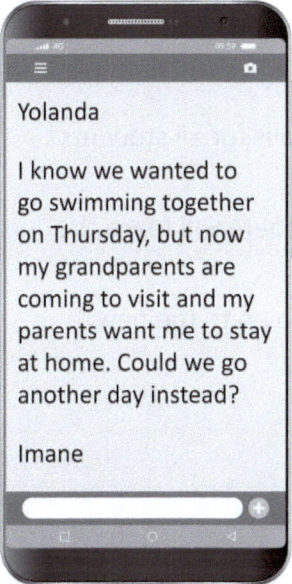

A   to suggest doing a different activity

B   to find out if Yolanda wants to meet her family

C   to change a plan that she and Yolanda have made

---

26   What are Kira and Nessim asking their classmates to do?

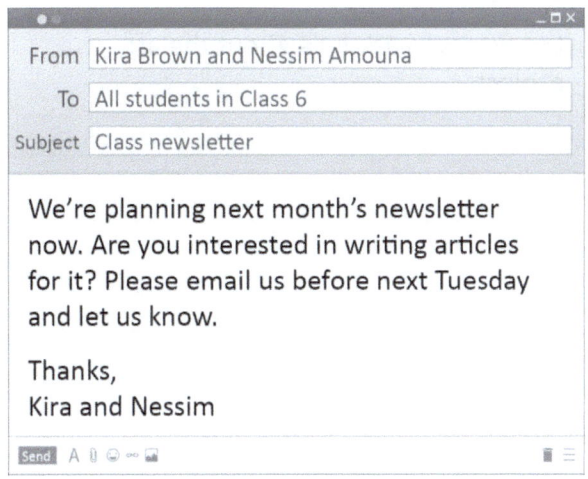

A   plan the magazine with them   [1]

B   send in a story for next month's magazine

C   tell them if they want to write something for the magazine

27

Art Museum
No shouting inside the museum.
Cameras are allowed.
Postcards in museum shop.
(Open every day 10 a.m.–5 p.m.)

A Museum visitors mustn't take photos. [1]

B Museum visitors shouldn't talk loudly.

C Museum visitors can't buy postcards today.

28

New school chess club!
Are you good at chess or would you like to improve? Or have you never played before and want to learn?
Everyone welcome!
Wednesdays after school in Room 10B.

A The new chess club is for all students who want to join. [1]

B The best club members will teach the beginners.

C All students have to go to the new chess club.

29

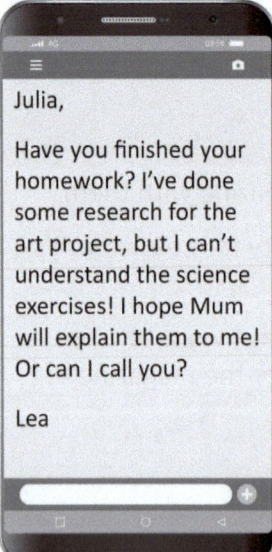

Julia,

Have you finished your homework? I've done some research for the art project, but I can't understand the science exercises! I hope Mum will explain them to me! Or can I call you?

Lea

A Lea is asking for help with her science homework. [1]

B Lea has asked her mother for some advice.

C Lea wants to ask Julia about the art project.

30

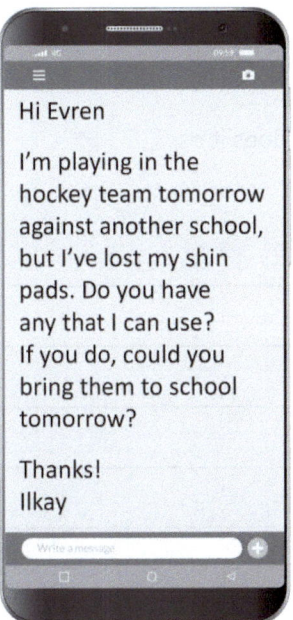

Hi Evren

I'm playing in the hockey team tomorrow against another school, but I've lost my shin pads. Do you have any that I can use? If you do, could you bring them to school tomorrow?

Thanks!
Ilkay

A Ilkay left something at Evren's house. [1]

B Ilkay wants to give Evren something.

C Ilkay needs something for a match.

Writing

31 Write about an animal.

What type of animal is it? What does it look like? Where does it live? What does it eat?

Write about 100 words.

_____

_____

_____

_____

_____

_____

_____

_____

_____

_____

_____

_____

_____

_____

_____

_____

_____

_____

_____

_____

_____

[Total: 20 marks]

Acknowledgements

The authors and publishers acknowledge the following sources of copyright material and are grateful for the permissions granted. While every effort has been made, it has not always been possible to identify the sources of all the material used, or to trace all copyright holders. If any omissions are brought to our notice, we will be happy to include the appropriate acknowledgements on reprinting.

Text excerpt from *The Lost Frost Girl (A Girl Called Owl)* by Amy Wilson. Text Copyright by Amy Wilson 2017. Used by permission of HarperCollins Publishers and Macmillan Children's Books; Extract from *Off Side* by Tom Palmer. Used with the permission of Random House Group Limited; Extract from *Song for a Whale* by Lynne Kelly. Text copyright Lynne Kelly, 2019. First published in the UK by Bonnier Books UK Ltd; Extract from *Billionaire Boy* by David Walliams, published by HarperCollins Children's Books. Used with the permission of Independent Talent Group Limited and Illustrations by Tony Ross, © 2010 Reprinted by permission of HarperCollins Publishers Ltd; 'You can be anything' by Teri Hopkins; 'Thank-You Letter' by Eric Finney from *Loony Letters & Daft Diaries: Poems chosen by Paul Cookson*, Macmillan Children's Books published 2003; Abridged extract from *Jurassic Park* by Michael Crichton, Copyright © 1990 by Michael Crichton, published by Alfred A. Knopf, an imprint of the Knopft Doubleday Publishing Group, a division of Penguin Random House LLC. All rights reserved; Extract and illustrations from *Willow* by Denise Brennan-Nelson and Rosemarie Brennan. Used with the permission of Sleeping Bear Press.

Thanks to the following for permission to reproduce images:

Cover: by Omar Aranda (Beehive Illustration); Inside: K. Menzel Photography/Getty Images; GlobalP/Getty Images; Design Pics/David Ponton/Getty Images